MW01056627

Narrative Worlds and the Texture of Time

This book brings together a model of time and a model of language to generate a new model of narrative, where different stories with different temporalities and non-chronological modes of sequence can tell of different worlds of human – and non-human – experience, woven together (the 'texture of time') in the one narrative. The work of Gerald Edelman on consciousness, J.T. Fraser on time, and M.A.K. Halliday on language is introduced; the categories of systemic functional linguistics are used for detailed analysis of English narrative texts from different literary periods. A summary chapter gives an overview of previous narrative studies and theories, with extensive references. Chapters on 'temporalization' and 'spatialization' of language contrast the importance of time in narrative texts with the effect of 'grammatical metaphor', as described by M.A.K. Halliday, for scientific discourse. Chapters on prose fiction, poetry and the texts of digital culture chart changes in the 'texture of time' with changes in the social context: 'narrative as social semiotic'.

Rosemary Huisman is Honorary Associate Professor in English at The University of Sydney. She is the author of *The Written Poem, Semiotic Conventions from Old to Modern English*, six chapters in *Narrative and Media*, and numerous articles on literary and legal language; she is also a published poet.

Routledge Interdisciplinary Perspectives on Literature

For more information about this series, please visit: https://www.routledge.com/Routledge-Interdisciplinary-Perspectives-on-Literature/book-series/RIPL

Narrative Worlds and the Texture of Time

A Social-Semiotic Perspective

Rosemary Huisman

Routledge
Taylor & Francis Group

NEW YORK AND LONDON

First published 2023
by Routledge
605 Third Avenue, New York, NY 10158

and by Routledge
4 Park Square, Milton Park, Abingdon, Oxon, OX14 4RN

*Routledge is an imprint of the Taylor & Francis Group, an
informa business*

© 2023 Rosemary Huisman

The right of Rosemary Huisman to be identified as author of this
work has been asserted in accordance with sections 77 and 78 of
the Copyright, Designs and Patents Act 1988.

Library of Congress Cataloging-in-Publication Data
Names: Huisman, Rosemary, 1941- author.
Title: Narrative worlds and the texture of time : a social-semiotic perspective /
Rosemary Huisman.
Description: New York, NY : Routledge, 2023. | Series: Routledge interdisciplinary
perspectives on literature ; 1 | Includes index.
Identifiers: LCCN 2022015715 (print) | LCCN 2022015716 (ebook) | ISBN
9781032260013 (hardback) | ISBN 9781032349411 (paperback) | ISBN
9781003324584 (ebook)
Subjects: LCSH: English literature--History and criticism. | Space and time in literature.
| Space and time in language. | Narration (Rhetoric) | LCGFT: Literary criticism.
Classification: LCC PR149.S75 H85 2023 (print) | LCC PR149.S75 (ebook) | DDC
820.9/23--dc23/eng/20220720
LC record available at https://lccn.loc.gov/2022015715
LC ebook record available at https://lccn.loc.gov/2022015716

ISBN: 978-1-032-26001-3 (hbk)
ISBN: 978-1-032-34941-1 (pbk)
ISBN: 978-1-003-32458-4 (ebk)

DOI: 10.4324/b23121

Typeset in Sabon
by SPi Technologies India Pvt Ltd (Straive)

for Tony Blackshield
man of law, literature and song

Contents

Figures

Tables

Acknowledgements

As the Preface implies, this book owes the generation of its basic ideas to the work of two scholars, the late M.A.K. Halliday and the late J.T. Fraser. Fraser I met once at an ISST conference; Halliday I had the privilege of knowing personally as well as professionally, especially in his later years. In their publications, both combine intellectual acuity with a practical focus on the application of their models of time and of language. I acknowledge their fundamental contribution to my thinking. Christian M.I.M. Matthiessen, who was a close collaborator with Halliday, is someone whose erudite and witty plenaries I have enjoyed in many parts of the globe. I acknowledge my debt to him particularly in his scrupulous accumulation of detailed analyses and examples (as in the fourth edition of *Halliday's Introduction to Functional Grammar*), to which I turn when flummoxed by some SFL detail.

In the last century (!), in the English department of the University of Sydney, I taught systemic functional grammar with Terry Threadgold, narrative and media studies with Helen Fulton, and reading and writing practices with Judy Quinn (all three women have gone on to senior roles in British universities); I'd like to acknowledge their continuing friendship and academic stimulation. Geoff Williams in Education joined Terry and me for post-graduate courses using SFL; more recently Annabelle Lukin and David Butt have involved me in their linguistics teaching at Macquarie University, Sydney (zooming through 2020 and 2021). I am fortunate to have had all these people as both intellectual colleagues and friends. Locally, many (especially women) who have contributed strongly to SFL in the field of Education remain valued friends. I particularly thank Sally Humphrey for involving me in her courses on language and literacy at ACU (the Australian Catholic University) in Sydney.

The SFL community is widespread; my two most recently published articles, referencing SFL, were first delivered as plenaries in China (at the Guangdong University of Foreign Studies, Guangzhou) and in India (Osmania University, Hyderabad). My thanks, respectively, to Professors Alex Peng and Geoff Williams, and to Dr Mohammad Ansari for these invitations, and to the editors of the journals, *Language, Context and*

Text and the *Nalsar Student Law Review*, in which those papers later appeared. The annual international SFL Congress and the annual conferences of national SFL associations have been important places for trying out and extending new ideas; my thanks to the indefatigable organizers of these events.

I must also acknowledge the importance of the ISST community of scholars to the development of my work. I participated in several ISST tri-ennial conferences and inter-conference symposia held in many parts of the world. In particular, Raji Steineck, Claudia Clausius, Sabine Gross, Steve Ostovich, Dennis Costa and Arkadiusz Misztal, all editors of my writing on time published in book chapters and journal articles, have contributed to my thinking. My special thanks to Jo Alyson Parker (Vice-President of ISST) and Emily DiCarlo (Editor of *Times News*, the society's newsletter) for help with elusive permissions.

This has been an interdisciplinary project and my involvement in other scholarly associations has also contributed to its development; in particular, I acknowledge the relevant focus of PALA, the Poetics and Linguistics Association.

Writing this, I think of my parents, long deceased, who raised me in a home full of books and conversation. Now Penny Huisman (daughter) and her husband, Brian Mariotti, have a similar home, warm and welcoming. I am grateful. A special thanks should be given to their son, Emmett (14 at the time of writing), a helpful adviser on some aspects of digital culture, discussed in Chapter 11.

And Tony Blackshield. He once told me his English teacher told him he was 'an Augustan who wanted to be a Romantic'. His favourite poem is Hopkins' *Wreck of the Deutschland* (he wrote a legal article on a constitutional case in the style of the poem ...); he can sight-read out loud Joyce's *Finnegan's Wake*. For me, he exceeds any literary (or other) categorization.

Finally, I must acknowledge the many voices that speak in quotations in this book. The author and the publisher wish to thank the copyright holders for their permission to reproduce from the following material:

From *Bright Air, Brilliant Fire: On the Matter of the Mind*, by Gerald Edelman, copyright © 1992. Reprinted by permission of Basic Books, an imprint of Hachette Book Group, Inc.

From 'Gerald M. Edelman (1929–2014)' by Giuilo Tononi, in *Science* copyright © 27 June 2014. Published by The American Association for the Advancement of Science.

© M.A.K. Halliday, ed. Jonathan J. Webster, 2003; 2005; 2007, *Works of M.A.K. Halliday*. Continuum Publishing, an imprint of Bloomsbury Publishing Plc.

From *Time and Time Again: Reports from a Boundary of the Universe*, by J.T. Fraser, copyright © 2007. Published by Brill.

Excerpts from 'The Origins of Language and Narrative Temporalities', by Rosemary Huisman. In *Origins and Futures: Time Inflected and Reflected*, edited by Raji C Steineck and Claudi Clausius, copyright © 2013. Published by Brill.

Figure 5.3 on page 216 and Table 1.4 on page 20 in *Halliday's Introduction to Functional Grammar*, 4th edn by M.A.K. Halliday revised by Christian M.I.M. Matthiessen, © 2014. Published by Routledge. Reproduced by permission of Taylor and Francis Group.

Excerpt(s) from AGAINST THE DAY by Thomas Pynchon, copyright © 2006 by Thomas Pynchon. Used by permission of Penguin Press, an imprint of Penguin Publishing Group, a division of Penguin Random House LLC. All rights reserved. (US Rights).

Against the Day by Thomas Pynchon. Copyright © Thomas Pynchon. Reproduced by permission of the author c/o Rogers, Coleridge & White Ltd, 20 Powis Mews, London W11 1JN.

Excerpt(s) from HAG-SEED: WILLIAM SHAKESPEARE'S THE TEMPEST RETOLD: A NOVEL by Margaret Atwood, copyright © 2016 by O.W. Toad Ltd. Used by permission of Hogarth, an imprint of Random House, a division of Penguin Random House LLC. All rights reserved. (US Rights).

From *Hag-Seed* by Margaret Atwood published by Hogarth. Copyright © Margaret Atwood 2016. Reprinted by permission of The Random House Group Limited.

From *Language in the Inner City, Studies in the Black English Vernacular* by William Labov, © 1972, Extract example number 18 on pp. 367–368. Reprinted with permission of the University of Pennsylvania Press.

Picador Australia: Extract from *Burial Rights* by Hannah Kent reprinted by permission of Pan Macmillan Australia Pty Ltd. Copyright© Hannah Kent, 2014.

Excerpts from THE MEMBER OF THE WEDDING by Carson McCullers. Copyright © 1946 by Carson McCullers, renewed by 1973 by Floria V. Lasky, Executrix of the Estate of Carson McCullers. Reprinted by permission of Mariner Books, an imprint of HarperCollins Publishers.

Excerpts from *The Cookbook Collector* by Allegra Goodman. Copyright © 2010, pp. 134 and 329. Reproduced with permission of the Licensor through PLSclear. (UK Rights).

Approval of 249 words on pp. 134 and 329 from *The Cookbook Collector* by Allegra Goodman. Copyright © 2000 Penguin Random House. (US Rights).

From The Crying of Lot 49 by Thomas Pynchon. Copyright (c) 1965, 1966 by Thomas Pynchon. Copyright renewed 1993, 1994 by Thomas Pynchon. Used by permission of HarperCollins Publishers.

Preface

In 2002 I presented a paper at the International Systemic Functional Linguistics (SFL) Congress in Liverpool, arguing against the relevance of much narrative theory to some texts which, nevertheless, have been called 'narratives'. My PhD, done many years before, had studied Old English poetry, with a focus on the long poems known as *Beowulf* and *Andreas*. The vellum manuscripts of these early poems record the text continuously across the page; that had motivated me to ask the (naïve?) questions, 'when did we and why do we (usually) print poems in lines?' – which led to the publication of a book, *The Written Poem, Semiotic Conventions from Old to Modern English* (1998), which traced the development of visual display as meaningful in English poetry. Now my problem in applying narrative theory to those early texts led me to ask not 'why is this text an inadequate narrative' but 'what does narrative theory assume that is not relevant to this text?' In that 2002 paper, I concluded: it is the assumption that narrative is axiomatically concerned with 'time'. (Patently, I was wrong or this book would not be written!) But this 'time' was one of chronological sequence (even in Paul Ricoeur's subtle discussion, 'real time', 1985, 25; 100–101). In SFL, an important system of 'Transitivity' describes choices of meaning in the grammatical clause. These choices imply three 'worlds' of human experience and chronological sequence is characteristic of only one of these worlds, the external and physical world of human experience. Hence I was presenting my arguments on time and narrative to an audience expert in this modelling of meaning and world (though not necessarily thinking about the meaning of 'time').

However, two years later (2004), staying in Cambridge, I (almost accidentally) attended the tri-ennial conference of the International Society for the Study of Time (ISST) and was introduced to the polyvalence of time, to temporalities, explored in papers from diverse fields in the sciences and the humanities (subsequently, I was to use this polyvalence in my study of both legal and literary texts). A different temporality, I realized, might enable a different mode of sequence. And so began, for me, the meaningful juxtaposition of SFL and ISST concepts in my thinking about narrative, now recorded in this book.

SFL was initially developed from the work of M.A.K. Halliday (1925–2018). The subtitle of this book, 'a social-semiotic perspective', comes from Halliday's understanding of the relation of language and the social system: 'the social system [is] a social semiotic: a system of meanings that constitutes the "reality" of the culture. This is the higher-level system to which language is related: the semantic system of language is a realization of the social semiotic' (Halliday 2007, 197). An early collection of his papers, written between 1972 and 1976 and, in Halliday's words, 'linked by a common theme', is entitled *Language as Social Semiotic, the Social Interpretation of Language and Meaning* (1978). In the last 40-odd years, Halliday's modelling of language, with its focus on meaning as functional within social context, has developed into 'systemic functional linguistics' (SFL) and to wider applications to non-linguistic modalities. Chronicles of this development are now written, extending into the past and future: for example, see Lukin's account of the relevant work of scholars preceding Halliday (Chapter 2, 'The Quest for Meaning in Twentieth-Century Linguistics', in *War and Its Ideologies, a Social-Semiotic Theory and Description*, 2019) and Jewitt, Bezemer and O'Halloran's account of work extending a social semiotic approach beyond language (Chapter 4, 'Social Semiotics', in *Introducing Multimodality*, 2016). Most closely associated with Halliday in the detailed grammatical development of the linguistic theory is Christian M.I.M. Matthiessen; in this book I take my theoretical linguistic bearings from the work, singular and joint, of Halliday and Matthiessen. Beautiful minds, both of them, in action in the world.

ISST is similarly born from the initiative of a profoundly thoughtful scholar, J.T. Fraser (1923–2010), an engineer and inventor, who in 1966 founded the international society. I had the privilege of being introduced to his ideas by his own talk at the Cambridge conference and was struck by his easy movement between the sciences and the humanities, in explanation and examples. The audience was similarly eclectic and one consequence – I realized when writing my own contributions to later ISST conferences and publications – was that one could assume an educated hearing/reading but not the jargon of one's own disciplinary discourse. Fraser had emigrated from Europe to the United States after WWII and his motive in establishing a society focused on 'time' was at least to promote interdisciplinary communication and cooperation through a concept given meaning in many scholarly contexts. ISST publications include the annual journal, *Kronoscope*, and the book series, *The Study of Time*, published by Brill (Volume 17 in 2021).

In bringing a juxtaposition of SFL and ISST concepts to bear on narrative theories I had not anticipated a reverse effect: that narrative concepts would bear upon my understanding, in particular, of SFL. As discussed in Chapter 2, on 'spatialization' in language, Halliday did considerable work on 'grammatical metaphor', which effectively removes/reduces meanings of time. This strategy Halliday studied initially as it emerged in scientific discourse; more generally it is important in literate writing practices and has been incorporated into some teacher education. 'Everyday language' uses this strategy less and this can give the impression that such language is inherently 'simpler'. But narrative theorists sometimes talk about different ways of 'knowing and being', and it struck me that the language of narrative, for which temporal meanings are so important, enables different, not simpler, ways which deserve close attention. Chapter 6, on 'temporalization' in language explores such ways.

Because my academic location has been in an English department, the texts discussed in this book are in English and are, for the most part, the 'highly valued' works of prose fiction and poetry. Because I was in that area of the department that taught both mediaeval literature and language of any period, the historical sweep of 'narrative as social semiotic' particularly interests me; I principally use my model of 'narrative worlds and the texture of time' to compare the texture of narratives from different contexts of English cultural history.

Dramatic changes in language technology produce consequences that those in the changing social context have not predicted. Like Darwinian evolution, they can be described only retrospectively. The first is the change from oral to literate culture, the second the change from manuscript to print culture, the third the change from print to digital culture. The *Beowulf* poem I studied is the written record we have of what, in part, originated in pre-literate culture, its stories spoken and respoken. Yet the questions of narrative and temporalities provoked by that study turn out to be relevant to later and different social contexts – even, lightly touched on in Chapter 11, to the still evolving digital culture that we humans will adapt even as it adapts us.

Rosemary Huisman (née Lowe)
Sydney, January 2022

References

Fraser, J.T. 2004. 'List of Fraser's Works on Time to 2004'. *KronoScope* 4: pp. 185–196.

Halliday, M.A.K. 1978. *Language as Social Semiotic, The Social Interpretation of Language and Meaning*. London: Edward Arnold.

Halliday, M.A.K. 2007 [1975]. 'Language as Social Semiotic: Towards a General Sociolinguistic Theory'. In *Language and Society*. Volume 10 in the Collected Works of M.A.K. Halliday, ed. Jonathan J. Webster. London and New York: Continuum.

Huisman, 1998; 2000. *The Written Poem, Semiotic Conventions from Old to Modern English*. London and New York: Cassell; Continuum.

Jewitt, Carey, Jeff Bezemer and Kay O'Halloran. 2016. *Introducing Multimodality*. London and New York: Routledge.

Lukin, Annabelle. 2019. *War and its Ideologies: A Social-Semiotic Theory and Description*. Singapore: Springer.

Ricoeur, Paul. 1985 [1984]. *Time and Narrative*, Volume 2. Chicago and London: The University of Chicago Press.

1   Human consciousness and the dual experience of time felt and time understood

Scholars of narrative have agreed that time is of the essence – Chapter 4 explores this assertion – yet what is understood by 'time'? St Augustine of Hippo (354–430 CE), the early Christian theologian and philosopher, famously considered this question, devoting Book 11 of his *Confessions* to a personal exploration of Latin *tempus*. In Chapter 14 he muses:

> For what is time? Who can easily and briefly explain it? Who even in time can comprehend it, even to the pronouncing of a word concerning it? But what in speaking do we refer to more familiarly and knowingly than time? And certainly we understand when we speak of it; we understand also when we hear it spoken of by another.
>
> (Augustine n.d.)

Augustine then repeats his question and confesses his confusion:

> *quid est ergo tempus? si nemo ex me quaerat, scio; si quaerenti explicare velim, nescio.*
>
> (2014, 238)

> What then is time? If no one inquires of me, I know; if I should like to explain to one inquiring, I do not know.
>
> (author's translation)

Even now, it is worth considering the implications of his words, for they gesture towards important and contemporary topics: time in consciousness and time in language. Augustine studies time through introspection; interrogating his own consciousness, he is aware that he both knows and does not know. However, in the detail of his comment, he makes explicit the differing contexts of this contradiction. Augustine describes a clear contrast between two situations: the first situation of 'knowing' is that of a solitary one of personal experience, of self-awareness; the second situation of 'not knowing' is that of a shared social experience, of dialogue

DOI: 10.4324/b23121-1

between inquirer and explainer in question and answer by those sharing the same language.

A review paper published in 2013 credits Augustine with insights foundational for the current discipline of neuropsychology in that the discipline talks about 'subjective time': the inter-relation of an awareness of 'time and self' (Manning et al. 2013). However, equally Augustine talks about inter-subjective time, time that can be talked about between speakers but not explained. Inasmuch as Augustine's method of questioning is one of introspection, his answer, of knowing and not knowing, points towards the dual nature of human understanding: through personal awareness and through shared language. These fundamental human attributes of self-consciousness and language remain central to the understanding of human 'time', as later scholars echo Augustine's 'confused' answer.

Some fifteen hundred years later, the American philosopher and psychologist William James (1842–1910) begins to describe 'the introspective study of the adult consciousness':

> **The Fundamental Fact.** – The first and foremost concrete fact which everyone will affirm to belong to his inner experience is the fact that consciousness of some sort goes on. 'States of mind' succeed each other in him. If we could say in English 'it thinks,' as we say 'it rains' or 'it blows,' we should be stating the fact most simply and with the minimum of assumption. As we cannot, we must simply say that thought goes on.
>
> (James 1892)

Augustine, as earlier quoted, claims that we refer to time 'familiarly and knowingly', and that 'certainly we understand when we speak of it; we understand also when we hear it spoken of by another'. Thus, in James' comments above, we understand words of temporal meaning without difficulty: 'states of mind *succeed* each other' – succession is sequence in time. Foreshadowing this book's account of 'grammatical metaphor' in Chapter 2, James would prefer the activity of consciousness to be signified by a verb (as a process), 'it thinks', rather than by a noun (as a thing), 'thought goes on'.

James continues:

> **Four Characters in Consciousness.** – How does it go on? We notice immediately four important characters in the process, of which it shall be the duty of the present chapter to treat in a general way:
>
> 1. Every 'state' tends to be part of a personal consciousness.
> 2. Within each personal consciousness states are always changing.

3. Each personal consciousness is sensibly continuous.
4. It is interested in some parts of its object to the exclusion of others, and welcomes or rejects – chooses from among them, in a word – all the while.

(1892)

Again the temporal meanings are obvious, though distributed through different grammatical forms and meanings: 'states are always *changing*' (verb for process); 'consciousness is sensibly *continuous*' (adjective for attribute); '*all the while*' (nominal group for circumstance).

James then channels Augustine's dilemma in his choice of words:

> When I say every 'state' or 'thought' is part of a personal consciousness, 'personal consciousness' is one of the terms in question. Its meaning we know so long as no one asks us to define it, but to give an accurate account of it is the most difficult of philosophic tasks.
>
> (1892)

Nevertheless, James is prepared to 'confront' this most difficult task, effectively founding the discipline of psychology as distinct from philosophy.

Gerald Edelman (1929–2014), bringing psychology into relation with biology in the discipline of neurobiology, begins his discussion of consciousness by repeating James' echoes of Augustine:

> What is daunting about consciousness is that it does not seem to be a matter of behaviour. It just *is* – winking on with the light, multiple and simultaneous in its modes and objects, ineluctably ours. It is a process and one that is hard to score. We know what it is for ourselves but can only judge its existence in others by inductive inference. As James put it, it is something the meaning of which 'we know as long as no one asks us to define it'.
>
> (1994, 111)

To define consciousness, Edelman suggests, one should start from a consideration of its properties, which he explicitly paraphrases from James' list, above, with its temporal focus:

> Consider what I call its 'Jamesian' properties … It is personal (possessed by individuals or selves); it is changing, yet continuous; it deals with objects independent of itself; and it is selective in time, that is, it does not exhaust all aspects of the objects with which it deals.
>
> (1994, 111)

It is clear that the explanation of Augustine's human time, subjective and intersubjective, will be inter-related with the explanation of human consciousness, and it is in Edelman's account of consciousness through his theory of 'neural Darwinism' that this complex explanation can be pursued. Edelman's theory is referred to, approvingly, by both M.A.K. Halliday (in his theory of language) and J.T. Fraser (in his modelling of time), and the work of these two scholars is central to the discussion and suggestions of this book. For this reason – if at the risk of stepping well outside my own disciplinary expertise – in this chapter I offer a summary introduction to Edelman's ideas.

In a 'Retrospective' for Edelman, published in 2014 after his death, Giulio Tononi, restates 'the essence of his theory':

> [First] the basic principles of selectionism: There must be mechanisms to generate diversity, mechanisms to sample a changing environment, and mechanisms to differentially amplify those variants that fit the environment well. It was long assumed that species are what they are immutably and by design, and it took Darwin to imagine that they may evolve by variation and selection. Similarly, it was first thought that antibodies had to be 'instructed' by antigens into the appropriate shape, until Edelman and others proved that antibodies, too, are produced by variation and selection. And the same was thought true for the brain: Most people implicitly assume that the world comes prelabeled into fixed categories—whether faces, animals, objects, or anything else—and that the brain 'processes information' about such inputs. Instead, insisted Edelman, 'the world is an unlabeled place', and the brain, too, is a selectionist system: There is a preexisting repertoire of variations, albeit constrained by evolutionary history and developmental processes; there is the unique history of encounters of a brain with its environment; and there is the differential amplification, usually through the strengthening of synapses, of those brain circuits that work best in that environment. Of course, just as evolution includes sexual selection and immunity requires tolerance, neural selection too has its special features, such as neuronal groups and 'reentry'. These were discussed in *Neural Darwinism* and in later work that expanded the theory of neuronal group selection to address consciousness and higher brain functions.
>
> (Tononi 2014)

The following discussion of Edelman's work on 'consciousness and higher brain functions', and its relevance to a concern with 'time', draws heavily on the account in his publication, *Bright Air, Brilliant Fire, On the Matter of the Mind*. This is a book intended for a general rather than scientific audience, which Edelman describes as designed 'to explain some rather technical matters to nonspecialist readers' (1994, xiii). Edelman is careful to provide an intellectual context for assessing his theory: in Part I he discusses 'problems' with earlier accounts of 'mind'; in Part II he argues for the necessity of 'putting psychology on a biological basis'; by Part III, he can write: 'we are now in a position to use what we know about biology, psychology and philosophy to postulate a theory of consciousness that will be an essential part of a theory of how the brain works' (1994, 71). Edelman then describes the basic duality of his theory: that human consciousness is of two kinds: primary consciousness and higher-order consciousness.

Primary consciousness results from the evolved inter-relation of the two major kinds of nervous system organization: the evolutionary earlier limbic-brain system and the later thalamocortical system; this relation is both in the evolution of strong links between the two systems and in the evolution of 'continual re-entrant signalling' (a 're-entrant circuit') between them.

The earlier organization combining the brain stem and the limbic system is 'concerned with appetite, sexual and consummatory behaviour, and evolved defensive behaviour patterns. ... Together [they] regulate heart and respiratory rate, sweating, digestive functions,... as well as bodily cycles related to sleep and sex' (1994, 117). These regularities and cycles are temporal experiences of the body. Edelman describes them as 'of the interior'; they did not evolve to respond to 'large numbers of unanticipated signals from the outside world'. This is a 'value system' (1994, 117), that is, 'the driving forces of animal behaviour are thus evolutionarily selected value patterns that help the brain and the body maintain the conditions necessary to continue life' (1994, 94).

In the later thalamocortical system, the thalamus and the cortex act together. In contrast to the earlier system, the cerebral cortex has evolved to receive signals from the outside world 'through many sensory modalities simultaneously – sight, touch, taste, smell, hearing, joint sense (feeling the position of your extremities)' (1994, 118). It permitted 'increasingly sophisticated motor behavior, and the categorization of world events'. In addition, the cortical appendages – 'cerebellum, basal ganglia, and hippocampus' – evolved along with the cortex. These dealt with succession 'both in actual motion and in memory', that is as both spatial and temporal experience.

During evolution, these two systems, limbic-brain stem and thalamo-cortical, were closely linked, a critical step for 'learning'. In Edelman's words,

If the cortex is concerned with the categorization of the world and the limbo-brain stem system is concerned with value ...then learning may be seen as the means by which categorization occurs on a background of value to result in adaptive changes in behaviour that satisfy value.

(1994, 118)

In some animals, 'learning' enables what Edelman calls 'a scene': 'a spa-
tiotemporally ordered set of categorizations of familiar and nonfamiliar
events, *some with and some without necessary physical or causal connections to others in the same scene*' (Edelman's italics. 1994, 118). In this
way, events that have been significant to the animal's learning in the past
can be related to new events, even if those events are not causally related,
that is:

> the salience of an event is determined not only by its position and
> energy in the physical world but also by the relative value it has been
> accorded in the past history of the individual animal as a result of
> learning.
>
> (1994, 118)

The result of this repeated interaction of the two systems of nervous
organization is primary consciousness (1994, 120). In notes to a figure
(numbered 11–1), Edelman summarizes his model of primary consciousness thus:

> Past signals related to value (set by internal control systems) and
> categorized signals from the outside world are correlated and lead to
> memory in conceptual areas ... This memory, which is capable of
> conceptual categorization, is linked by re-entrant paths to current
> perceptual categorization of world signals ... This results in primary
> consciousness. When it occurs through many modalities (sight,
> touch, and so forth) primary consciousness is of a 'scene' made up of
> objects and events, some of which are not causally connected. An
> animal with primary consciousness can nonetheless connect these
> objects and events through memory via its previous value-laden
> experience.
>
> (1994, 120)

Primary consciousness is necessary for the evolution of Edelman's second
kind of consciousness, **higher-order consciousness**, that which is associated with human experience. His explanation of the difference between
the two states is given in temporal terms: he refers to primary consciousness as 'the remembered present', one lacking the temporal sense that
gives rise to human selfhood:

> [Primary consciousness] is limited to a small memorial interval
> around a time that I call the present. It lacks an explicit *notion* or a
> concept of a personal self, and it does not afford the ability to model
> the past or the future as part of a correlated scene.
>
> (1994, 122)

Edelman illustrates primary consciousness with a picturesque comparison:

> An animal with primary consciousness sees the room the way a beam of light illuminates it. Only that which is in the beam is explicitly in the remembered present; all else is darkness.
>
> (1994, 122)

In Edelman, the momentary experience of primary consciousness is one humans share with all conscious animals, but from this primary consciousness evolved the higher-order consciousness of the human brain, in which time before and time after are understood.

In summary, 'an animal with primary consciousness alone is strongly tied to the succession of events in real time' (1994, 125). It is capable of learning and so living in a 'remembered present', but it lacks a 'symbolic memory', that is a memory for symbols and their associated meanings. Higher-order consciousness 'requires the continued operation of the structures serving primary consciousness', but to go beyond this remembered present 'new forms of symbolic memory and new systems serving social communication and transmission' must evolve for the animal/ human (Edelman acknowledges the chimpanzee may share some of the features of higher consciousness). With a symbolic memory, the animal/ human with higher-order consciousness has 'the ability to construct a socially based self-hood and to model the world in terms of the past and the future' (1994, 125). With higher-order consciousness comes self-awareness, that is the animal/human is 'conscious of being conscious' (1994, 131). 'In its most developed form', Edelman concludes, 'this means the evolutionary acquisition of the capability for language' (1994, 125).

The linguist M.A.K. Halliday (1925–2018) refers approvingly to Edelman's work (see, for example, Halliday 2003, 390–397), seeing parallels with his own account of language development. For the latter, Halliday describes three temporal perspectives: that of phylogenesis, the development of language in the human species, that of ontogenesis, the development of language in the individual human child, and that of logogenesis, in the unfolding of an individual text. In the following explanation, Halliday refers to the 'instantiation' effect, which he previously illustrated by the relation of 'weather' and 'climate':

> I myself am aware of various changes that have taken place in my own grammar of English during my adult lifetime – including three or four within the verbal group, starting (and perhaps remaining) as changes in relative frequency but still restructuring the system in subtle and significant ways. This is the 'instantiation' effect referred to earlier whereby each instance (which means, in this context, each utterance received by and produced by the individual) perturbs the

probabilities of the system: rather as each day's weather perturbs the probabilities of the climate system, except that in a semiotic system, as opposed to a physical one, this effect takes place in three time dimensions – three 'histories' at once, the **social-semiotic process** ('the language' as observed from a distance), the **individual brain** (the neuronal group networks), and the **text** ('the language' as observed from close at hand).

(Halliday 2003, 411)

Phylogenetically, in Edelman's account, the first important development is 'the assumption of bipedal posture by hominids' (1994, 126); walking upright is followed by changes in the 'basicranial structure of the skull':

[This enabled] the evolution of a uniquely human piece of anatomy, the supralaryngeal tract or space ... As part of this evolutionary development, the vocal folds emerged and the tongue, palate, and teeth were selected to allow fuller control of air flow over the vocal cords, which in turn allowed the production of coarticulated sounds, the phonemes.

(1994, 126)

Edelman describes the evolution of the brain which accompanies, or follows, these changes:

special cerebral cortical regions emerged on the left side, that are now known as Broca's and Wernicke's areas. These cortical regions linked acoustic, motor, and conceptual areas of the brain by re-entrant connections. Through these connections, Broca's and Wernicke's areas served to coordinate the production and categorization of speech. Most importantly, they provided a system for the development of a new kind of memory capable of recategorizing phonemes (the basic units of speech) as well as their order.

(1994, 127)

While Edelman points to the correlation of biological evolution and language development in the species (phylogenesis), Halliday describes the ontogenetic correlation of moving (material action) and meaning (semiotic action) in the development of the individual child. Learning to mean in the adult mother tongue (the higher-order semiotic system) is correlated with the child's walking upright, but before that the child is learning to mean in developing complexity as s/he cries, reaches and grasps, rolls over, sits up and crawls. Each physical accomplishment becomes associated with increased functional, that is meaningful, expression, with the child developing its own mono-functional protolanguage before its eventual move into the multifunctional adult language (see the discussion of 'metafunctions' in Chapter 5). Halliday describes these complex develop-ments in detail in his book *Learning How to Mean – Explorations in the Development of Language* (1975).

Both Halliday and Edelman are in agreement: linguists must abandon 'any notion of a genetically programmed language acquisition device' (Edelman 1994, 126). Rather, it is necessary to account for speech 'in epigenetic as well as genetic terms'. In terminology, Halliday rejects the word 'acquisition', as if of something externally packaged, speaking instead of the child 'learning how to mean', an internalized activity (1975, 1–4). So, using Halliday's phrasing to describe Edelman and Halliday's agreement: the evolved biological capability (the genetic capability) of a human child is its potential for learning language. However, the child's learning 'how to mean' emerges epigenetically in human interaction.[1]

J.T. Fraser (1923–2010), a renowned scholar of time (his work is the principal topic of Chapter 3), acknowledges the work of Edelman and his Neurosciences Research Institute in studying the evolution of the human brain 'as the most complex system known' (Fraser 2007, 2). Edelman's neurobiological perspective for human consciousness (both primary and higher-order consciousness) yields two types of temporalities for the dual nervous systems of the brain, and Fraser devises terms for this duality, *time felt* and *time understood*. The first phrase, *time felt*, refers to the temporal experience of primary consciousness. *Time felt* is quintessentially personal: in Fraser's words: 'We can write volumes about pain, love making or the experience of time's passage, but the experiences themselves remain of the character of personal knowledge' (2007, 262). This is the evolutionarily earlier experience of time which humans share with all conscious animals. As already described in Edelman's account, the temporal experience aris-ing from the inter-relation of the limbic-brain system and thalamocortical systems is complex, that is multi-dimensional. (For studies relating time and consciousness, on different perceptions of time by individuals, and on research examining how bodily processes, especially the heartbeat, may give us an internal sense of 'felt time', see Wittmann 2016.)

In contrast to *time felt* of the older levels of the brain, Fraser uses *time understood* of the temporal dimensions of the evolved level of higher-order human consciousness. Like Edelman, Fraser recognizes the centrality of human language to human consciousness, and hence to time understood. He writes: 'The tasks of the new regions of the brain are those of speech and associative functions. … [time understood] includes our awareness of our aging and eventual death, as well as an appreciation of societies and cultures' (2007, 262). And again: 'Only for the uniquely human level of the brain does time possess open horizons of past and future, populated by long-term individual intentions and memories' (2007, 261). In the time understood of higher-order consciousness, remembered events past, and imagined or predicted events future, can be brought into present awareness.

As many a narrative of human experience tries to tell us, the human consciousness of that experience is inherently conflicted. As primary consciousness continues to underwrite higher-order consciousness, an individual human experiences both time felt, in the temporalities of her/his bodily systems, and time understood, in the symbolic configurations of language. As Augustine's knowing and not knowing acknowledged, time felt and time understood cannot be simply reconciled. In Fraser's words:

> the human experience of time, in its everyday sense, is a balancing act between these two extremes … It is a permanent call for watchfulness to protect our integrity as individuals, such as by maintaining the conflict between time felt and time understood, without becoming unthinking zombies or abstract heads unfit to survive.
>
> (2007, 264)

We have now reached a partial answer to Augustine's question or rather his dual response. When Augustine does not have to communicate his knowledge of time to another, there is no problem. His primary consciousness 'knows' time felt directly. However, he does not know time understood directly, though his higher-order consciousness, with the use of language, enables him to talk about temporal matters with others ('certainly we understand when we speak of it; we understand also when we hear it spoken of by another'). But in the very asking 'what is time?', the one who inquires has silenced Augustine. The word 'time' is a symbol in language; what does it mean to 'explain' that symbol? As the next chapter elaborates, the very language used to pose the question ('what is time?') makes it impossible for Augustine to 'know' an answer.

Note

1 Epigenetics literally means 'above' or 'on top of' genetics. 'In its modern sense, epigenetics is the term used to describe inheritance by mechanisms other than through the DNA sequence of genes. It can apply to characteristics passed from a cell to its daughter cells in cell division and to traits of a whole organism. It works through chemical tags added to chromosomes that in effect switch genes on or off' (Cowell, n.d.). Edelman includes, for example, the complex behaviours of bird song, which have both genetic and epigenetic components (1994, 46–47).

References

Augustine, Saint. n.d. *Confessions*, trans. J. G. Pilkington. Logos Virtual Library. Accessed 18 February 2019. www.logoslibrary.org/augustine/confessions/1114.html
Augustine, Saint. 2014. *Confessions*. Loeb Classical Library. Cambridge, MA: Harvard University Press.

Cowell, Ian. (n.d.) 'Epigenetics – It's Not Just Genes That Made Us'. Written for the British Society for Cell Biology. Accessed 13 March 2019. https://bscb.org/learning-resources/softcell-e-learning/epigenetics-its-not-just-genes-that-make-us/

Edelman, Gerald. 1994 [1992]. *Bright Air, Brilliant Fire: On the Matter of the Mind*. London: Penguin Books.

Fraser, J.T. 2007. *Time and Time Again, Reports from a Boundary of the Universe*. Leiden and Boston: Brill.

James, William. 1892. 'The Stream of Consciousness'. In *Psychology: Briefer Course*, Chapter 11. London: Macmillan & Co. Reproduced by The Project Gutenberg, released 4 August 2017. www.gutenberg.org/files/55262/55262-h/55262-h.htm

Halliday, M.A.K. 1975. *Learning How to Mean – Explorations in the Development of Language*. London: Edward Arnold.

Halliday, M.A.K. 2003. *On Language and Linguistics*. Volume 3 in the Collected Works of M.A.K. Halliday, ed. Jonathan J. Webster. London and New York: Continuum.

Manning, Liliann, Daniel Cassel, and Jean-Christophe Cassel. 2013. 'St. Augustine's Reflections on Memory and Time and the Current Concept of Subjective Time in Mental Time Travel'. *Behavioral Sciences* (Basel) 3 (2): pp. 232–243. Published online 2013 April 25. https://doi.org/10.3390/bs3020232

Tononi, Giulio. 2014. 'Gerald M. Edelman (1929–2014): A Great Biologist Made Fundamental Discoveries and Conceived a Selectionist Theory of the Brain'. *Science* 344(6191): pp. 1457–1457. www.jstor.org/stable/24744756

Wittmann, M. 2016. *Felt Time, The Psychology of How We Perceive Time*, trans. Erik Butler. Cambridge, MA and London: The MIT Press.

2 'Spatialization' and scientific discourse, taking time out of language

Benjamin Whorf's 'configuration of experience' and M.A.K. Halliday's 'grammatical metaphor'

As Edelman's account of the brain makes clear, to the extent that 'time' can be talked of in language, it will be 'time understood', as Fraser put it. This immediately raises the question: how do languages talk of time? And conversely – because it will develop as a feature of scientific discourse – how can language be used so as to efface talk of time? The latter question is primarily focused on in this chapter, with particular reference to the work of Benjamin Whorf on language difference and of M.A.K. Halliday on grammatical metaphor. First, however, it is helpful to describe the foundational observations given by John Ellis in his book *Language, Thought, and Logic*[1] (1993), for these observations emerge as relevant to the work of both Whorf and Halliday.

Ellis begins with a masterly overview of work in different disciplines on the theory of language. He describes the confusion among and between these many studies, before going on to identify what he sees as 'virtually universal' in such theorizing: three initial 'missteps'. The first misstep – and 'perhaps' the most important is 'the assumption that the purpose of language is communication', an assumption that immediately 'misdirects' the development of subsequent theorizing about language (1993, 15):

> Nothing seems more reasonable than the assumption that the purpose of language is communication. But there is a subtle trap here: granted a particular act of language use may result in communication between two people, but much must have happened before they could get that far. Suppose that the two were without a language; do they lack simply the means of communicating or something more? Surely the latter: without a language they barely have anything to communicate.
>
> (1993, 17)

Ellis can now propose a different direction for the study of language:

> Because the really distinctive features of language lie in such things as the creation of the possibility of information and the implicit

DOI: 10.4324/b23121-2

decisions as to what will count as information, linguistic theory
should begin with them ...

(1993, 18)

And this focus leads him to what he judges 'the most central issue in linguistic theory: categorization':

> Categorization, not syntax, is the most basic aspect of language, and
> it is a process that must be understood correctly if anything else
> (including syntax) is to be understood, and categorization, not com-
> munication, is the most important function of language, one that is
> prior to all others.

(1993, 27)

Ellis's book is published by a university press in the United States; the
repetition of 'syntax' in the previous quote points to the approach to
linguistic study of which he is most critical, that of (as he calls it) the MIT
tradition associated with Noam Chomsky and the development of generative grammar. Ellis explicitly associates this tradition with his second
'initial misstep': the assumption that one should begin with simple cases
and generalize from them to derive principles that can 'be used to break
down the hard cases', as in beginning with syntactic analysis because it is
easier to 'systematize' syntactic patterns than semantic ones (1993, 21).
Ellis associates this misstep with a mistaken understanding of scientific
method: science does not necessarily build on what is known, from easy
to difficult cases, but 'new knowledge may profoundly change our understanding of old knowledge'. He writes plainly: 'Generative grammar was
founded, therefore, not on scientific method, but on a then popular delu-
sion about science that had been especially common among humanists'
(1993, 22).

The third and last misstep Ellis identifies is 'the assumption that linguistic categories group like things together' (1993, 24). Now turning
from the three missteps he has identified, Ellis can begin 'stepping' in a
new direction: 'we grasp the essence of the process of categorization only
when we see it as the grouping together of things that are not the same in
order that they will count as the same' (1993, 25).

For Ellis, 'the central task of linguistics' is 'surely never to concern less
than the nature and function of language' (1993, 23), and he finds categorization central to this central task, calling his Chapter 3, 'The Heart of
Language: Categorization'. I paraphrase from this chapter: processes of
categorization and abstraction must have gone on before the individual
categories of a particular language can arise; the facts of experience are
infinitely variable (no two situations are alike): to say something about a
situation is to place it among other possible situations, which requires a
system of categories; language functions as the instrument of human

knowledge and communication because it simplifies the complexity of experience; what is communicated is not the facts of the situation but its place within the categories of the particular language. Ellis speaks of 'the imposition of equivalence', the reduction of the variety of experience so that for speakers of a language, all structures categorized in a certain way are treated 'as if there was no difference between them'. The source of the principles of equivalence and difference is the purposes of the speakers, so that equivalence is a functional principle:

> [L]inguistic categories are primarily the reflection of the collective purposes of the speakers of a language rather than direct reflections of the structure of the world.
>
> (Ellis 1993, 34)

As discussed in Chapter 1, Edelman also described a 'categorization' process. Is this an accident of word choice or can Ellis' categorization be linked to that described by Edelman? (Edelman does not appear in Ellis' *Bibliography*.) Edelman writes of two processes of categorization, associated with the two evolutionary levels of consciousness in the human species. In primary consciousness, the thalamocortical nervous system enabled the categorization of events; the cortical appendages enabled the memory of succession in spatial and temporal experience. In higher-order consciousness, the evolution of new areas in the brain (the Broca's and Wernicke's areas) enabled the production and categorization of speech, including a new kind of memory that could recategorize phonemes and remember their order (Edelman 1994, 127). We recall that, in the (transcribed) account of his basic structuralist model, Ferdinand de Saussure described language as composed of both signification and value: for his linguistic sign, signification refers to the arbitrary association of sound-image (signifier) and meaning (signified); value refers to the relation of signifier to signifier, and signified to signified. Thus, paradigmatically, the signifiers of a particular language (its phonemes) contrast in sound-image with each other; the signifieds (meanings) contrast in meaning with each other (de Saussure 1959, 114–115; Thibault 1997, 163–186). The importance of categorization – from both primary and higher-order consciousness – as a pre-condition of these developments is evident.

Ellis praises four scholars as moving away from the axiomatic missteps he has described (1993, 20). Three, Saussure, Peirce and Wittgenstein, he sees as partially but incompletely successful, but the fourth, Benjamin Whorf, he praises most, devoting a later chapter to Whorf's defence (1993, 55–65).

In reviewing Ellis' book, M.A.K. Halliday in turn praises Ellis' insight into the systemic categorization of language and its functional motivation, and his sympathetic reading of Whorf's work (the review is first published in *Functions of Language* 2.2 (1995, 249–267) and reprinted as Chapter 11 in Halliday 2003). At the same time, Halliday regrets that Ellis was not familiar with systemic functional linguistics (SFL), the theory associated with Halliday's own work and one that is compatible with Ellis' 'new direction' for the theory of language. That SFL is called 'functional' draws attention to a significant divergence in linguistic theorizing, and ironically a divergence that may be less familiar to some English-speaking linguists, particularly those in the United States. In a brief historical account elsewhere, Halliday describes two perspectives on the study of language, the 'logical-philosophical' and the 'ethnographic-descriptive'. 'They are not really impossible to reconcile with one another', he writes, '[b]ut from time to time in the history of linguistics they drift exaggeratedly apart … and this is what happened in the mid-twentieth century, leading to an almost total breakdown of communication between the two' (Halliday 1984, 4–5). Philosophical grammar tries to explain the system of language without regard to its use, to study the code in isolation from behaviour;[2] this perspective has been dominant in the United States, most famously with the work of Chomsky on 'competence'. Effectively a parallel discipline of 'pragmatics' had to be established for the study of 'performance', language in use, but Halliday suggests that both logical-philosophical linguistics and its associated pragmatics are constrained by the 'organizing concept of rule':

> The code is represented in terms of rules of grammar; and where the focus shifts on to behaviour, the rule leaps over the gap and we have rules of interpretation and rules of use.
>
> (Halliday 1984, 5)

In contrast, ethnographic theories tend to interpret language as a resource. Halliday cites as modern examples the work of 'Boas and Sapir, the Prague School, Malinowki and Firth, and in the glossematics theories of Hjelmslev and Uldall' (1984, 4). It is notable that these scholars are for the most part European, their publications perhaps less accessible to the more monolingual world of native English-speakers. Rather than set up an opposition between the system and its use, these theories attempt to bring code and behaviour together. The code is 'a potential for behaviour'; behaviour is an instance, an 'actualization', of that potential. A consequence of this ethnographic perspective for Halliday's systemic linguistic theory is its view of 'natural' grammar: that '[t]he form of the code [the resource for behaviour] has been determined in the course of linguistic evolution by the patterns of its use, so that the system is organized internally on a functional basis' (Halliday 1984, 7). This is eminently compatible with Ellis' theorizing: that the principle of equivalence is a functional principle; in his words already quoted: '[L]inguistic categories are primarily the reflection of the collective purposes of the speakers of a language rather than direct reflections of the structure of the world' (Ellis 1993, 34).

Both Ellis and Halliday describe approvingly the 1930s work of Whorf, whose writing has been misrepresented – or at least not understood – when read in the context of the formal (Chomskian) linguistics, which Ellis criticizes and which Halliday does not pursue. To his chapter on Whorf's work (Chapter 5), Ellis appends 36 endnotes, many of which are devoted to excoriating criticism of previous scholarly comments and assumptions about Whorf (Ellis, 1993, 138–142). If, on the other hand, Whorf's work is read in the context of Edelman's description of human consciousness and Halliday's functional theory of language, his account is illuminating. Accordingly, from here on this chapter interweaves the work of Halliday and Whorf.

Benjamin Lee Whorf (1897–1941) died before he could complete the publication of his linguistic work. In 1956, John B. Carroll edited a 'Selected Writings of Benjamin Lee Whorf', under the title *Language, Thought, and Reality*. It is on this selection that many commentaries have been based, together with the so-called 'Sapir-Whorf Hypothesis', a straw man for casual dismissal (for example, by Gomel, 2014, 4, in an otherwise engaging discussion). In 1996, Penny Lee published the monograph, *The Whorf Theory Complex, A Critical Reconstruction*, and in a section titled 'Misread, Unread and Superficially Treated' (1996, 14–23), she refers to several variously egregious dismissals of Whorf.[3] In her 'critical reconstruction', Lee exhaustively re-examines Whorf's evidence and arguments. Most significantly, as an appendix (1996, 251–280), Lee publishes for the first time what she labels 'The Yale Report', a '17 page handwritten draft document, together with nine finalized typed pages which comprise a little more than the first seven of the draft' (1996, 250 fn 1). The second edition of *Language, Thought, and Reality* also includes the 'Yale Report', again as an appendix, with Lee's annotations as footnotes (Whorf 2012, 345–376). In the comments below, I make most use of this late published text, titled, in Whorf's original, 'Report on Linguistic Research in the Department of Anthropology of Yale University for the Term Sept. 1937 – June 1938'. (The report says, 'By B. L. Whorf and G.L. Trager', but, in Tragers' absence in Europe, 'was conceived and undertaken' by Whorf; Lee 1996, 253.) Whorf's study of American Indian languages, like Halliday's experience in studying and teaching Mandarin Chinese (Halliday 2009; Halliday and Matthiessen 1999, 297–319) – that is, the experience of a language outside the Indo-European family – considerably enlarged his thinking about the possibilities of language.

Halliday (1925–2018) has left us many published books and papers. The latter, edited by Jonathan Webster, are gathered in the 11 volumes of Halliday's *Collected Works*, published from 2002 to 2018 (volumes 3, 5 and 8 are referenced for this chapter). The primary reference for the grammar of systemic functional theory, *Introduction to Functional Grammar*, was published in first (1985) and second (1994) editions by

Halliday alone, and in the third (2004a) and fourth (2014) editions with Christian Matthiessen.

In a 1987 paper, 'Language and the Order of Nature', Halliday tries, as he puts it, 'to enumerate some features of natural language, as embodied in our everyday informal discourse from earliest childhood, that constitute for us a theory of reality' (2003, 127–128).

Here he sets out six general terms for such features, suggesting that, though 'each language presents its own particular mix', the following features are 'common to all languages':

- Clausal structures
- Projection
- Expansion
- Transitivity
  i.   different types of process
  ii. two models of processes, transitive and ergative
- Tense and Aspect.

The first feature, clausal structures, refers to the organization of meanings as 'wording'. Halliday describes the clause as:

> the gateway through which meanings are brought together and realized in ordinary grammar ... the clause nucleus is a happening (Process + Medium ...). So natural languages represent reality as what happens, not as what exists; things are defined as contingencies of the flow.
>
> (2003, 127)

In a later paper (1989), Halliday associates this 'ordinary grammar' with ontogenesis ('children learn first to talk in clauses'). He also correlates it with phylogenesis (the development of a language) but with more specific focus: 'In English, and other languages of Europe, the oldest pattern is the clausal one: and it is based on certain principles of wording'. He lists these principles as:

1. processes (actions, events, mental processes, relations) are expressed by verbs;
2. participants (people, animals, concrete and abstract objects that take part in processes) are expressed by nouns;
3. circumstances (time, place, manner, cause, condition) are expressed by adverbs and by prepositional phrases;
4. relations between one process and another are expressed by conjunctions.

(Halliday 2004b, 173)

As Halliday acknowledges, these correlations of meaning and grammar are those assumed to be 'natural' in the Indo-European family of languages. With similar insight 50 years previously, Whorf wrote of the non-Indo-European languages he had studied:

> It is impossible to break up the flow of events in a non-arbitrary manner into 'subject', 'actor', 'predicate', etc, as if there existed external realities of this sort. We, to be sure, may analyse a phenomenon as 'boy runs', but another l[angua]ge is capable of analysing it 'run manifests as boy'.
>
> (Lee 1996, 259; Whorf 2012, 354)

In the 'Yale Report', Whorf classifies the discipline he is describing as 'Configurative Linguistics'. Under a subtitle, 'The configuration of experience as seen in language', he discusses the 'segmentation of experience', and he appears to understand this phrase in a way similar to Ellis' use of the word 'categorization'. Whorf writes (I expand some of his contractions):

> The flux of experience may be classified and 'chopped up' differently by different languages: this is most readily seen by going outside of Indo-European, American Indian languages providing some of the greatest contrasts. These differences in 'segmentation' – in what is treated as 'one' aspect, phenomenon, substance or quasi-whole, isolated out of the mass of presentation and fitted together with other such segmentation to make the mosaic representation of life which the language and culture takes for granted – these differences may apply not only to the large outlines of the cosmic picture …, where they are at their most subtle and hard to appreciate, but also in countless small matters of detail, where they are much more easily seen.
>
> (Lee 1996, 261; Whorf 2012, 356)

This is reminiscent of Charles Sanders Peirce's semiotics in his account of objectivity. Peirce's triadic model of signification has primary sign (roughly comparable to Saussure's signifier) referring to secondary object and signifying tertiary interpretant (roughly Saussure's signified). Unlike Saussure's dyadic sign of sound-image and concept, in Peirce's triadic model the subjective interpretant is linked to the objective world of the interpreter, that is to the interpreter's experience of the world. But this semiotic objectivity is not simply equivalent to an external objectivity (Deely 1990, 54–55). The segmentation of a language does not apply directly, as Whorf put it, 'to the conformation of reality itself', though to monolingual native speakers of a particular language, reality can appear to be so conformed. Although Saussure's sign was of internal

consciousness, a signifying sound-image associated with an idea or concept, his understanding of *la langue* implied a recognition similar to
Peirce's semiotic objectivity. Thus, in *Re-reading Saussure*, Paul Thibault
can quote from Saussure's published *Course in General Linguistics*,
'There are no pre-established ideas, and nothing is distinct before the
appearance of the language system'. Thibault continues (making a reference to Edelman's work, as discussed in Chapter 1):

> That is, Saussure rejects the assumption that the categories of the
> world are pre-specified, and that the organism is pre-programmed to
> respond to these. Semiotically, the individual selectively attends to an
> open-ended environment and further elaborates this through the
> available social-semiological resource systems.
>
> (Thibault 1997, 171)

For systemic functional theory, Halliday and co-author Christian
Matthiessen foreground this non-intuitive direction of language and
experience when they entitle one publication, *The Construal of Experience
through Meaning* (1999).

Whorf begins his analysis of non-Indo-European languages with linguistic configurations that sound familiar (nouns, verbs) but points out
that one cannot assume a common meaning for these terms:

> The task of formal grammar ends when the analysis of all linguistic
> configurations is completed, but the characteristics of a language are
> by no means fully accounted for then. It still remains to indicate the
> type of experience and kinds of referents referred to by different
> grammatical classes, for languages may here differ widely. Our [that
> is Indo-European] ordinary ways of classifying referents, as being
> 'things', 'objects', 'actions', 'states' etc. are quite unsuitable for this
> work, as they are themselves names for partitionings of experience
> resulting after it has been grammatically classed, and circular defini-
> tions or mere confusion will result from applying them as if they
> referred to the conformation of reality itself.
>
> (Lee 1996, 259; Whorf 2012, 354)

Looking for a 'non-linguistic' (that is, not inherently Indo-European) way
of talking about language, Whorf became impressed by the theorizing of
'visual perception' in early twentieth century Gestalt psychology:

> The basic principle is the contrast of figure and ground, involving the
> differing degrees of organization, stability, and fixity in figures of out-
> lines of all sorts. ... [One can consider] whether the referent <u>has an
> outline</u> or has not, and next, how much of an outline, a definite or a

vague outline, a fluctuating or a stable outline, a quality of ground or field as more important than outline, ...

(Lee 1996, 259–260; Whorf 2012, 355)

He gives examples in English, and then in several American Indian languages, finishing with Hopi.

Hopi is indeed rich in highly figured verbs, with no counterpart in English. If the experience is also momentary or fluctuating it <u>must</u> be a verb reference, no matter how outlinish, unlike English; hence our nouns 'wave', flash', 'blow' (striking), 'splash', 'lightning', 'meteor' cannot be translated by nouns in Hopi, but the same experiences are there denoted by verbs. This pattern even prohibits the reifying or 'nounizing' of such momentarily outlined experiences by roundabout linguistic devices such as participles: 'shooting star' is ruled out in favour of 'star moves', 'sunset' in favour of 'sun sets' (literally, 'sun interiorizes'), 'running dog' is permissible only when used like a dependent relative clause, and 'it is a running dog' is ruled out in favour of 'a dog runs'.

(Lee 1996, 260; Whorf 2012, 356)

In a paper written in 1939 for a more general audience, 'The Relation of Habitual Thought and Behavior to Language' (possibly the best known of Whorf's writings), Whorf describes the nominalization of temporal cycles in (what he refers to as) SAE, 'Standard Average European':

Such terms as 'summer, winter, September, morning, noon, sunset' are with us nouns, and have little formal linguistic difference from other nouns. They can be subjects or objects, and we say 'at sunset' or 'in winter' just as we say 'at a corner' or 'in an orchard'. They are pluralized and numerated like nouns of physical objects ...

(Whorf 2012, 183)

In contrast, in Hopi, Whorf writes:

all phase terms, like 'summer, morning,' etc., are not nouns but a kind of adverb, to use the nearest SAE analogy. They are a formal part of speech by themselves, distinct from nouns, verbs, and even other Hopi 'adverbs'. ... It means 'when it is morning' or 'while morning-phase is occurring.' These 'temporals' are not used as subjects or objects, or at all like nouns. One does not say 'it's a hot summer' or 'summer is hot'; summer is not hot, summer is only WHEN conditions are hot, WHEN heat occurs.

(Whorf 2012, 184)

Thus, for Hopi, and unlike for SAE, Whorf can argue that 'there is no objectification' of temporal meanings:

> Nothing is suggested about time except the perceptual 'getting later' of it. And so there is no basis here for a formless item answering to our 'time'.
>
> (Whorf 2012, 184)

In the Foreword to the second edition of Whorf's writings (Whorf 2012), Stephen Levinson notes that Malotki, in 1983, published a lengthy study on the temporal concepts in Hopi grammar and texts, arguing that Whorf's claims were 'empirically wrong in most details'. Levinson comments that 'Whorf, it seems, was definitely wrong about the lack of spatial metaphors for time in Hopi', but he adds an interesting parenthesis, '(although we must remember that Whorf was working a half century earlier, when Hopi was less influenced by English)' (Whorf 2012, xii). Levinson adds that Malotki does, however, support some of Whorf's comments on words of temporal meaning: he 'admits' that the word for *day* is 'quite remarkable'. It is 'both nominal and verbal'. But Whorf had put such words in a special class, as described above – and it is used with ordinal numbers, not cardinal, which, as Whorf pointed out, implies that, in Hopi, unlike SAE, a temporal *day* is not configured as a thing like a spatial *bottle* that can be grouped and counted (*three bottles*), but as a succession of the same (*the third day*) (Whorf 2012, 180).

Whorf was misinterpreted by those who did not understand his 'configurative linguistics', or perhaps more simply by those who conflate meaning and grammar. He did not suggest the Hopi had no temporal understanding. He did assert that their language did not objectify/reify that understanding in the grammatical word class of a noun – the word class that to speakers of SAE signifies a 'thing'. (See Panos Athanasopoulos et al. 2017 for the study of 'spatio-temporal metaphors' in many different cultural contexts.) To explore just how SAE languages have configured experience through such nominalization I return to the writing of M.A.K. Halliday.

In a 1995 paper, 'Language and the Reshaping of Human Experience', Halliday takes the ontogenetic perspective (Halliday 2004b, 7–23). He describes the child moving into the adult language through three stages of development: first, from protolanguage (the precursor to the mother tongue) to generalization in the pre-school child (for example, from proper to common nouns), second, to non-sensory abstraction in the primary school ('they can construe entities that have no perceptual correlate, like *worth* and *due* and *habit* and *intend* and *price*'), as in learning to write with abstract symbols, and third to grammatical metaphor as encountered in the secondary school disciplines, where the wording of 'ordinary grammar' is reworded:

> [T]his later phase, that of technical knowledge, the discourse of the specialized disciplines, depends on metaphor: metaphor in the grammatical sense, the wholesale recasting of the relationship between the grammar and the semantics. Instead of:

> *If a fire burns more intensely it gives off more smoke*

> we now say

> *The intensity has a profound effect on smoke injection*
> (Halliday 2004b, 19)

From the phylogenetic perspective (the development of a language), Halliday suggests that grammatical metaphor 'started, or at least first reached a significant scale, with nominalization: decoupling "qualities" and "processes" from their congruent realizations as adjectives and verbs and recoupling both these meanings with nouns'. He notes that this recoupling between grammatical classes was happening already in the Bronze and Early Iron Ages, in the classical languages of Chinese, Greek and Sanskrit (Halliday 2004b, xvi).

From my own observation, Old English (English before c. 1100 CE) added the suffix -th (in modern spelling), sometimes with vowel stem change, to translate many adjectives to nouns. These survive into Modern English as, for example, long/length; true/truth; deep/depth; whole/health, or with transfer of -th to t, high/height. Each nominalization expresses a complex meaning: the semantic junction of the quality meaning of the adjective and the nominal meaning of 'entity' or 'thing'. The suffix -ness was similarly used (happy/happiness, heavy/heaviness, light/lightness), though most such formations are first recorded in Middle English. There is some evidence of Old English verb to noun relation with -th/-t, as survives in the Modern English verb *see* and noun *sight* (the junction of process meaning and the meaning 'entity' or 'thing'), but generally it is in Middle English that verb to noun translation proliferates, deriving its morphology from the romance languages (an accelerating development from the so-called twelfth century renaissance on). Thus, first recorded about 1275 CE, the English verb *move* comes from Anglo-Norman *mover*, while the noun *motion* ('partly a borrowing from French, partly a borrowing from Latin') is recorded with the meaning 'agitation or disturbance of a physical substance (esp. of water)' by 1398 (OED Online 2021).

In 'everyday discourse', as Halliday describes it, each clause is centred on a verb; but when the meaning of the verb is translated into a noun, as with grammatical metaphor, wordings which were sequences of clauses turn into nominal groups, which can now function as elements of a single clause. In his historical study of the language of science, Halliday describes the 'semogenic power' of this rewording:

> The birth of science ... is realized semiotically by the birth of grammatical metaphor ... [This rewording] construes these phenomena as if they were **things**. The prototypical meaning of a noun is an object ... Where the everyday 'mother tongue' of commonsense knowledge construes reality as a balanced tension between things and processes, the elaborated register of scientific knowledge reconstrues it as an edifice of things. It holds reality still, to be kept under observation and experimented with; and in so doing, interprets it not as changing with time (as the grammar of clauses interprets it) but as persisting – or rather persistence – through time, which is the mode of being of a noun.
>
> (Halliday 2004b, 216–217)

Recall Ellis' words: 'linguistic categories reduce an infinite world of experience to a finite and thus make knowledge possible' (Ellis 1993, 40). The categories of natural grammar still allow a more complex world of temporal experience, but nominalization, thing-making, reduces that world for the functional purpose of increasing scientific knowledge. As Halliday puts it, 'Symbolically, this kind of discourse is holding the world still, making it noun-like (stable in time) while it is observed, experimented with, measured and reasoned about' (2004b, 21). By the twentieth century to do science was to talk the language of science.

So – grammatical metaphor leaches temporality from meaning. The spacetime reality of human experience, in which things are understood as '(spatial) contingencies of the (temporal) flow' is reconfigured as a spatial reality in which things exist. I refer to this as 'spatialization'.

Halliday has described the sequential emergence of spatialization in terms of both phylogenesis (the development of the language) and ontogenesis (the development of the individual). In Halliday's principles of wording for 'natural language', the second principle states that participants are expressed by nouns. Four types of participant are listed: 'people, animals, concrete and abstract objects that take part in processes', and of these the first three types of participants occupy external three-dimensional space but the fourth – abstract objects – emerges in the second stage of child development, that of abstraction. By the third stage of child development, that of grammatical metaphor, any meaning can be construed as spatial. It has been suggested – for example, by David Olson (1994, 238–239) – that, phylogenetically, in the cultural change from orality to literacy, the external recognition of language in writing lead to the postulation of 'mind' as the internal 'mental space' where 'ideas' are held. (Remember James: in English we have to say 'thought goes on' though he'd prefer 'it[consciousness] thinks'.1892).

Grammatical metaphor is not, however, just a matter of nominalization. Rather, the drift of semantic function that Halliday has described for grammatical metaphor, and which I call spatialization, is a drift towards 'thingness', a 'move towards the concrete' (Halliday 2004b, 77). This drift is made possible because of the stratified nature of language (the SFL dimension of stratification is discussed more fully in Chapter 5). Semiotically, language is not a simple relation of expression (speech or writing) to semantics (meaning); between these two levels is the wording, the level of lexicogrammar (grammar and vocabulary). Halliday goes so far as explicitly to relate Edelman's 'higher order [sic] consciousness' to stratification:

> I assume an account of the evolution of human consciousness along the lines worked out by Gerald Edelman (1992); but interpreting his 'higher order consciousness' as consciousness based on grammar – on a stratified semiotic system. (Stratification is the decoupling of grammar from semantics.)
>
> (Halliday 2004b, 118)

The congruent pattern of relationships between the grammar and the semantics is that in which the two levels first co-evolved, phylogenetically and ontogenetically. Table 2.1 describes the congruent relation of particular semantic/meaning functions and the grammatical unit of the class word.

Table 2.2 describes the congruent relation of semantic functions and grammatical units higher in rank than the word (rank scale and the SFL

Table 2.1 Congruent relation: semantic function and grammatical unit word

semantic function	construed by grammatical class
relator (in sequence)	conjunction
minor process (in circumstance)	preposition
process	verb
quality	adjective
entity ('thing')	noun

(Halliday 2004b, 75).

Table 2.2 Congruent relation: semantic function and higher units

semantic function	grammatical realization
sequence	clause nexus
figure	clause
element	group/phrase

(Halliday 2004b, 40).

dimension of structure are discussed in Chapter 5). A clause complex is built up by a chain of tactic relations; in that complex, any one pair of clauses related by interdependency, or 'taxis', is referred to as a clause nexus (Halliday 2014, 441–442).

However, the 'decoupling' of grammar from semantics, illustrated in Figure 2.1, enables the phenomenon of semantic drift, in which a semantic function may be realized, incongruently, by various grammatical structures. Figure 2.1 is reduced from Halliday's original diagram (the numbering refers to his original examples); the drift of grammatical metaphor is to be read from left to right, with the drift lines beginning from the relator in a clause complex, that is, from the clausal structure of 'natural language'. This example shows the drift of the semantic function of a *causal* relation, with its congruent realization as a clause nexus in which the relator meaning is realized by a conjunction ('this happened (**and**) so that happened'), to its maximal incongruent realization as a nominal group with head noun ('**result**').

The drift can be more or less extensive. Grammatical metaphor is not an either/or dichotomy, and some drift may not reach final nominalization as noun. For example, Halliday gives the example of the drift from 'poverty increases' to 'increasing poverty' (Halliday 2004b, 41), a drift of grammatical verb/process meaning to grammatical adjective/quality meaning. The less drift across this continuum, the less spatialization of language.

Chapter 1 began with Augustine of Hippo's questions about the meaning of time and here, at last, Halliday's account of grammatical metaphor may cast further light on that dilemma. Figure 2.2 describes the drift of *temporal* meaning from the sequence of the clause nexus to the static quality and entity of the nominal group.

Relator	Circumstance (10)	Process (9)	Quality (7)	Entity (4)	Modifier
Clause Nexus	Clause		Nominal Group		

(a happened)

so (x happened)

——————————————————————————————→ 4 the result (of happ'g a)

——————————————————————————→ 7 the resultant (happening of x)

——————————————————————→ 9 (happening x) resulted from (happening a)

——————————→ 10 (x happened) as a result of (happening a)

Figure 2.1 Semantic drift: 'decoupling' of grammar and semantics, causal sequence.

Source: (Halliday 2004b, 76–77).

Relator	Circumstance (10)	Process (9)	Quality (7)	Entity (4)	Modifier
Clause Nexus	Clause		Nominal Group		

(a happened)

and then (x happened)

———————————————————————————————→ 4 the time (of happ'g x)

——————————————————————————→ 7 the subsequent (happening of x)

———————————————————→ 9 (happening x) followed (happening a)

——————————→ 10 (x happened) after (happening a)

Figure 2.2 Semantic drift: 'decoupling' of grammar and semantics, temporal sequence.

Source: (based on Halliday 2004b, 76).

It is possible to add a further block to the left of this diagram, that is to the left of 'clause complex'. Here, beyond grammatical structure, we could include the cohesive logical relation between separate sentences in the one text, as in 'A happened. Then b happened'. (The punctuation of clause complexes as sentences is of course a graphic realization of the written mode.) In summary, we can discern a semantic drift of temporal meaning from one grammatical extreme of unrelated clauses/clause complexes to the other extreme of nominal group, with ultimate drift to the head word noun. Halliday uses the phrase 'semantic junction' to describe the meaning function of the word 'heat' in Classical Greek; it is an early technical term from the classical period as 'a quality ["hot"] construed as a thing' (Halliday 2004b, 38). The word 'time' is another such semantic junction, of ancient lineage, although of a relation construed as a thing. (The discussion in this chapter, on 'spatialization of language', has focused on 'time' as the nominalization of the meaning of logical sequence. 'Time' is also understood as duration; the realizations of that meaning are discussed in Chapter 6 on 'temporalization' of language.)

Given the stratification of language that enables this recoupling of word and meaning in grammatical metaphor, it is now clear that Augustine of Hippo needed to answer two questions. When asked 'what is time?' he would have to answer: 'it is a noun'. And if then asked 'but what does it mean?', he might answer 'my understanding of one experience happening after another' – that is, in congruent language it is a clausal relation of sequence, but it is certainly not 'a thing'.

As Halliday notes in various papers, it is unsurprising that the prestige of science and technology in the so-called 'knowledge economy' of developed nations has led to this nominalized discourse being taken up as inherently more impressive in other domains.

Here's a statement from a review of education in Australia – it refers to parents' being involved in education:

> This will be further enhanced through the work currently underway to develop <u>an evidence-informed definition of parent engagement</u>, which will allow for <u>a core set of agreed measures aligned to the definition</u> to be established and used to drive <u>improvements in policies and practice</u>.
>
> (*Sydney Morning Herald*, 7 May 2018, 19)

The nominal results of grammatical metaphor are underlined. You will also note the careful omission of human participants with agency.

Or from a letter by the Attorney-General of the Australian Government:

> The Turnbull government does not consider that there exists any *persuasive evidence* indicating *an insufficiency in the current multi-faceted approach to combating corruption*.
>
> (*The Guardian*, 23 May 2018, www.theguardian.com/au)

Is this language functionally helpful? Halliday comments:

> This sort of discourse has served well for the natural sciences, ... But this sort of synoptic vision is less relevant to other realms of our experience; and it may be positively obstructive in certain contexts, when it becomes a means of obscuring the critical issues and a vehicle for maintaining the *status quo ante* of power.
>
> (Halliday 2004b, 21)

Halliday sees extreme cases of 'obfuscation in the language of military strategy'. Such insight is central to Annabelle Lukin's book-length study, *War and Its Ideologies*, in which Lukin traces the divergent language used to construe 'war' from that used to construe 'violence' (2019).

Ironically, for some scientists, by the early twentieth century the 'spatialization' of meaning in scientific discourse was becoming obsolete, an impediment to construing reality as science was coming to understand it.

In 1908, Hermann Minkovski (Einstein's former teacher) wrote:

> The views of space and time which I wish to lay before you have sprung from the soil of experimental physics, and therein lies their strength. They are radical. Henceforth space by itself, and time by itself, are doomed to fade away into mere shadows, and only a kind of union of the two will preserve an independent reality.
>
> (Kennedy 2003, 80)

Halliday was well aware of these stresses on scientific language, and in the last pages of the last paper in the volume of his collected works on science, he confronts this 'problem and paradox', to use his words. He explains:

> In adapting natural languages to the construction of experimental science, the creators of scientific discourse developed powerful new forms of wording; and these have construed a reality of a particular kind – one that is fixed and determinate, in which objects predominate and processes serve merely to define and classify them. But the direction of physics in C20 has been exactly the opposite: from absolute to relative, from object to process, from determinate to probabilistic, from stability to flow.
>
> (Halliday 2004b, 223)

This, as Halliday points out, is a theorizing of reality much closer to the theory of reality construed by natural language, as he first described it, and so he suggests that 'while still functioning at the technical and abstract level of scientific discourse', the grammar of science needs to move closer to spoken language, 'recasting the nominal mode into a clausal one while developing the verbal group as a technical resource' (Halliday 2004b, 224). Effectively, Halliday is arguing that 'time' be restored to the grammar of scientific discourse.

But what is the meaning of 'time' in scientific discourse? The next chapter explores one model of polyvalent temporalities.

Notes

1 Ellis' title, *Language, Thought, and Logic*, recalls A. J. Ayer's *Language, Truth and Logic* (1952); Ellis criticizes Ayer's theory of language while respecting the central importance Ayer gives to language. Ellis' title also references Benjamin Whorf's late papers, 'Languages and Logic' and 'Language, Mind, and Reality', published in the year of his death, 1941. For the posthumous editions of Whorf's papers, the latter title is paraphrased as *Language, Thought and Reality* (1956, 2012). Ellis devotes a chapter 'Language and Thought', to Whorf's work.

2 In *Re-reading Saussure*, Paul Thibault discusses such focus on 'code' in isolation as a misreading of Saussure's *la langue* (language system) and *parole* (individual language activity): 'the crucial factor in Saussure's view is the role played by the language system. *Langue* is a transindividual social-semiological system. It is not a matter of external sensations or sensory inputs being "associated" with ideas by internal neural activity. ... No association between concept and acoustic image can take place in the absence of a socially shared system of semiological values. That is why Saussure shifts the explanatory basis away from his starting point – the individual act – to the "social fact" of *langue*' (1997, 141).

3 Perhaps the most notable dismissal Lee discusses is that by Steven Pinker in *The Language Instinct* (1994). Lee describes it as a 'diatribe', with errors of

attribution and oversimplification (1996, 19). More recently, Daniel Casasanto demonstrates the logical fallacy in Pinker's argument, in which Pinker equates 'We think in language' (from George Orwell's *1984*) with Whorf's claim, 'Language shapes thought' (2008: 64–66).

References

Athanasoupoulos, Panos, Steven Samuel and Emanuel Byland. 2017. 'The Psychological Reality of Spatio-temporal Metaphors'. In *Studies in Figurative Thought and Language*, edited by Panos Athanasoupoulos. Amsterdam and Philadelphia: John Benjamins.

Ayer, A.J. 1952 [1936] *Language, Truth and Logic*. New York: Dover Publications.

Casasanto, Daniel. 2008. 'Who's Afraid of the Big Bad Whorf? Crosslinguistic Differences in Temporal Language and Thought'. In *Time to Speak: Cognitive and Neural Prerequisites for Time in Language*, edited by Peter Indefrey and Marianne Gullberg. Maiden: Wiley-Blackwell.

Deely, John. 1990. *Basics of Semiotics*. Bloomington and Indianapolis: Indiana University Press.

de Saussure, Ferdinand. 1959 [1916]. *Course in General Linguistics*, translated Wade Baskin, edited by Charles Bally and Albert Sechehaye with Albert Riedlinger. New York: McGraw Hill.

Edelman, Gerard. 1994 [1992]. *Bright Air, Brilliant Fire: On the Matter of the Mind*. London: Penguin Books.

Ellis, John M. 1993. *Language, Thought, and Logic*. Evanston, IL: Northwestern University Press.

Gomel, Elana. 2014. *Narrative Space and Time, Representing Impossible Topologies in Literature*. London and New York: Routledge.

Halliday, M.A.K. 1984. 'Language as Code and Language as Behaviour: A Systemic Functional Interpretation of the Nature and Ontogenesis of Dialogue'. In *The Semiotics of Culture and Language, Volume 1: Language as Social Semiotic*, edited by Robin P. Fawcett, M. A. K. Halliday, Sydney M. Lamb, and Adam Makkai. London and Dover, NH: Frances Pinter.

Halliday, M.A.K. 1985. *An Introduction to Functional Grammar*. 1st ed. London: Edward Arnold.

Halliday, M.A.K. 1994. *An Introduction to Functional Grammar*. 2nd ed. London: Edward Arnold.

Halliday, M.A.K. 2003. *On Language and Linguistics*. Volume 3 in the Collected Works of M.A.K. Halliday, ed. Jonathan J. Webster. London and New York: Continuum.

Halliday, M.A.K. 2004a. *An Introduction to Functional Grammar*, revised by Christian M.I.M. Matthiessen. 3rd ed. London: Arnold.

Halliday, M.A.K. 2004b. *The Language of Science*. Volume 5 in the Collected Works of M.A.K. Halliday, ed. Jonathan J. Webster. London and New York: Continuum.

Halliday, M.A.K. 2009. *Studies in Chinese Language*. Volume 8 in the Collected Works of M.A.K. Halliday, ed. Jonathan J. Webster. London and New York: Continuum.

Halliday, M.A.K. 2014. *Halliday's Introduction to Functional Grammar*, revised by Christian M.I.M. Matthiessen. 4th ed. London and New York: Routledge.

Halliday, M.A.K. and Christian M.I.M. Matthiessen. 1999. *Construing Experience Through Meaning, a Language-Based Approach to Cognition*. London and New York: Continuum.

Kennedy, J.B. 2003. *Space, Time and Einstein, an Introduction*. Montreal and Kingston; Ithaca NY: McGill-Queen's University Press.

Lee, Penny. 1996. *The Whorf Theory Complex: A Critical Reconstruction*. Amsterdam and Philadelphia: Benjamins.

Lukin, Annabelle. 2019. *War and Its Ideologies: A Social-Semiotic Theory and Description*. Singapore: Springer.

OED Online. December 2021. Oxford University Press. 'move, v.'. https://www-oed-com.ezproxy.library.sydney.edu.au/view/Entry/123027?rskey=AZYKEr& result=2&isAdvanced=false; 'motion, n.'. https://www-oed-com.ezproxy.library. sydney.edu.au/view/Entry/122693?rskey=Wo0fHF&result=1 (accessed 16 January 2022).

Olson, David R. 1994. *The World on Paper: The Conceptual and Cognitive Implications of Reading and Writing*. Cambridge and New York: Cambridge University Press.

Pinker, Stephen. 1994. *The Language Instinct*. New York: William Morrow and Company.

Thibault, Paul J. 1997. *Re-reading Saussure: The Dynamic of Signs in Social Life*. London and New York: Routledge.

Whorf, Benjamin Lee. 1956. *Language, Thought and Reality: Selected Writings of Benjamin Lee Whorf*, ed. John B. Carroll. Cambridge, MA: M.I.T. Press.

Whorf, Benjamin Lee. 2012. *Language, Thought and Reality: Selected Writings of Benjamin Lee Whorf*, eds. John B. Carroll, Stephen C. Levinson, and Penny Lee. Cambridge, MA: M.I.T. Press.

3 Levels of nature and worlds of time

J.T. Fraser's model of five levels of natural complexity associated with six worlds of different temporalities in the extended human umwelt

As described in Chapter 2, Halliday's account of 'semantic drift' in the linguistic potential of grammatical metaphor establishes that the temporal meaning of 'sequence' can be realized in diverse ways in the wording of the lexicogrammar. In the extreme realization of nominalization, temporal sequence is reduced to the noun 'time'; this one word realizes the meaning of a 'moment' (in SAE, to use Whorf's acronym, often metaphorically spatial as a point on a line) in the context of a variable sequence: of physical events, historical periods, geological eras and so on. (In Chapter 6, the potential meaning of the noun will be extended to include temporal duration as well as sequence.) In contrast to the assumptions of 'everyday language', grammatical metaphor demonstrates that a grammatical noun cannot be assumed to mean 'a thing'. Rather, the noun 'time' and the different grammatical realizations of group and clause associated with it realize a similar temporal meaning of sequence. This is one kind of complexity, the realization of meaning in grammar, which is internal to the potential of language. This chapter now turns to another kind of complexity: that of different understandings of temporal meaning so that one can now talk of different temporalities and, consequently, different types of temporal sequence associated with each. From this perspective, the nominalization 'time' is singular in grammatical number but not monovalent in meaning. Paradoxically, as will be discussed in later chapters, this complex polyvalence of time will enable us to clarify – even simplify – the discussion of narrative sequence and textual coherence.

In 1966, J.T. Fraser (1923–2010) founded the International Society for the Study of Time (ISST). Originally an engineer and inventor, but a genuine polymath, Fraser was interested in the humanities and social sciences as well as the natural sciences. Given that M.A.K. Halliday was also catholic in his interests, studying language in diverse social contexts, it is not surprising that Fraser's study of time and Halliday's study of language are in some ways complementary. (This topic, centrally relevant to my theorizing of narrative, is the focus of Chapter 7.) Moreover, as

DOI: 10.4324/b23121-3

mentioned in Chapter 1, Fraser, like Halliday, makes explicit reference to Edelman's account of the human brain.

> Since 1981, Gerald Edelman and members of his Neurosciences Research Institute in La Jolla, California, have carried out extensive research on the intricate dynamics of the human brain and made interesting suggestions about its neural population. What they found supports the idea that the human brain is the most complex system known. Thus to the variables of length, time, velocity, mass and temperature, was added the variable of complexity.
>
> (Fraser 2007, 2)

The variables Fraser lists are those traditionally associated with the study of 'nature'. Employing the added variable of complexity, Fraser now uses 'algorithmic information theory' in order to develop a 'measure of complexity' and from such calculations he is able to compare the complexity of 'physical structures and processes, organic structures and processes and the human brain and minding'. For Fraser, the term 'minding' resonates with the functions of Edelman's higher-order consciousness:

> By 'minding' in this context is meant the ability to create symbolic transformations of experience, to create and maintain self-awareness, the ability to speak a language and to perceive the world in terms of open-ended futures and pasts.
>
> (Fraser 2007, 2)

The human brain is remarkable not only in the organization of its component parts but even more so, Fraser writes, 'in the much larger immensity of the different ways in which those parts may be interconnected so as to form distinct brain states'. He quotes Edelman: 'the human brain is the most complicated object in the universe' and his calculations of complexity support the claim: the human brain is not just complicated but is also 'the most complex known object of the universe' (Fraser 2007, 240). Such calculations make it possible to identify a scale of complexities in nature, with boundaries for each level. The human brain, Fraser suggests, 'constitutes a natural boundary to complexity possible to achieve by biological means'. He concludes:

> As humans, we live at prohibitive distance from the physical limits of speed, density, temperature, size and duration, and also from the cosmic horizons. But because we possess human brains, we are at the complexity boundary of nature. More precisely: our brains are.
>
> (Fraser 2007, 240)

It is from the boundaries between levels of complexity in nature that Fraser develops his hierarchical theory of time. He identifies five 'nested integrative' levels of nature. These levels are hierarchically nested in that each level emerges from the previous; they are also integrative in that each earlier level continues to co-exist with those that have later emerged. Each level is sufficiently stable to have characteristic properties of causation and temporality. As each level determines a qualitatively different temporality, its emergence adds new, unresolvable conflicts to the level/s below it (a point to be elaborated later). Thus time is 'not a single unitary feature of the universe', not 'an apparently homogenous universal aspect of nature', rather, time is 'a dynamic, developing, and open-ended hierarchy of temporalities', an evolutionary sequence of temporal levels associated with different natural worlds (Fraser 1982, 22; 181; and see Fraser 1999, 26–43; Fraser 2007, 153–174). Table 3.1 represents my reading of Fraser's model.

In Table 3.1, Fraser's five nested integrative levels of nature are listed in the left-hand column. Note that levels one to four correspond, in the right-hand column, to four 'worlds', and each of these worlds is associated with one temporality and causation. However, Fraser's fifth and most recently evolved level of nature, that of human minding (comparable to Edelman's 'higher-order consciousness') is associated with two worlds,

Table 3.1 J.T. Fraser's model of the development and evolution of temporalities

	nested integrative levels of nature	*temporality*	*causation*	*world*
▲ 5.	human 'minding'	sociotemporal	collective intentionality/ historical causation	social world/ society
		nootemporal	individual long-term intentionality	mental world of individual human
4.	living matter *(organic being)*	biotemporal	short-term intentionality	physical world of living organism
3.	matter *(material being)*	eotemporal	deterministic lawfulness	inorganic physical world
2.	particles + mass *(stochastic being)*	prototemporal	probabilistic lawfulness	wave-particle world
1.	photons no mass *(becoming)*	atemporal	none – chaos	electro-magnetic radiation

each with its characteristic temporality and causation. The implications of this model are now drawn out in detail.

Fraser refers to the 'canonical forms of causation' and 'the canonical forms of time'. These are the different particular types of causation and temporality associated with each integrative level of nature, and these then constitute the particular environment, or world, for its natural inhabitants. This is comparable to the species-specific universe *Umwelt*, the term used by the German biologist Jakob von Uexküll, and also taken up in modern psychology ('the circumscribed portion of the environment which is meaningful and effective for a given species'[1]) (Fraser 1999, 23; 2007, 154). Thus Fraser uses 'umwelt' for the spatio-temporal 'reality' experienced by the inhabitants of each level. For example, one can speak of the umwelt of an object travelling at the speed of light, which exists only in the level one world of electromagnetic radiation. ('Umwelt' also has currency in Peircean semiotics, Deely 1990, 59–62; more recently David Herman has suggested its relevance to narrative study, 2011, 265–266.)

From the point of view of human existence, all the five levels of nature always co-exist, as each level is nested within the previous. However, explicit human awareness of the earlier levels is recent. Until the end of the nineteenth century the last two levels, with their three associated worlds of biotemporality, nootemporality and sociotemporality, constituted the human umwelt, reality as understood from the experience of human life on earth. It is in the context of this natural human umwelt that the emergence – in Halliday's terms, the phylogenesis – of human language took place and traces of that umwelt are realized in language. This will be discussed further in Chapter 5.

Yet Fraser's identification of temporalities goes beyond those described for the human umwelt. Von Uexküll had pointed out that an animal's understanding of its world was determined by its receptors and effectors. (A receptor detects the stimulus and converts it into an impulse, for example a light receptor in the eye which detects changes in light in the environment. An effector converts the impulse into an action, for example a muscle, Biology Tutor n.d., online.) For the human species, however, through the development of technology and through the abstract thinking of mathematics, the environmental reality can be extended beyond that experienced through the natural human animal. Fraser calls this the *extended umwelt principle* (Fraser 2007, 39–49). By this principle, humans have access to the evolutionarily earlier worlds, Fraser's worlds 1, 2 and 3 (as in Table 3.1), as well as to the umwelts of other species: for example, seeing the patterns on butterflies wings with ultra-violet light (Fraser 2007, 19–20). As Fraser puts it, the extended umwelt principle 'amounts to equating epistemology with ontology'. He compares this understanding to the oppositional positions of traditional metaphysics:

> Philosophers have long sought normative criteria for a categorical definition of reality. For our purpose all that is necessary and

sufficient is to have established a working concept of reality – the extended umwelt principle – and to note that as our knowledge of the world expands, so does our reality. This amounts to equating epistemology with ontology: the world is the way we find it to be through the many forms of human knowledge, even if some of its features appear to be counterintuitive. ...

The generalised umwelt principle resembles but is not identical to realism, because it does not maintain that our senses and thoughts present us with details of a world whose furnishings are independent of the knower. Water is for fishes something quite different from what it is for cats. The generalized umwelt principle also resembles but is not identical to idealism, for it rejects the notion that ultimate reality resides in a transcendental realm.

(Fraser 1999, 25)

So things 'are' as we 'know' them to be. This is a view compatible with a Peircean semiotics of an 'objective', rather than external, reality, as remarked on in Chapter 2.

Because, as later chapters discuss, the extended umwelt principle has particular application in the writing and study of narrative, this chapter now describes in more detail the five different levels of nature and six associated worlds of Fraser's model of time, as identified in Table 3.1. (For non-specialists, like myself, Kennedy (2003) gives a brief and accessible introduction to the science of earlier levels. Elana Gomel gives a relevant 'sketch of the changing scientific picture of the world' in the 'Introduction' to her book, *Narrative Space and Time*, though her focus is primarily on 'Space', 2014, 1–25.)

Level 1 is the world of electro-magnetic radiation, a world inhabited by photons with no mass, always on the move at the speed of light. Their world is characterized by atemporality, where everything happens at once, a world of becoming ('pure Heraclitean becoming', in Fraser's words) rather than being, lacking a form of causation. This is the reality of a chaotic world, as described by the special theory of relativity.

Level 2 is the world inhabited by wave-particles with mass, travelling at speeds less than that of light. Fraser calls its time prototemporality, 'proto' meaning the first in a series, and this being the world in which the possibility of time emerges. Its causation or lawfulness is probabilistic; it is not possible to point to the exact instant when a particle is emitted, only to the probability of its having been emitted, as, for example, in the half-life of radioactive material. In this world, the reality of being is stochastic, possible, but not identifiable; this is the world described by quantum theory.

Level 3 is the world of inorganic physical matter, the world of galaxies, the world of material being. Fraser calls its time eotemporality, for the dawn of time (Eos was the Greek goddess of dawn). Its value can be measured, though the value will depend on the measurer's spatial location and so its temporality is not directional, is even reversible. Its causation is that of deterministic lawfulness; its inhabitants exist in a reality of determinable cause and effect. Significantly, this is a world without 'now':

> The eotemporal world does not contain structures capable of protecting and maintaining their identities as living organisms do. Nothing among eotemporal functions can correspond, therefore to simultaneities of need or intent. It follows that in the eotemporal world no meaning can be attached to the concept of 'now'. Coincidences do occur but they must remain simultaneities of chance. As futurity and pastness make sense only in terms of a present to which they are referred, it further follows that eotemporality is a directionless time, one of pure succession. It is a completely symmetrical time. Purely cyclic processes are eotemporal as is an ideal clock.
>
> (Fraser 1982: 30–31)

This is the world of the general theory of relativity, also called space-time theory.

Level 4 is the world of living organisms, of organic being, including, of course, the physiological world of the human species. Its time, biotemporality, makes sense to us in our human experience. Biotemporality is directional, moving from birth to death for the individual organism. It is the first temporality to which the concept of 'the present' is relevant, as the time at which the organism feels or satisfies its need. Fraser calls its canonical form of causation short-term intentionality, referring to the organism's intention to satisfy its needs of survival and reproduction. For those organic beings with primary consciousness, as in Edelman's account, this is the time of the remembered present, as discussed in Chapter 1. For humans, it is the time of 'time felt', as directly known by Augustine.

Fraser's final integrative level of nature, level 5 in the nested hierarchy, is that peculiar to the evolution of the human species, Fraser's human 'minding'. It is associated with the most complex evolutionary development, that of the human brain, 'a boundary of the universe'. In Edelman's terminology, it is the level of higher-order consciousness, which he associates with the human development of language. Thus this level gives rise to two worlds of human experience, both essential for language: that internal to the individual consciousness, with its particular memories, predictions and fantasies, and that of social interaction and consensus in myth, ritual, social identities and attributes and historical understanding.

The time of the individual mental world Fraser calls nootemporality (from *noos*, Greek for 'mind' or 'thought'), with the associated causation that of individual long-term intentionality. Fraser describes the hallmarks of nootemporality as 'open temporal horizons and the necessary reference to a "you" and "me" and to a mental present with its continuously changing temporal boundaries and cognitive content' (Fraser 1982, 29). This description makes clear the inter-relation of temporal sense and consciousness, as William James suggested. Characteristically, in the nootemporal world, events are connected through the individual's intentionality being directed toward concrete or symbolic goals and serving the continued integrity of the self. The congruence of Edelman, Halliday and Fraser's work is here most evident. As discussed in Chapter 1, Edelman speaks of the symbolic translation characterizing human mental life and Fraser elaborates on this symbolic strength:

> The noetic umwelt is created by our capacity to produce symbolic transformations of experience and then manipulate them as part and parcel of reality.
>
> (Fraser 1982, 29)

The time of the social world, the society of the human group, Fraser calls sociotemporality, with the associated causation that of collective or social intentionality, also described as historical causation. Sociotemporality is

> the way a culture represents time ... It is a social consensus necessary for the survival of a society, a definition of that society's way of being. ... It is a collective evaluation of time, the ethical rules guiding society in view of its history and future goals.
>
> (Fraser 1999, 37–38)

It is the public institutional time in which a society understands the social identity of its historical periods, political movements, literary innovations.

Fraser formulates his model of the levels of nature within the advances of modern physics in extending the human umwelt (the human understanding of reality), as implied in the theories of special relativity (level 1), quantum theory (level 2) and general relativity (level 3). This formulation (already described as 'equating ontology with epistemology') also implies that Fraser's model is empirically open: further extension of the human umwelt through science and technology can add further levels. For example, like the dual temporal worlds of Fraser's level 5, human minding, one could argue for dual worlds at level 4, that of organic being: one the biotemporal world of the individual, the other the temporal world of the genome, which persists beyond the individual organism.

The description of the levels of nature as 'hierarchically nested' has several important implications. That the 'individual' human is, rather, a living, thinking and social being made of matter means that, in Fraser's words, 'each person shares some of the potentialities and all of the restraints of these organizational levels' (Fraser 1999, 28). There are many possible consequences from this polyvalent existence, but here I focus on the implications for temporality and causation. First, causation.

Though processes characteristic of each of these levels function with different types of causation 'the different types of causations can never be found in pure forms; all processes are amalgams of qualitatively different causal links organized in a nested hierarchical fashion' (Fraser 1999, 31). ('Process' here includes structures: a structure differs from what is usually called a process only by its rate of change.) Thus, for example, at the sociotemporal level, the processes of human history display collective intent but also necessarily include noetic and biological intentionality, as well as deterministic, probabilistic, and chaotic elements. Fraser explains:

> The contributions from chaos (*ie* absolute unpredictability) take different forms at the different integrative levels: the laws of nature serve as filters; For instance, chaotic events in quantum physics, unpredictable from the probabilistic laws of the quantum world, differ in kind from chaotic, unpredictable events in mutations in mice, [or] unpredictable behaviour of a person, or unpredictable events in history.
>
> (Fraser 1999, 31)

Or in Robbie Burns' words: *The best laid schemes o' Mice an' Men, / Gang aft agley.* (See Greenspan, 2003, on the role of randomness in biology, with a critique of determinism.)

Second, consider the implications for temporality of 'hierarchically nested' levels of nature, where evolutionary earlier temporalities are not replaced but subsumed by later ones. This implies talk about 'time' uses a term for a synthesis of temporalities, not reducible to one simple understanding. Chapter 2 ended with Halliday's comments on the spatialized language of scientific discourse: that it served the purpose of emerging science from the sixteenth through the nineteenth century, but that it is now not adequate for the demands of contemporary disciplines. Fraser makes much the same observation about the extended human understanding of temporalities:

> Because of nature's nested hierarchical organization, the canonical forms of time never appear in pure forms; all processes take place in amalgams of qualitatively different temporalities. This view distinguishes the hierarchical theory of time from the Platonic dichotomy

between time and the timeless and from its elaboration by Christianity. That elaboration made the Renaissance birth of science and the subsequent rise of the scientific-industrial civilization possible. The very science born of the Platonic and Christian views of time and the timeless, however, made the dichotomy unacceptable for a post-Darwinian, post-Freudian and post-Einsteinian world. The hierarchical theory of time allows for a synthesis of the different temporalities into the totality of what is ordinarily called time, provided one gives up the belief that the experiential time of humans is appropriate for all the lower levels of complexity that inorganic and organic evolution have created.

(Fraser 1999, 38–39)

Temporal complexity has further consequences. As each natural level determines a qualitatively different temporality, for one conscious individual, there are two forms of 'nowness': that of the mental (noetic) present and that of the physiological (biotemporal) present. For the human individual, the physiological present (of time felt) has given rise to, and remains coexistent with, the mental present (of time understood) (Fraser 2007, 34). As every child rebuked in class for 'daydreaming' learns, and every adult who walks into a barricade while thinking of something else belatedly recognizes, these two experiences of time require a balancing act by the individual. I have already quoted Fraser's warning, that we humans need 'to protect our integrity as individuals, such as by maintaining the conflict between time felt and time understood, without becoming unthinking zombies or abstract heads unfit to survive' (Fraser 2007, 264). And yet it may be just this capacity to be in two 'nows' simultaneously that gives us the taste for story, for being mentally other than where we materially are.

Even more generally, given the qualitative temporal difference between the natural levels, Fraser warns that 'each level adds new, unresolvable conflicts to those of the level or levels below it'. Consider the temporalities of the one human individual:

A *person* is a member of our species who possesses a stable identity. The process that creates and maintains that identity involves a continuous reintegration of the neural population of the cortex …but the whole story is that of a ceaseless conflict between the processes that create that identity and the social and biological perturbations that oppose it. The opposing trends are coordinated in the mental present.

What conflicts are peculiar to personhood? Those between the desired and the possible. Those between the simultaneous awarenesses of living and dying. [Many apt literary quotes can illustrate

these statements: Fraser quotes Freud, Goethe, St Augustine.] ...
[T]he conflicts themselves may be seen as constitutive of personhood: an individual is a human being with a family of conflicts
that distinguishes him or her from other individuals.

(Fraser 1999, 39–40)

Even at the one natural level of 'human minding', there are 'unresolvable'
conflicts between sociotemporal and nootemporal experience. Fraser
describes these in dramatic terms:

A permanent reconciliation between collective and individual interests is impossible because of the mind's unbounded imaginative power
and its subsequent ever-new demands on the community, as well as
the community's ever-new demands on the individual. People may
still exist if the conflicts cease, but their society will have collapsed.

(Fraser 1999, 39)

Fraser's book of 1999 is entitled *Time, Conflict, and Human Values,* and
it is clear Fraser sees his theory of time has important implications for
human values constitutive of human health, individually and socially:

Since in the mind of man there can be no closure to the conflicts
between time felt and time understood, no civilization can be maintained without the benefit of its arts, letters, and sciences continuously mediating these conflicts.

(Fraser 2007, 265)

Gerald Edelman also describes what he sees as the role of art in this
mediation:

What is perhaps most extraordinary about conscious human beings
is their art – their ability to convey feelings and emotions symbolically and formally in external objects such as poems, paintings or
symphonies. The summaries of conscious states constrained by history, culture, specific training, and skill that are realized in works of
art are not susceptible to the methods of scientific analysis. Again
there is no mystification in this denial, for understanding and
responding to these objects requires reference to *ourselves* in a social
and symbolic mode. No external objective analysis, even if possible,
supplants the individual responses and intersubjective exchange that
takes place within a given tradition and culture.

(Edelman 1994, 176)

It is noticeable, in the previous quote, that Edelman implies a semiotic
level (meaningful 'external objects' of art) evolving from the social level

('a social and symbolic mode'), as does Halliday when he, like Fraser, discusses relations of complexity. In an introduction written for a collection of his earlier papers, Halliday is explaining general assumptions he has made within those papers – in his words, what 'sorts of things about language are being taken for granted'. He begins with the basic assumption that 'a language is a system of meaning – a semiotic system' and then assumes that there are three other kinds of system: physical, biological and social.

> A physical system is just that: a physical system. A biological system, on the other hand, is not just that; it is a physical system (or an assembly of physical systems) having an additional feature – let us say 'life'. A social system, in turn, is an assembly of biological systems (life forms) having a further additional feature – which we might call 'value': it is what defines membership; so an assembly of life forms with a membership hierarchy. So a social system is a system of a third order complexity, because it is social and biological and physical. We could then think of a semiotic system as being of a fourth order of complexity, being semiotic and social and biological and physical: meaning is socially constructed, biologically activated and exchanged through physical channels.
>
> (Halliday 2003, 2)

In general terms, both Fraser and Halliday describe 'levels of nature' and 'systems' in comparable ways: they are nested in that each emerges from the previous, and they are integrative in that each earlier level or system continues to co-exist with those which have later emerged. Each elaborates in areas of his particular focus. Fraser's level 4 of organic being is comparable to Halliday's biological systems but Fraser describes three physical levels in nature (levels 1, 2 and 3 in Table 3.1) where Halliday mentions one. In contrast, in the worlds of human experience, where Fraser describes one natural level (5 of human minding) to accommodate two worlds of (mature) human experience (as an individual and as a social being), Halliday, a linguist – and especially one who has described the child's socialization into the adult language as 'learning how to mean' (Halliday 1975) – sees the experience of social systems as a necessary context for the individual's entry into the semiotic systems of human culture. But this is a difference of emphasis, not understanding; the social context of Edelman's human with 'higher-order consciousness', a being evolved to Fraser's natural level of 'human minding', is necessarily a semiotic context ('language as social semiotic'). For Fraser, a scientist given to quoting poetry in his conference papers (as I personally have heard), the shared significance of the preoccupations of higher-order consciousness is essential for human survival. Having elaborated the importance of the arts and letters (in a continuing evolution of semiotic modes: through dance, music, language, painting, sculpture, architecture, film ...), Fraser adds:

> To the store of humanities let me, therefore, add the forms of knowledge known as the sciences. ... They share with the humanities their spirit of exploration, their search for coherence by plot that is, by meaning (known as hypotheses) and their readiness to mine the imagination. To the immense store of imaginary scenarios offered by the arts and letters, the sciences add their tests – with their validities forever challenged and subject to change – as to what is possible, difficult or impossible for humans made of matter, possessing life and possessed by ideas.
>
> (Fraser 2007, 265)

Unlike the nested understanding of temporalities just described, European philosophy, from the nineteenth century through the twentieth, has often focused more exclusively on the concept of 'becoming'. In her introduction to the book, *Becomings* (a collection by different authors), the editor Elizabeth Grosz writes:

> [this collection] explicitly focuses on and develops out of the work of a privileged few who have insisted on the fundamental openness of time to futurity – who have resisted all attempts to reduce time to the workings of causality, and who have seen in it the force of becoming – Nietzsche, Bergson, and Deleuze. ... Others could be considered philosophers of becoming, among them Heidegger, Merleau-Ponty, Derrida, Foucault, Klossowski, and Irigaray.
>
> (1993, 3)

Grosz also acknowledges the central importance of Darwin, although the book does not discuss his work. Despite the hyper-modernity of this philosophical approach, there is the danger of once again reducing the recognition of time to one temporality (*viz* the third paragraph on page 5 of *Becomings*), from, say, a structuralist monovalent biotemporality (as classified in the next chapter) to a poststructuralist monovalent atemporality. In contrast, Fraser's inter-disciplinary model has an open and evolutionary understanding of time, including the atemporality of becoming and including its co-existent persistence in the levels later developed.

Note

1 Fraser takes this definition of *Umwelt* from Horace B. English and Ava Champney English, *A Comprehensive Dictionary of Psychological and Psychoanalytic Terms*, New York: McKay, 1964, s.v. 'Umwelt'.

References

Biology Tutor. n.d. Accessed 11 March 2020. www.mytutor.co.uk/answers/13025/GCSE/Biology/What-is-the-difference-between-a-receptor-and-an-effector-in-the-nervous-system/

Deely, John. 1990. *Basics of Semiotics*. Bloomington and Indianapolis: Indiana University Press.

Edelman, Gerald. 1994 [1992]. *Bright Air, Brilliant Fire: On the Matter of the Mind*. London: Penguin Books.

Fraser, J.T. 1982. *The Genesis and Evolution of Time, A Critique of Interpretation in Physics*. Amherst: Massachusetts University Press.

Fraser, J.T. 1999. *Time, Conflict, and Human Values*. Urbana and Chicago: Illinois University Press.

Fraser, J.T. 2007. *Time and Time Again, Reports from a Boundary of the Universe*. Leiden and Boston: Brill.

Gomel, Elana. 2014. *Narrative Space and Time, Representing Impossible Topologies in Literature*. London and New York: Routledge.

Grosz, Elizabeth, editor. 1993. *Becomings, Explorations in Time, Memory, and Futures*. Ithaca, New York: Cornell University Press.

Greenspan, Ralph J. 2003. 'Darwinian Uncertainty'. *Kronoscope* 3 (2): pp. 217–225.

Halliday, M.A.K. 1975. *Learning How to Mean – Explorations in the Development of Language*. London: Edward Arnold.

Halliday, M.A.K. 2003. *On Language and Linguistics*. Volume 3 in the Collected Works of M.A.K. Halliday, ed. Jonathan J. Webster. London and New York: Continuum.

Herman, David. 2011. '1880–1945: Re-minding Modernism'. In *The Emergence of Mind, Representations of Consciousness in Narrative Discourse in English*, edited by David Herman, pp. 241–272. Lincoln and London: University of Nebraska Press.

Kennedy, J.B. 2003. *Space, Time and Einstein*. Montreal and Kingston, Ithaca: McGill-Queen's University Press.

4 Narrative studies and time

A summary account of 'scientific' and 'philosophical' understandings of temporal meaning in narrative theory and narratology

The meaning of narrative is explored in many disciplinary contexts, serving many different purposes. Yet one assumption runs through most disciplinary modelling: that narrative narrates time. For William Labov, in his sociolinguistic description of spontaneous oral narratives, this was the basic criterion: 'a minimal narrative is defined as one containing a single temporal juncture' (1972b, 361). A concern with time may not be sufficient, but it is of the essence in identifying a semiotic instance as narrative. Thus, when Marie-Laure Ryan lists examples of 'previous definitions of narrative', she includes among the basic statements which 'a definition should support, even entail': 'narrative is about the temporality of existence' (Ryan 2007, 23–24). Definitions of narrative become entwined with human experience, existentially. To the philosopher Paul Ricoeur, 'Time becomes human time to the extent that it is organized after the manner of narrative; narrative in turn is meaningful to the extent that it portrays the features of temporal existence' (1984, 3). More recently, H. Porter Abbott asks 'what does narrative do for us?' and answers 'many things', but then adds (Abbott's italics):

> But if we had to choose one answer above all others, the likeliest is that *narrative is the principal way in which our species organizes its understanding of time*. This would seem to be the fundamental gift of narrative with the greatest range of benefits. And it certainly makes evolutionary sense. As we are the only species on earth with both language and a conscious awareness of the passage of time, it stands to reason that we would have a mechanism for expressing this awareness.
>
> (Abbott 2008, 3)

We see here the blurring of talk of time and consciousness, as we saw in Edelman's quoting of William James' quoting of Augustine of Hippo. We could also reverse the direction of Porter Abbott's last sentence, as Ricoeur did in his rhetorically balanced structure, to express the

DOI: 10.4324/b23121-4

co-existent emergence of higher-order human consciousness and temporal understanding: 'we become aware of time as we tell narratives'.

The study of 'narrative' has been variously theorized during the twentieth century, but there is a notable flurry of retrospective survey and summary publication in the first decade of the twenty-first century. In 2003, Ansgar Nünning maps many approaches in the article, 'Narratology or Narratologies? Taking Stock of Recent Developments, Critique and Modest Proposals for Future Usages of the Term'. David Herman, Monika Fludernik and Brian McHale describe their versions (including denials) of histories of narrative theory in the 'Prologue' to *A Companion to Narrative Theory*, published in 2005 (Phelan and Rabinowitz 2005, 19–71). James Phelan adds a chapter, 'Narrative Theory, 1966–2006: A Narrative', to the 2006 revised edition of *The Nature of Narrative* (Scholes et al. 2006, 283–336). *The Routledge Encyclopedia of Narrative Theory* is published in 2005 (Herman et al. 2005). The last, in its 'Introduction', describes 'an exponential growth of research and teaching activity centring around narrative' and notes the wide disciplinary spread of this interest (Herman et al. 2005, ix). On a more limited scale, Martin Cortazzi, wanting to help teachers find useful techniques from various studies of narrative, had earlier described the modelling of narrative, through theory and practice, in the disciplines of sociology and sociolinguistics, psychology, literary study and anthropology (Cortazzi, 1993). And for each discipline the list of publications could continue, taking the understanding of 'narrative' into different contexts of relevance and levels of significance. Thus Russell Meares, in the field of psychiatry discussing 'the development of self', sees '[the self's] principal contribution to survival of the species may be its potentiation of a social group who share in the creation of a culture, the fabric of which is made up of a network of stories' (2016, 8). This 'capacity for narration' is most advantageously evolved in the dual structure of myth (Meares 2016, 164–66), and Meares invokes this structure in the therapeutic interplay of patient and therapist (2016, 185–194).

In this chapter, I discriminate broadly between two temporal orientations to narrative study; I identify these loosely as the 'philosophical' and 'scientific' orientations. Admittedly, using this simple dichotomy effaces important differences in the one category. Thus the first orientation might be extended as philosophical /metaphysical /theological/psychological ... an open-ended list. Labelling the second orientation: scientific/linguistic/ sociological is perhaps less misleading. On the whole, it is to studies in the latter orientation that the term 'narratology' has been applied, or, more restrictively, the phrase 'structuralist studies of narrative'. My basic criterion for discrimination is derived from two of Fraser's temporalities (as described in Chapter 3). In the scientific orientation, despite complexities of theory, temporal sequence is assumed to be chronological and in Chapter 7 this sequence will be uniquely associated with biotemporality, the time of Fraser's world 4. In contrast, in the understanding of the philosophical orientation, time is – or is at least understood to include – nootemporality, the time associated with the individual consciousness of Fraser's world 5. I discuss each of these orientations in turn, skimming lightly over some areas of scholarship (typically those well-rehearsed elsewhere) while lingering over others.

The scientific orientation effectively begins diversely with the French-speaking Swiss linguist Ferdinand de Saussure (1959) and the Russian literary formalists (Erlich 2012), whose work comes together in the 'linguistic poetics' of the Prague Linguistics Circle, one member, Sergej Karcevskij, having been a student of de Saussure (Graffi 2019). The life of Roman Jakobson, harried by twentieth century politics and war, tells a personal story of this intellectual trajectory. Jakobson (1896–1982), a young man attracted by Italian Futurism and experimentalism in the arts, in 1915, as a first year undergraduate, is a co-founder of the Moscow Linguistic Circle – from which, along with the Petersburg Circle ('The Society for the Study of Poetic Language'), the literary concerns of Russian Formalism emerge. Jakobson moves to Czechoslovakia in 1920 and in 1926 is a co-founder of the Prague Linguistic Circle; in 1939 he escapes to Scandinavia (meeting linguists of the Copenhagen School) and thence by 1941 travels to the United States. (For the posthumous publication of eleven essays which Jakobson himself collated as an introduction to his work on linguistics and poetics, see Jakobson 1985.) In New York he is a founding member of the *École Libre des Hautes Études,* which has been described as a university-in-exile for French academics (Rutkoff and Scott 1983). Another member was Claude Lévi-Strauss. Jakobson's intimate knowledge of Saussurean structuralism, with its two axes of paradigmatic 'selection' and syntagmatic 'combination', influenced Levi-Strauss, who is famously known for his work on 'structural anthropology', including the structural analysis of myth (Lévi-Strauss 1977, 206–231).

The formalist Vladimir Propp published his study of the Russian folk tale in 1928 (Propp 1968). Thirty years later, the Bulgarian Tzvetan Todorov translated the work into French and its approach was disseminated, belatedly, more widely. In general, the Russian formalists looked for what is different in literary language, but Propp's concern is with what is 'the same' in the folk tale. His analysis offers a formalist but not structuralist account: its 'functions', the narrative role of events in the tale told, are analysed on the syntagmatic axis of sequence only (not also on the paradigmatic, unlike Lévi-Strauss' later structuralist analysis of myth). The explicit structuralist analysis of narrative effectively begins with Roland Barthes, with the publication of his influential paper, in French, in 1966; in 1975 it was published in English as 'An Introduction to the Structural Analysis of Narrative'. In that paper,

Barthes acknowledges the work of Propp (and of Todorov), Lévi-Strauss and Jakobson, together with other contemporaries, including the French linguist Émile Benveniste and the narrative theorist A.J. Greimas. A functional modelling of language, such as that of Halliday's SFL (discussed in Chapter 5), can extend linguistic study directly to the semantic unit of the text. However, Barthes assumes a non-functional view of the discipline 'linguistics' when he writes, 'As everyone knows, linguistics stops at the sentence' (Barthes 1975, 239). This assumption leads him to propose the study of 'narrative language' in a way analogous to the study of the sentence, analysing 'narrative language' in terms of structuralist paradigm and syntagm. Thus, under the sub-heading 'Functional syntax', Barthes can ask 'How, according to what "grammar," are the different units linked together in the narrative syntagm?' (1975, 251). This question exemplifies the assumed objectivity of structuralism in its search for formal patterns in the text, an activity which will become the focus of post-structuralist critique. It is notable that, five years before his quintessentially structuralist paper was available in English (1975), Barthes had already moved towards a more post-structuralist perspective on narrative. In his study, *S/Z*, of a Balzac short story (1974 in English; first published in French in 1970), the codes are identified subjectively, dependent on the reader's (that is Barthes') interpretation. (On the general move from structuralism to poststructuralism, see Huisman 2005, 28–44).

In a structuralist approach, the narrative is assumed to have a dualism of level perceived and level inferred but only one meaning of 'time'. The reader/listener perceives the surface telling of the particular text in which the chronology of events may be disordered but infers/understands an underlying sense of the story told in which chronological progression is restored. In his *Dictionary of Narratology*, Gerald Prince lists five understandings of the lemma '**story**', three of which relate to this structuralist dualism: story as narrated content (what) versus the expression or discourse of narrating (how); story as *fabula*, the basic material, as opposed to *sjuzet*, its arrangement into plot; story as *histoire*, the object of the enunciation, versus *discours*, 'the situation of enunciation', which 'implies a sender and receiver' (Prince 2003, 93). (John Pier makes a detailed comparison of these terms and describes the tendency to collapse the different dualisms into one story/discourse dualism, Pier 2003.) This 'scientific' orientation continues through French and French-influenced structuralism to its apotheosis in Gérard Genette's study of Marcel Proust's *A la recherche du temps perdu* (1972), translated from the French into English as *Narrative Discourse* (1980 – again note the time-lapse for monolingual English scholars). So Genette begins Chapter 1 of *Narrative Discourse* discussing this narrative duality with the German terms '*erzäahlte Zeit* (story time)' and '*Erzählzeit* (narrative time)'. He quotes Christine Metz (1974) on narrative in 'film language': that the time of the thing told is 'the time of the signified' and the time of the narrative is 'the time of the signifier' (Genette 1980, 33); the Saussurean heritage is explicit. He does express some quibbles – in effect, adding the biotemporality of the reader to the structuralist duality of the text. In his remarks, below, I am reminded of Whorf's comments on the metaphoric translation of time to space characteristic of SAE (discussed previously in Chapter 2):

> The temporality of written narrative is to some extent conditional or instrumental; produced in time, like everything else, written narrative exists in space and as space, and the time needed for 'consuming' it is the time needed for crossing or *traversing* it, like a road or field. The narrative text, like every other text, has no other temporality than what it borrows, metonymically, from its own reading.
>
> (Genette 1980, 34)

This gives Genette three, rather than two, dimensions (Mieke Bal also unusually uses three: *fabula*, story and text, Bal 1997). However, Genette then accepts textual duality as 'part of the narrative game' (1980, 34), and devotes the first three of his five chapters to studying 'three essential determinations' of relations between, what he calls, 'the time of the story and the (pseudo) time of the narration':

> connections between the temporal *order* of succession of the events in the story and the pseudo-temporal order of their arrangement in the narrative; ... connections between the variable *duration* of these events or story sections and the pseudo-duration (in fact, length of text) of their telling in the narrative – connections thus of speed ...; finally, connections of *frequency*, that is (to limit myself to an approximate formulation), relations between the repetitive capacities of the story and those of the narrative, ...
>
> (1980, 35)

It is clear that, in this account, the sequence of 'real' time, as opposed to 'pseudo-time', is chronological, one lived event after another. Again, this is the time of Fraser's world 4 of living organisms, in which one event follows another in the organic 'now' in a directed movement from birth to death. To repeat: for the structuralist study of narrative following the 'scientific' orientation, the 'real time' which relates the two levels of the text is monovalent, and, in Fraser's terms, assumed to be that of biotemporality.

Before leaving what I have called the 'scientific' orientation to narrative, I turn to a (socio)linguistic, rather than literary, development of narrative studies. William Labov began his introduction to *Sociolinguistic Patterns* (1972a) by lamenting the way in which, during the 1960s 'the great majority of linguists had resolutely turned to the contemplation of their own idiolects'. His aim in his early work, he wrote, was 'to avoid the inevitable obscurity of texts, the self-consciousness of formal elicitations, and the self-deception of introspection' (1972a, xix). (Labov elaborates on these 'problems' in 'What Is a Linguistic Fact?', 1975.) Against such introspection, Labov asserted:

> that there is a growing realization the basis of intersubjective knowledge in linguistics must be found in speech – language as it is used in everyday life by members of the social order, that vehicle of communication in which they argue with their wives, joke with their friends and deceive their enemies.
>
> [It is perhaps salutary to remind ourselves of how recently women have joined the 'social order'!]

This quote suggests several of Labov's aims and assumptions: the 'scientific' aim to derive conclusions by an empirical method of induction; his use of 'texts' to mean 'written texts'; the assumption that the presence of the speaker may inhibit obscurity; the assumption that spontaneous language instantiates linguistic knowledge. From all these, Labov concludes that the linguist's object of study must be spontaneous speech. There is also an echo in that phrase 'intersubjective knowledge' of Bakhtin's 'interact' (Todorov 1984: 30): that meaning is negotiated between speakers in social interaction, rather than inherent in codes internalised by individuals – though the term 'knowledge' is somewhat contradictory, associated as it is with the cognition of the individual speaker.

To explore his assertion – that the linguist should study everyday speech – Labov collected responses from speakers in specific social environments, in New York and Philadelphia. In his earliest work, his research method used simple questions which – it was hoped – would elicit the required detail in answer. (Michael Kak, who assisted him in 1963 in New York, tells of the frustration in trying to elicit the word 'bad' in order to check on its vowel choice – people just didn't like to use the word! Kak, 1997.) But, as Labov tells us in his book, *Language in the Inner City*:

> In the course of our studies of vernacular language, we have developed a number of devices to overcome the constraints of the face-to-face interviews and obtain large bodies of tape-recorded casual speech. The most effective of these techniques produce *narratives of personal experience*, in which the speaker becomes deeply involved in rehearsing or even reliving events of the past.
>
> (1972b, 354–355)

In Labov's later book *Principles of Linguistic Change* (1994), 'narratives' in the index sends you to a chapter in which just the raw data of individuals' 'narrative of personal experience' are recorded.

Labov acknowledges the constraints of the interview situation: 'the form [the narratives] take is ... typical of discourse directed to someone outside of the immediate peer group of the speaker' but argues, 'because the experience and emotions involved here form an important part of the speakers' [*sic*] biography, he seems to undergo a partial reliving of that experience, and he is no longer free to monitor his own speech as he normally does in face to face interviews'. So the primary object of study to be elicited was spontaneous speech of personal experience, rather than narrative *per se*, but in a chapter entitled 'The Transformation of Experience in Narrative Syntax', Labov gives his analysis of 'the structural features' in these spontaneous narratives: a 'complete narrative begins with an orientation, proceeds to the complicating action; is suspended at the focus of evaluation before the resolution, concludes with the resolution, and returns the listener to the present time with the coda' (1972b, 369). He comments that evaluation may move throughout the narrative.

Labov explicitly defines narrative as 'one method of recapitulating past experience by matching a verbal sequence of clauses to the sequence of events which (it is inferred) actually occurred' (1972b, 360). In effect, the structuralist dualism of discourse telling and story told is collapsed into one dimension of story. This is a more limited conception of narrative than any other I'm aware of and, as Michael Toolan points out in his discussion of Labov and Joshua Waletzky's work, this conception sharply differentiates the Labovian concern from that of literary studies of narration (2001, 167–172). For some working with systemic functional theory, Labov's account of the 'structural features' of narrative has been influential though they extend it to written texts and elaborate it further in the staged analysis of different genres for literacy education (Martin and Rose 2008, 49–52). I also use systemic functional theory (with particular reference to Halliday and Matthiessen's writing) but apply it differently in my study of narrative.

I turn now to the 'philosophical' orientation, and its understanding of time to include nootemporality, the time associated with the individual human consciousness. Here again are those perennial questions raised in Chapter 1. The philosopher Genevieve Lloyd, in *Being in Time, Selves and Narrators in Philosophy and Literature*, offers a subtle account of the 'literary aspects of philosophical writing', beginning with Augustine's 'problem' of time (1993). The inter-related work of the American William James (on 'consciousness') and the Frenchman Henri Bergson (on *durée*) is still suggestive (Gunn 1920) and for this reason I elaborate on it most fully in the latter part of this chapter. Bergson's influence on the Russian Mikhail Bakhtin is significant (Rudova 1996), although Bakhtin himself moves into a more complex understanding of temporality in his theory of chronotopes, the different space-time characteristics of different narratives. (He explicitly acknowledges his borrowing of the term 'space-time' from Einstein's Theory of Relativity, Bakhtin 1981, 84.) The French metaphysical tradition perhaps reaches its fullest expression in the work of Paul Ricoeur, in his three volume opus, *Narrative and Time* (Ricoeur 1984, 85–88). Again, in this 'philosophical' orientation, we see a rereading of the earlier authors by more recent scholars: the American Gary Morson exploring the writing of Bakhtin (1986), the French Gilles Deleuze rehabilitating the study of Bergson. In English, Deleuze's work on Bergson is particularly taken up by the philosopher Elizabeth Grosz (see her extensive bibliography of his works, 2004, 2005).

The late nineteenth and early twentieth centuries were a time of considerable intellectual ferment, with the transformation of old disciplines and the emergence of new. For this period, in a discussion of time and narrative, the work of William James (1842–1910) and of Henri Bergson (1859–1941) is particularly central. Bergson published three major works: in 1889 *Time and Free Will: An Essay on the Immediate Data of Consciousness* (*Essai sur les données immédiates de la conscience*, Bergson 2002), in 1896 *Matter and Memory* (*Matière et Mémoire*, Bergson 2004), and in 1907 *Creative Evolution* (*L'Evolution Créatrice*, Bergson 1975). In 1890, James published *The Principles of Psychology*, which had taken him 12 years to write. Two years later, he published *Psychology* (1892, usually subtitled *Briefer Course*, a work reduced 'to make it more directly available for class-room use'; it is from this work that the material on 'stream of consciousness' was quoted in Chapter 1) and in 1907, *Pragmatism: A New Name for Some Old Ways of Thinking*. Alexander Gunn, author of *Bergson and his Philosophy*, published in 1920 at the height of Bergson's influence, is anxious to correct what he sees as 'erroneous ideas' about the historical and intellectual relation between James and Bergson (Gunn 1920, 4). James' investigations, says Gunn, 'had been proceeding since 1870', so the mere date of publication does not imply Bergson's ideas were prior. In turn, Bergson denied that the ideas of his first book, *Time and Free Will*, were influenced by an earlier, 1884, article by James ('On Some Omissions of Introspective Psychology'), which, in Gunn's words, 'deals with the conception of thought as a stream of consciousness, which intellect distorts by framing into concepts' (1920, 5). However, during at least the last seven years of James' life, each was well aware of the work of the other, through reading and correspondence (both were fluent in English and French, James having been to school in Geneva, Bergson's mother being English). In the Hibbert lectures of 1908, published as *A Pluralistic Universe*, James claimed that Bergson's influence had led him to realize that 'reality, life, experience, concreteness, immediacy, use what word you will, exceeds our logic, overflows and surrounds it' (James 2012, 112–113).

And to the French translation of James' *Pragmatism*, published posthu-
mously in 1911, Bergson wrote a 16-page introduction. Yet their ideas
certainly were not identical, and the following brief notes, focused on
understandings of time, trace out the views of each independently.

James' philosophy of pragmatism – derived from a principle that he
had heard from Charles Sanders Peirce in 1878 (James 2018, 18) – tried
explicitly to bridge the differences between an abstract rationalism and a
concrete empiricism. '[There is] no difference in abstract truth that doesn't
express itself in a difference in concrete fact and in conduct consequent
upon that fact, imposed on somebody, somehow, somewhere and
somewhen' (James 2018, 20). For James, this means that 'Science and
metaphysics would come much nearer together' because, while traditional
metaphysics rests when it uses the word that 'names the universe's
principle' (such as, he lists, 'God,' 'Matter', Reason,' 'Energy'), 'you', as
pragmatist, must 'set [each word] at work within the stream of your
experience' (James 2018, 20–21). The pragmatic method is '*The attitude
of looking away from first things, principles, "categories," supposed
necessities; and of looking towards last things, fruits, consequences, facts*'
(James' italics, 2018, 22). (All quotations in this paragraph are from
Lecture II, 'What Pragmatism Means', of his Boston/New York lectures
published as *Pragmatism*.)

How did the word 'time' respond to James' method? Lecture V of the
Boston/New York series, 'Pragmatism and Common Sense', speaks to his
understanding:

> Experience merely as such doesn't come ticketed and labelled …
> What we usually do is first to frame some system of concepts mentally
> classified, serialized, or connected in some intellectual way, and then
> to use this as a tally by which we 'keep tab' on the impressions that
> present themselves. Find a one-to-one relations for your sense-
> impressions *anywhere* among the concepts, and in so far forth you
> rationalize the impressions.
>
> (James 2018, 65–66)

(This sounds very similar to Ellis's discussion of Whorf on configuration
in language, as described in Chapter 2.) Various conceptual systems can
be used for such rationalization, but the most ancient and enduring way
of rationalizing sense-impressions acquires the status of 'commonsense'.
For James. 'Our fundamental ways of thinking about things are discoveries of exceedingly remote ancestors', and he lists 'the most important
concepts' of this transmitted common-sense as:

> Thing; The same or different; Kinds; Minds; Bodies; One Time;
> One Space; Subjects and attributes; Causal influences; The fancied;
> The real.

Yet despite the apparent solidity of these concepts, he claims, 'There is not a category ... of which we might not imagine the use to have thus originated historically and only gradually spread' (James 2018, 65–66).

James goes on to illustrate this assertion of his several concepts, and of Time and Space (his use of upper case) he writes:

> That one Time which we all believe in and in which each event has its definite date, that one Space in which each thing has its position, these abstract notions unify the world incomparably; but in their finished shape as concepts how different they are from the loose unordered time-and-space experiences of natural men! Everything that happens to us brings its one duration and extension, and both are vaguely surrounded by a marginal 'more' that runs into the duration and extension of the next thing that comes. But we soon lose all our definite bearings; and not only do our children make no distinction between yesterday and the day before yesterday, the whole past being churned up together, but we adults still do so whenever the times are large ... Cosmic space and cosmic time, so far from being the intuitions that Kant said they were, are constructions as patently artificial as any that science can show. The great majority of the human race never use these notions, but live in plural times and spaces, interpenetrant and *durcheinander* [English: mixed up, messy, muddled].
>
> (2018, 68)

At the very least, James' 'loose unordered time-and-space experiences', experiences of duration (time) and extension (space), are characteristic of Fraser's world 5, the world of nootemporality, the human mental experience of time. They are experiences internal to the individual. At the same time, I'd suggest James' duration and extension are also characteristic of Fraser's world 6, the world of sociotemporality, with its conflation and elevation of significance experienced in myth, religious ritual, the shared cultural understanding of a people, in which 'the whole past [is] churned up together'. Neither of these times correspond to the common-sense concept of just 'one Time', that is, a biotemporality of directed chronological sequence.

Like nootemporality, the biotemporality of world 4 is also a temporality of the individual organism, but it is external, physical, observable by others. It is the temporality that can be correlated with the temporality of others in shared activity. Thus when the concept of 'one Time' is conceived and taken into common sense, it is this temporality of world 4, the temporality which is external, that can be conceptualized as one 'objective' time, even while its origin is subjective, a concept of the oneness of congruent experience. In summary, James' understanding of time, in terms of Fraser's integrative levels, allows for the different temporalities of worlds 4, 5 and 6. As James wrote, 'The great majority of the human race ... live in plural times and spaces'. It is also worth noting that while 'one Time' is a concept of common sense, this does not exclude the possibility of other concepts of time being added to human understanding through further extension of the human umwelt, as Fraser's model explicitly describes. In this respect, I suggest, James's account of time is quite different from that of Bergson.

In *Time and Free Will*, the first of his three largest works, Bergson himself is primarily concerned with a debate traditionally important to metaphysics. In his Author's Preface, he writes:

> The problem which I have chosen is one which is common to metaphysics and psychology, the problem of free will. What I attempt to prove is that all discussion between the determinists and their opponents implies a previous confusion of duration with extensity, of succession with simultaneity, of quality with quantity ...
>
> (Bergson 2002, xix–xx)

However, although the last third of his book focuses on this 'problem', and the previous two thirds are described 'as an introduction' to its solution, it is the latter that proves to be of greater influence, with his concept, 'duration', central to the consideration of temporal meanings.

Bergson uses the concept 'duration' (in the original French *durée*, sometimes also translated 'durance'), to refer to a qualitative understanding of time, the time of human consciousness: 'Pure duration is the form which the succession of our conscious states assumes when our ego lets itself *live*, when it refrains from separating its present state from its former states' (2002, 100). We see the similarity between James' 'unordered' duration and Bergson's *durée,* as the latter writes:

> Pure duration might well be nothing but a succession of qualitative changes, which melt into and permeate one another, without precise outlines, without any tendency to externalise themselves in relation to one another, without any affiliation with number: it would be pure heterogeneity.
>
> (2002, 104)

For Bergson, explanations of time inevitably present a quantitative understanding, a substitution of the attributes of space for those of time (as for Whorf, a fundamental attribute of SAE, Standard Average European). These spatial attributes are those of extension and measurability, the counting of homogenous units, which are 'simultaneous' in the sense of being undifferentiated, qualitatively identical:

> ... in place of an organism which develops, in place of changes which permeate one another, we perceive one and the same sensation

stretching itself out lengthwise, so to speak, and setting itself in juxtaposition to itself without limit.

(2002, 107)

This is time measured, by the concrete regularities of clocks or the abstracted divisions of a calendar. For brevity, we can call this quantitative understanding, public time.

How does this distinction between qualitative and quantitative temporality relate to Fraser's model? On the face of it, duration must be the temporality of world 5, the mental world of humans, and public time the temporality of world 4, the physical world of organic beings. Certainly, public time enables the physical co-ordination of individuals for social purposes (as in clock time and calendar time: 'we'll all meet at 6pm on the 25th of this month'). But, as the earlier comment on 'explanation' implies, for Bergson language inevitably translates the qualitative duration of consciousness into the quantitative attributes of public time. The concepts/configurations of language segment what is continuous in experience, so any talk of consciousness is already quantitative. Narrative, being already a parcelling up of experience in language (or some other semiotic medium), cannot then tell duration directly, though narrative nootemporality can tell *about* duration, can return us to a greater awareness of our own consciousness (and Augustine of Hippo can be aware of his own confusion). Bergson briefly acknowledges this possibility:

> Now, if some bold novelist, tearing aside the cleverly woven curtain of our conventional ego, shows us under this appearance of logic a fundamental absurdity, under this juxtaposition of simple states an infinite permeation of a thousand different impressions which have already ceased to exist the instant they are named, we commend him for having known us better than we knew ourselves. This is not the case, however, and the very fact that he spreads out our feeling in a homogenous time, and expresses its elements by words, shows that he has arranged this shadow in such a way as to make us suspect the extraordinary and illogical nature of the object which projects it; he has made us reflect by giving outward expression to something of that contradiction, that interpenetration, which is the very essence of the elements expressed. Encouraged by him, we have put aside for an instant the veil which we interposed between our consciousness and ourselves. He has brought us back into our own presence.

(2002, 133–134)

'Bold novelists' did indeed take up the challenge. In the first decades of the twentieth century, Bergson's ideas, or at least his ideas as they were understood, had a considerable influence on literary production of the poetry and prose that came to be described as 'Modernism'.

The last 50-odd years have seen a renewed scholarly interest in charting this influence on both sides of the Atlantic. In *Bergson, Eliot and American Literature*, Paul Douglass sees authors appropriating Bergson as a defence of art (quality) against science (quantity):

> For consciously 'modern' writers in America during the period between the wars, technology and its muse, Science, seemed on a path toward spiritual impoverishment and disaster. As the gap between body and soul widened, that literature recorded the disso-ciations – the *deboublement* of the self – but it also held out hope of a path back to wholeness. This, at its simplest level, is what Bergson personified to American artists like Faulkner, William Carlos Williams, Frost, Wolfe, Henry Miller, and Gertrude Stein. They responded equally or more strongly than the generation of British artists considering the same sorts of problems: Joyce, Woolf, the later Yeats.
>
> (Douglass 1986, 167)

Ten years later, Mary Ann Gillies expressed surprise that a similar exten-sive study of Bergson's influence on British Modernism had not till then appeared (Gillies 1996, 3). Her book, *Henri Bergson and British Modernism*, gives detailed attention to the work of T.S. Eliot, Virginia Woolf, James Joyce, Dorothy Richardson and Joseph Conrad.

One phrase that became firmly associated with Modernist prose fiction was that of 'stream of consciousness'. The phrase was already used by James in 1890:

> Consciousness, then, does not appear to itself chopped up in bits. Such words as 'chain' or 'train' do not describe it fitly as it presents itself in the first instance. It is nothing jointed: it flows. A 'river' or a 'stream' are the metaphors by which it is most naturally described. In talking of it hereafter, let us call it the stream of thought, of con-sciousness, or of subjective life.
>
> (James 2007, 239)

And subsequently Bergson frequently used (in English translation) the word 'stream' when talking of duration ('we perceive duration as a stream against which we cannot go', 2002, 41). Shiv K. Kumar's 1962 mono-graph, discussing the work of Dorothy Richardson, Virginia Woolf and James Joyce, is titled simply, *Bergson and the Stream of Consciousness Novel*. Kumar notes (1962, 14, note 66 to Chapter 1) that the term was first brought into literary criticism in 1918 by May Sinclair; writing on Dorothy Richardson's novels in *The Egoist*, Sinclair said, 'there is no drama, no situation. no set scene. Nothing happens. It is just life going on and on. It is Miriam's stream of consciousness, going on and on' (Sinclair

1917, 58). The novelist Dorothy Richardson herself has said she was not directly influenced by Bergson (Kumar 1962, 36–37), but the reviewer May Sinclair was very familiar with his work. (Sinclair was a philosopher, dedicated to 'idealistic monism'; in her 'Introduction' to *A Defence of Idealism*, she writes that she finds it 'painful to differ from M. Bergson and from William James [whereas it is 'dangerous to differ from Mr. Bertrand Russell'] but differ she must' 1917, xiv.) It is no accident, surely, that the River Liffey is the (dis)organizing principle of James Joyce's *Finnegan's Wake*, the ultimate record of a modernist author's semantic, lexicogrammatical, phonic and graphic stream of consciousness.

It was after the publication in 1907 of Bergson's third major work, *Creative Evolution*, that he became, in the parlance of the twenty-first century, a celebrity. His work was disseminated in both academic and popular contexts, directly and indirectly, and could be described as part of 'the social contextualization of the arts' (Gillies 1996, 5). His influence is not therefore simply linear so that critical discussions must discriminate between 'Bergson and Bergsonism', as Paul Douglass (1986) does when describing various interpretations and apparent applications of Bergson's thought. Bearing these convolutions in mind, I return here to Bergson's own words.

In *Creative Evolution*, Bergson pushes his concept of duration further. He rejects attempts to give coherence to changing inner states by postulating a unifying ego:

> What we actually obtain in this way is an artificial imitation of the internal life, a static equivalent which will lend itself better to the requirements of logic and language, just because we have eliminated from it the element of real time.
>
> (1975, 4)

He extends duration from the conscious experience of time to life itself (James' conflation of time and consciousness was mentioned in Chapter 1):

> Continuity of change, preservation of the past in the present, real duration – the living being seems, then, to share these attributes with consciousness. Can we go further and say that life, like conscious activity, is invention, is unceasing creation?
>
> (1975, 24)

And he extends this understanding further, from the organic to the universal; for Bergson, 'exist' is no longer a synonym for 'be' but for 'becoming':

> We are seeking only the precise meaning that our consciousness gives to this word 'exist', and we find that, for a conscious being, to exist

is to change, to change is to mature, to mature is to go on creating oneself endlessly. Should the same be said of existence in general?...

(1975, 8)

Bergson offers an answer to his own question:

The universe *endures*. The more we study the nature of time, the more we shall comprehend that duration means invention, the creation of forms, the continual elaboration of the absolutely new. The systems marked off by science endure only because they are bound up inseparably with the rest of the universe.

(1975, 11)

For Bergson, 'real time, regarded as a flux, or, in other words, as the very mobility of being, escapes the hold of scientific knowledge' (1975, 355). Both science and language, he argues, use what he calls the 'cinematographic method', which, in photography, is 'to take a series of snapshots of the passing [event] and to throw these instantaneous views on the screen, so that they replace each other very rapidly' (1975, 322). And whereas 'intelligible reality', the reality of scientific laws of being ('constant relations between variable magnitudes' 1975, 352), is discerned by the human intellect, 'sensible reality', the experienced reality of becoming, may be apprehended by what Bergson calls 'intuition' (1975, 331). 'We do not *think* real time. But we *live* it' (1975, 49). Bergson's intuition is not the colloquial 'hunch': it might be glossed as attention, awareness. His description reminds me of the states of consciousness sought in some practices of meditation:

The feeling we have of our evolution and of the evolution of all things in pure duration is there, forming around the intellectual concept properly so-called an indistinct fringe that fades off into darkness.

(1975, 49)

This 'intellectual concept' is the sign of science and natural language (1975, 347). Effectively, Bergson contradicts the assumptions of neoplatonism, in which knowledge is of the 'ideal' persistent form, measured and counted in the nominalization of pre-Einsteinian scientific discourse (as Halliday traced in his account of grammatical metaphor, discussed in Chapter 2). To some of the 'bold novelists' previously mentioned, Bergson's ideas appeared to return to art an holistic function of the imagination. Though science effaces the fringe, perhaps literary art, even with its limitation as language, could give attention to that which is indistinct, liminal. Positively, this insight can encourage those hoping to dismantle the 'grand narratives' of constraint and repression (Lyotard 1984);

negatively, this focus can merely replace the monovalent intellectual 'being' with a monovalent intuitive 'becoming'. (Although in his earlier writing Bergson's *durée* seems most comparable to Fraser's nootemporality, the time of world 5 of human consciousness, his expansion of qualitative time to 'becoming' encompasses the time of Fraser's world 1, that of atemporality, thus collapsing the natural levels of Fraser's model. See also the last paragraph of Chapter 3.)

For narrative theory generally, one possible consequence of a different disciplinary focus, inclining to one temporal understanding or another, can be a different theoretical focus on product (text) or process (productive and interpretative strategies and their context). Thus in contrast to literate literary structuralism, classical classification of the spoken performance (as in Aristotle's *Poetics*; see Lowe 2000) based its generic descriptions on the process of the act of narration, rather than the narrative object told – that is, on the form of action, including speech, in the drama, versus the form of telling in the lyric poem, and both spoken and told in the mixed mode of the epic. Likewise, post-structuralist studies of narrative have foregrounded the process of narration, drawing attention to the ideological positioning of the interpreting subject in relation to the narrated object (Huisman 2005, 28–44). Thus poststructuralist literary approaches are more compatible with some of the work done in anthropological and psychological studies – for example, that the nature and purpose of narrative is differently understood in different cultural environments, or that story structures are distinguished by the 'affective function' to produce surprise, suspense or curiosity. The recent collection, *A Companion to Literary Theory*, with chapters by many eminent scholars of narrative, groups its papers by topic, not chronology, 'in order to highlight the relationships between earlier and most recent theoretical developments' (Richter 2018). Part I on 'Literary Form' thus includes chapters on 'Russian Formalism' and 'Structuralism and Semiotics', as well as a chapter by James Phelan on 'Contemporary Narrative Theory'; the latter discusses theories of non-mimetic ('Unnatural') narrative, of borders between fiction and non-fiction ('Fictionality'), of mind-reading ('Theories of Mind'), and feminist and queer narrative theories intersecting with narrative as theory and individual practice ('Intersectionality'). Phelan writes that he has 'construct[ed] this [chapter] as a companion piece to my chapter, "Narrative Theory – 1966–2006: A Narrative"', which appeared in the 2006 collection *The Nature of Narrative* (Scholes et al. 2006). In total, the seven general topics, Parts I to VII, of *A Companion to Literary Theory*, contain 36 chapters/contributors, demonstrating in their variety the spread of method and object of study in narrative theory, even when the latter is limited to what can be relevant to 'literary theory'.

The most recently published book on narrative that I have read moves beyond both literary texts and literary theory: this is *Fragmented*

Narrative, Telling and Interpreting Stories in the Twitter Age, by Neil Sadler (2022). Sadler's analysis widens even further the possibilities of the 'philosophical' orientation to narrative theory. To the contemporary fragmentation of text and the 'intuitive' engagement with stories 'in the mode of circumspection rather than thematic looking' (158), the author applies the concepts of Ricoeur, Gadamer and Heidegger (the book appends a 'Glossary of Heideggerian Terms', to explain his use of them, 163–166). (Sadler's book is referred to again in Chapter 11.)

It is possibly an act of hubris on my part for this book to offer just one chapter in such summary mode on the work of so many scholars, with so little discussion of many whose contribution is of obvious importance. Nonetheless, I hope it speaks to the heterologic value given to the field, and points to the continuing possibilities of narrative study.

References

Abbott, H. Porter. 2008. *The Cambridge Introduction to Narrative*. 2nd ed. Cambridge: Cambridge University Press.

Bakhtin, M. M. 1981. *The Dialogic Imagination, Four Essays*, edited by Michael Holquist. Austin: University of Texas Press.

Bal, Mieke. 1997. *Narratology: Introduction to the Theory of Narrative*. 2nd ed. Toronto: Toronto University Press.

Barthes, Roland. 1974 [1970 published in French]. *S/Z*. New York: Hill and Wang.

Barthes, Roland. 1975 [1966 published in French]. 'An Introduction to the Structural Analysis of Narrative'. *New Literary History* 6 (2): pp. 237–272.

Bergson, Henri. 2002 [1889]. *Time and Free Will, An Essay on the Immediate Data of Consciousness*. London and New York: Routledge.

Bergson, Henri. 2004 [1896]. *Matter and Memory*. Mineola, NY: Dover Publications.

Bergson, Henri. 1975 [1907]. *Creative Evolution*. Westport, CT: Greenwood Press.

Cortazzi, Martin. 1993, reprinted 2002. *Narrative Analysis*. London and New York: RoutledgeFalmer.

de Saussure, Ferdinand. 1959 [1916]. *Course in General Linguistics*, translated Wade Baskin, edited by Charles Bally and Albert Sechehaye with Albert Riedlinger. New York: McGraw Hill.

Douglass, Paul. 1986. *Bergson, Eliot and American Literature*. Lexington, KY: Kentucky University Press.

Erlich, Victor. 2012. *Russian Formalism: History – Doctrine*. Berlin, Boston: De Gruyter Mouton. https://doi-org.ezproxy.library.sydney.edu.au/10.1515/9783110873375

Genette, Gérard. 1980. *Narrative Discourse, An Essay in Method*. Ithaca, New York: Cornell University Press.

Gillies, Mary Ann. 1996. *Henri Bergson and British Modernism*. Montreal and Kingston: McGill-Queen's University Press.

Graffi, Giorgio. 2019. 'The Prague Linguistic Circle'. In Oxford Bibliographies Online in Linguistics. Accessed 18 February 2021. https://www-oxfordbibliographies-com.ezproxy.library.sydney.edu.au/view/document/obo-9780199772810/obo-9780199772810-0247.xml?rskey=33tVJP&result=221

Grosz, Elizabeth. 2004. *The Nick of Time. Politics, Evolution and the Untimely.* Crows Nest, NSW: Allen and Unwin.

Grosz, Elizabeth. 2005. *Time Travels, Feminism, Nature, Power.* Crows Nest, NSW: Allen and Unwin.

Gunn, J. Alexander. 1920. *Bergson and his Philosophy.* London: Methuen.

Herman, David, Manfred Jahn and Marie-Laure Ryan, editors. 2005. *The Routledge Encyclopedia of Narrative Theory.* London and New York: Routledge.

Huisman, Rosemary. 2005. 'The Basics of Narrative Theory'. In *Narrative and Media*, edited by Helen Fulton, Rosemary Huisman, Julian Murphet and Anne Dunn, pp. 11–44.

Jakobson, Roman. 1985. *Verbal Art, Verbal Sign, Verbal Time.* Oxford: Basil Blackwell.

James, William. 1892. *Psychology: Briefer Course.* London: Macmillan & Co. Reproduced by The Project Gutenberg. www.gutenberg.org/files/55262/55262-h/55262-h.htm

James, William. 2007 [1890] *The Principles of Psychology.* New York: Cosimo.

James, William. 2012 [1908]. *A Pluralistic Universe: Hibbert Lectures at Manchester College on the Present Situation in Philosophy.* Auckland: The Floating Press. Available from: ProQuest Ebook Central.

James, William. 2018 [1907]. *Pragmatism: A New Name for Some Old Ways of Thinking.* Mineola, NY: Dover Publications, Inc.

Kak, Michael B. 1997. 'Present at the Creation: A Reminiscence of the Summer of "63", *Towards a Social Science of Language*, Papers in Honor of William Labov, Volume 2, *Social Interaction and Discourse Structures*. Amsterdam and Philadephica: John Benjamin.

Kumar, Shiv K. 1962. *Bergson and the Stream of Consciousness Novel.* London: Blackie.

Labov, William. 1972a. *Sociolinguistic Patterns.* Philadelphia: University of Pennsylvania Press.

Labov, William. 1972b. *Language in the Inner City, Studies in the Black English Vernacular.* Philadelphia: University of Pennsylvania Press.

Labov, William. 1975. 'What Is a Linguistic Fact?' In *The Scope of American Linguistics*, edited by Robert Austerlitz, pp. 159–196. Lisse: Peter de Ridder Press.

Labov, William. 1994. *Principles of Linguistic Change.* Oxford and Cambridge, Massachusetts: Blackwell.

Lévi-Strauss, Claude. 1977 [1958 published in French]. *Structural Anthropology.* Harmondsworth: Penguin.

Lloyd, Genevieve. 1993. *Being in Time, Selves and Narrators in Philosophy and Literature.* London and New York: Routledge.

Lowe, N.J. 2000. *The Classical Plot and the Invention of Western Narrative.* Cambridge: Cambridge University Press.

Lyotard, Jean-François. 1984 [1979 in French]. *The Postmodern Condition, A Report on Knowledge*. Manchester: Manchester University Press.

Martin, J.R. and David Rose. 2008. *Genre Relations, Mapping a Culture*. London and Oakville, Connecticut: Equinox.

Meares, Russell. 2016. *The Poet's Voice in the Making of Mind*. London and New York: Routledge.

Metz, Christian. 1974. *Film Language: A Semiotics of the Cinema*. New York: Oxford University Press.

Morson, Gary Saul. 1986. *Bakhtin, Essays and Dialogues on His Work*. Chicago and London: The University of Chicago Press.

Nünning, Ansgar. 2003. 'Narratology or Narratologies? Taking Stock of Recent Developments, Critique and Modest Proposals for Future Usages of the Term'. In *What is Narratology?* edited by Tom Kindt and Hans-Harald Müller, pp. 238–275. Berlin and New York: Walter de Gruyter.

Phelan, James and Peter J. Rabinowitz, editors. 2005. *A Companion to Narrative Theory*. Malden, MA and Oxford: Blackwell.

Pier, John. 2003. 'On the Semiotic Parameters of Narrative: A Critique of Story and Discourse'. In *What Is Narratology?* edited by Tom Kindt and Hans-Harald Müller, pp. 74–97. Berlin and New York: Walter de Gruyter.

Prince, Gerald. 2003. *Dictionary of Narratology*. Lincoln and London: University of Nebraska Press.

Propp, Vladimir. 1968 [1928]. *Morphology of the Folktale*. 2nd ed. Austin: Texas University Press.

Ricoeur, Paul. 1984–1988. *Time and Narrative*, Volumes 1–3, translated by Kathleen Blamey and David Pellauer. Chicago: The University of Chicago Press.

Richter, David, editor. 2018. *A Companion to Literary Theory*. Chichester, West Sussex: John Wiley & Sons.

Rudova, Larissa. 1996. 'Bergsonism in Russia: The Case of Bakhtin.' *Neophilologus* 80: pp. 175–188.

Rutkoff, Peter M. and William B. Scott. 1983. 'The French in New York: Resistance and Structure.' *Social Research* 50 (1): pp. 185–214.

Ryan, Marie-Laure. 2007. 'Towards a Definition of Narrative'. In *The Cambridge Companion to Narrative*, edited by David Herman, pp. 22–35. Cambridge: Cambridge University Press.

Sadler, Neil. 2022. *Fragmented Narrative, Telling and Interpreting Stories in the Twitter Age*. London and New York: Routledge.

Scholes, Robert, James Phelan and Robert Kellogg, editors. 2006. *The Nature of Narrative*. 2nd ed. Oxford and New York: Oxford University Press.

Sinclair, May. 1917. *A Defence of Idealism*. London: Macmillan.

Todorov, Tzvetan. 1984. *Mikhail Bakhtin, The Dialogical Principle*. Manchester: Manchester University Press.

Toolan, Michael. 2001. *Narrative: A Critical Linguistic Introduction*. 2nd ed. London and New York: Routledge.

5 Language and worlds of experience

The basic concepts of M.A.K Halliday's model of functional grammar, and its system of transitivity relating meaning to worlds of experience

In Chapter 2, the linguistic work of M.A.K. Halliday was introduced as it was relevant to his discussion of 'grammatical metaphor' and (what I have termed) the 'spatialization' of language, that is, taking time out of meaning. The next chapter, Chapter 6, explores the 'temporalization' of language, that is, keeping time in meaning, with detailed textual examples. First, however, this chapter must return to Halliday's model of language in systemic functional linguistics (SFL) to explain some features of its general 'architecture' and terminology. These concepts underpin the particular aspects discussed in Chapter 6. The latter part of this chapter also describes in detail one SFL topic directly relevant to the theorizing of 'narrative worlds': that of the system of transitivity. This material will be taken up again in Chapter 7, along with J.T. Fraser's model of worlds of different temporalities.

'The architecture of language' in systemic functional linguistics (SFL): dimensions of language and the concept of text

In the third and fourth editions of *An Introduction to Functional Grammar*, Halliday and Matthiessen describe five dimensions, or forms of order, in language (Halliday 2004a, 19–31; Halliday 2014, 20–31). These are the dimensions of **structure, system, stratification, instantiation** and **metafunction,** as indicated in Table 5.1 (Halliday 2004a, 2014, 20). Table 5.1, from Table 1–4 in Halliday 2014, is reproduced with permission.

Consider dimension 5, that of metafunction. In the right-hand column, three orders of metafunction are given: the ideational, the interpersonal and the textual, the ideational having two sub-orders, the logical and the experiential. In the social-semiotic assumptions of SFL, 'function' denotes meaning and individual functions/meanings are grouped under one or other of these metafunctions (Halliday 2002, 173–195). It is the experiential metafunction – later further discussed – which has a particular resonance with Fraser's 'worlds' of different temporalities and so with the worlds of narrative.

DOI: 10.4324/b23121-5

Table 5.1 The dimensions (forms of order) in language and their ordering
principles

	dimension	principle	orders
1	structure (syntagmatic order)	rank	clause – group or phrase – word-morpheme (lexicogrammar) tone group – foot – syllable – phoneme (phonology)
2	system (paradigmatic order)	delicacy	grammar – lexis (lexicogrammar)
3	stratification	realization	semantics – lexicogrammar – phonology – phonetics
4	instantiation	instantiation	potential – sub-potential or instance type – instance
5	metafunction	metafunction	ideational [logical – experiential] – interpersonal – textual

Halliday explains metafunction in terms of the phylogenesis of language,
that is, from the development of language in the evolution of (Edelman's
higher-order) human consciousness: 'language is as it is because of the functions in which it has evolved in the human species' (Halliday 2004a; Halliday
2014, 31). At the most general level, language evolved in two complementary functions: 'construing experience, and enacting social processes'
(Halliday and Matthiessen 1999, xi; Halliday 1978, 2; 2004a, 29–30; 2014,
30). Halliday refers to the former as the ideational metafunction, the latter as
the interpersonal metafunction. As language evolves, a third function weaves
the first two together as 'text'; Halliday calls this the 'textual metafunction'.
In summary, the ideational meanings of language (language as reflection)
enable humans to talk about happenings, the interpersonal meanings (language as action) enable humans to interact and express attitudes, the textual
meanings enable humans to produce coherent messages.

From these three metafunctions, Halliday infers three elements of the
context of situation in which language is used: field, tenor and mode,
as described in Table 5.2 (Halliday 2014, 33–34; Halliday 1978,
142–145).

The ideational metafunction, with the function of construing experience, gives rise to the field of social action: what is going on in the situation as, first, the nature of the social and semiotic activity and, second, the

Table 5.2 Metafunctions and the context of situation

context of situation	field of social action	tenor of situation	mode of message
Semantic metafunctions (meaning)	Ideational function: Experiential and Logical functions	Interpersonal function	Textual function

domain of experience this activity relates to. For a narrative this domain is the subject matter; thus a narrative has at least one semiotic action of telling and a subject matter told. (This may of course be recursive, as in Chaucer's *Canterbury Tales*.) This distinction is well recognized in the 'Subject' of French linguistic and semiotic study, as in Emile Benveniste's Subject of the enunciation, the telling, and Subject of the enounced, the told, to which film studies adds a third Subject: the subject position of the camera (Silverman 1983); verbally this can be comparable to Genette's 'focalization' (1980, 189–194). (The complex possibilities of narrative 'voice' are discussed in Chapter 6.)

The interpersonal metafunction, with the function of enacting social processes, gives rise to the tenor of situation: who is taking part in the situation as, first, the roles played by those taking part in the sociosemiotic activity (of status, of familiarity and so on) and, second, the values (neutral or loaded, positively or negatively) that those interacting give to the domain/subject matter. Thus, for example, typically the narrator has a role of 'information giver', varying in power (omniscient, unreliable, etc.) and characters in dialogue can alternate roles of questioner and answerer, can express attitudes and so on.

Finally, the textual metafunction, with the function of weaving a text coherent with the environment, gives rise to the mode of the message. that is, to what role is being played by language and other semiotic systems in the situation. This can be elaborated at length, as in the following list (Halliday 2014, 33–34):

(i).   the division of labour between semiotic activities and social ones (ranging from semiotic activities as constitutive of the situation to semiotic activities as facilitating);
(ii).   the division of labour between linguistic activities and other semiotic activities;
(iii). rhetorical mode: the orientation of the text towards field (as for example informative, didactic, explanatory, explicatory) or tenor (for example, persuasive, exhortatory, hortatory, polemic);
(iv).   turn: dialogic or monologic;
(v).   medium: written or spoken;
(vi).   channel: phonic or graphic.

The focus of my later discussion is on field. The meanings of the transitivity system, significant for the juxtaposition of Halliday's model of language and Fraser's model of time, belong to the experiential metafunction that gives rise to field – though it is obvious the other parameters of the context of situation, tenor and mode, are relevant to a rich discussion of narrative.

Returning to Table 5.1, consider SFL dimension 3, that of stratification. As Chapter 2 discussed, it is the stratified nature of language that enables grammatical metaphor in the phenomenon of 'semantic drift' as there is not an immediate one to one relation of expression and meaning (so also for lexical metaphor, touched on in Chapter 6). The strata/levels of this dimension are illustrated in Table 5.3.

The 'ordering principle' of this dimension is 'realization': in Table 5.3, the downward arrow represents the realization 'direction' of producing text (for example, the field of the context of situation is realized – in the language familiar to the speaker/writer – by choices of ideational meaning in the text); the upward arrow represents the realization direction of interpreting text (for example, the wording of a visually displayed text, print or digital, is understood from the graphic choices displayed – assuming the interpreter is familiar with the language deployed). In Halliday's words:

> Realization is probably the most difficult single concept in linguistics. It is the relationship of 'meaning-&-meant' which, in semiotic systems, replaces the 'cause-&-effect' relation of classical physical systems. Unlike cause, realization is not a relationship in real time. It is a two-way relationship that we can only gloss by using more than one word to describe it: to say that wordings (lexicogrammatical formations) *realize* meanings (semantic formations) means both that wordings **express** meanings and that wordings **construct** meanings.
>
> (Halliday 2003, 210)

More usually, Halliday continues, he uses the word *construe* rather than *construct*, which he glosses as '*construed* – that is, constructed in the semiotic sense'.

Each of the different levels of stratification has its own structure; these are described in the SFL dimension 1: Structure, which is depicted in Table 5.4 (each level in **bold**).

Structure refers to language on the syntagmatic axis of sequence, 'what goes with what'. The ordering principle of structure is that of rank; a rank hierarchy is made up of units of structure, as indicated in Table 5.4. The level of semantics/meanings has only one unit, that of the text, while the level of lexicogrammar/wording has a rank hierarchy of units of clause, group or phrase, word and morpheme. The level of expression is divided

Table 5.3 Dimension 3: Stratification (ordering principle of realization)

extra-linguistic concept	context of situation	↑
linguistic concepts	semantics: meanings	
	lexicogrammar: wordings	
	expression: phonology & graphology	↓

Table 5.4 Dimension 1: Structure (ordering principle of rank)

semantics / meanings
text
lexicogrammar / wordings
clause
group or phrase
word
morpheme
expression

graphology (written language)	phonology (spoken language)
perimeter	tone group
block	foot (rhythm group)
line	syllable
character	phoneme

into two: graphology and phonology, each with its own hierarchy of units of structure. (The units of graphology listed derive from my own work on the graphic realization of poetry, Huisman 1998, 2016.) In the simplest structure, units of higher rank are made up of those below, thus clauses are made up of groups or phrases; in more complex structures, units can be 'rank-shifted', such as a clause embedded in another unit (for example, the traditional 'defining relative' or 'adjectival clause' embedded in a nominal group, or a clause functioning as subject embedded in another clause).

Formal linguistics (such as generative theories) focus on the study of grammar and its formal highest unit, the 'sentence'. In SFL, the highest unit of lexicogrammar is the clause; in writing, the graphically punctuated sentence usually realizes a single clause or a clause complex (clauses linked, typically by a conjunction). But as a functional linguistics, SFL also studies the higher stratum of semantics. The one unit of semantics is the text. What is 'text' in SFL? In their book-length study of textual 'cohesion', Halliday and Hasan write:

> The concept of texture is entirely appropriate to express the property of 'being a text'. … a text derives this texture from the fact that it functions as a unit with respect to its environment …
>
> (Halliday and Hasan 1976, 2)

Here, the word 'environment' is a deliberately wide and inclusive word, textually and contextually. To describe what is involved in 'texture', here the property of being a text, SFL investigates three aspects: theme and information; cohesion; register. The first two enable the study of the internal organization of the individual text, the third places the one text in a wider context of other texts. A few introductory words on these three aspects follow.

Halliday and Matthiessen (2004a, 2014, Chapter 3) describe the Theme and Information systems as choices of textual meaning that realize the mode of the context of situation (as in Table 5.2). They thus link the organization of a message to its environment of use. Theme is realized in the wording of the clause (the lexicogrammatical level): in English thematic meanings are placed at the beginning of the clause. For example, in an on-going conversation an English speaker typically puts information that is already shared, or that is recoverable from the verbal or physical environment, at the beginning of the grammatical clause. The information system, on the other hand, is realized in spoken language only; speakers give more emphasis to new information, which typically, but not necessarily, falls towards the end of their utterances. (Writers occasionally resort to idiosyncratic means to indicate the spoken focus of their information, using bold, italics, underlining, highlighting …)

Cohesion is also the study of textual meanings: the study of cohesive relations between different sentences of the text, that is between language that is not linked by grammatical structure but is linked by meaning. In a book-length study, *Cohesion in English*, Halliday and Hasan identify four types of cohesive tie: reference; substitution and ellipsis; conjunction; lexical relations (1976). An analysis of the cohesive ties in a text shows how the text is coherent with respect to itself, and therefore cohesive. (In an alternative development of SFL, J.R. Martin offers a 'reinterpretation' of cohesion as 'discourse semantics', in which cohesion is 'reformulated as a set of discourse semantic systems at a more abstract level than lexicogrammar, with their own metafunctional organization', 2002, 53–55. The account here continues to follow that of Halliday and Hasan.)

Finally, register. In Halliday's words:

> A register can be defined as the configuration of semantic resources that the member of a culture typically associates with a situation type. It is the meaning potential that is accessible in a given social context.
>
> (Halliday 2007, 182)

Here the phrase 'semantic resources' implies the inclusion of all metafunctions, that is, ideational (experiential and logical), interpersonal and textual meanings. ('Register', variously extended, continues to be a significant focus of study in SFL, Matthiessen 2009, 24–48; 2015; Huisman 2019).

The mention of 'potential' and 'situation type' introduces another of the five SFL dimensions, Dimension 4: Instantiation. This dimension enables the individual text and context to be considered in a wider environment, as depicted in Table 5.5 (Halliday 2014, 27–29).

Table 5.5 Dimension 4. Instantiation (ordering principle: the cline of instantiation)

		context of situation
	institution – situation type	*instance*
context of culture	*subpotential - instance type*	specific text
potential	*repertoire of registers –* text type	
system of language		

The column on the right represents the instance of both language and context, such as the choices of language in a particular literary text and a particular context of situation of field, tenor and mode construed from those choices. This is no structuralist relation of objective interpretation: potential and instance are individually experienced. Those with a similar context of culture, with similar predictive expectations, will tend to construe a similar understanding of the text. (At the limit of subjective variation, the context of situation may be understood as the field, tenor and mode construed by an individual reader in the instance of a particular reading.) The column on the left represents the full potential of both language and context, what is fully available. On this dimension, the context of situation of a text instantiates the potential situations in the context of culture, and the text instantiates the potential choices of language in the system of language. However, as represented in the central column, this panoramic view can be reduced to more specific social contexts, such as the situation types within the institution of the law, and the 'repertoire of registers' that constitute legal text types (Maley 1994, 16). The basic focus of this book could be said to be the study of the 'repertoire of registers' that constitute temporal text types, as elaborated in Chapter 6.

Halliday's modelling of text and context, his theoretical approach, endorses the narrative theorists' focus on time. Consider yet again Porter Abbot's answer to the question, 'what does narrative do for us?': 'first many things ... [but] if we had to choose one answer above all others, the likeliest is that *narrative is the principal way in which our species organizes its understanding of time*' (Porter Abbott 2008, 3). Compare this opinion with the following comment by Halliday, made when he is introducing the language of science and grammatical metaphor (as discussed in Chapter 2) as 'the power that a language has for theorizing':

All use of language embodies theory: ... the grammar of every language contains a theory of human experience: it categorizes the elements of our experience into basic phenomenal types, construing these configurations of various kinds, and these configurations into logical sequences.

(2004b, xvii)

Halliday is speaking here of the clause and the clause complex, but his inclusive 'all use of language' goes further than grammar and I take it to include the construal of text, such as a narrative text. So we can infer the following: that a narrative text embodies theory (Halliday) and that that theory is (at least) a theory of time (Abbott). It is not that time organizes narrative – but rather that narrative (a use of language) organizes/ theorizes time, so that a different organization of the narrative can mean a different understanding of time. This topic is a particular focus of Chapter 7, when Halliday's theorizing on language is brought together with Fraser's theorizing on time.

One more dimension of systemic functional grammar remains: Dimension 2: System with the ordering principle of 'delicacy'. Whereas structure refers to the syntagmatic axis of language sequence (*what goes with what*), system refers to the paradigmatic axis of choice (*what could be chosen instead of what*). The following offers a very brief introduction to this technical area of the theory.

> A text is the product of ongoing selection in a very large network of systems – a system network. Systemic theory gets its name from the fact that the grammar of a language is represented in the form of system networks, not as an inventory of structures. Of course, structure is an essential part of the description; but it is interpreted as the outward form taken by systemic choices, not as the defining characteristic of language. A language is a resource for making meaning, and meaning resides in systemic patterns of choice.
>
> (Halliday 2004a, 2014, 23)

Halliday's compound name for the inter-stratum between expression and semantics – lexis plus grammar to give 'lexicogrammar' – relates to 'delicacy', the ordering principle of dimension 2. The choices of meaning in a system can be described more or less fully, in expanding branches as one choice becomes the entry point for further choices. At that stage where systemic description ends (is most delicate) and the description of the meaning of individual words begins, the description has changed from one of grammar to one of lexis (vocabulary). Just how delicate description needs to be depends on the needs and purposes of the researcher.

The system of transitivity: meaning and construing worlds of experience

In their co-authored book, *Construing Experience through Meaning* (1999), Halliday and Matthiessen write (as already quoted) that language evolved in two complementary functions: 'construing experience, and enacting social processes'. The book, as its title denotes, is concerned with the first of these functions; it describes how the language function of 'construing experience' constructs the 'ideation base':

> By virtue of its unique properties as a stratified semiotic system, language is able to transform experience into meaning. (1999, xi); [and]

> experience is the reality that we construe for ourselves by means of language.
>
> (1999, 3)

This account implies a direction of modelling:

> in modelling the meaning base we are building it 'upwards' from the grammar.
>
> (1999, 2)

This direction is compatible with Ellis' account of 'categorization' and Whorf's concept of 'configuration' through 'segmentation', discussed in Chapter 2, and the authors comment that it contrasts with that of the more usual assumption, in cognitive science, of a knowledge base, in which prior knowing of concepts and categories is used to interpret experience.

Beginning then with the grammar of the clause, SFL builds upwards to the construal of ideational meaning and thence to experience, the construed reality. Ideational meaning has two sub-meanings: experiential meaning built up from one clause; logical meaning built up from the grammatical joining of more than one clause in a clause complex. As already discussed, from these two types of ideational meaning is 'built up' the field of the context of situation (for example, the characters and events of a narrative). It is obvious that a clause complex will build up a more complex meaning (a complex of experiential meanings linked by logical meanings), which will in turn build up a more complex experience of reality.

In Chapter 2, I quoted Halliday's terms for the 'theory of reality' embodied in everyday use of language: Clausal structures; Projection; Expansion; Transitivity (i) different types of process and Transitivity (ii) two models of processes, transitive and ergative; Tense and Aspect. In that list, projection and expansion name the two types of logical meaning distinguished in SFL; these meanings will be further discussed in Chapter 6 (logical expansion of causation and of temporal relation have already been mentioned in Chapter 2). On the other hand, the two types of Transitivity, together with Aspect and Tense (for the most part), are terms for choices of experiential meaning, the meaning 'built up from' the individual clause. As Halliday wrote, 'the clause nucleus is a happening (Process + Medium ...)', and the temporal meanings of that happening, here the central concern of a focus on narrative, are primarily built up from the grammar of the verbal group which realizes the nuclear process.

Within the grammatical verb group, all words are of the word class verb. However, it is the final (or only) word, sometimes referred to as the 'lexical verb', which realizes the meaning of the process. In SFL, a system of meaning choices is realized in a particular grammatical choice; thus different process meanings, realized in the lexical verb, make up the choices of the transitivity system. The system is illustrated in a figure labelled 'The grammar of experience: types of process in English' (here reproduced as Figure 5.1), which appears in several editions of Halliday's *Introduction to Functional Grammar* (1994, 108; 2004a, 172; 2014, 216) and, in colour, on the cover of the second edition (1994). Figure 5.1, from Fig. 5–3 in Halliday 2014, is reproduced with permission.

Halliday and Matthiessen write:

> [Figure 5.1] represents process types as a semiotic space, with different regions representing different types. The regions have core areas and these represent prototypical members of the process types; but the regions are continuous, shading into one another, and these border areas represent the fact that the process types are fuzzy categories.
>
> (Halliday 2004a,172; 2014, 216)

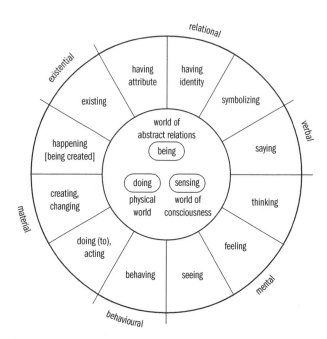

Figure 5.1 The grammar of experience: types of process in English.

Process types are written around the outside of the circle. Notice the reference to 'core areas' and 'prototypical members of the process types' or major process types: these are the three process types of material, relational and mental processes. These three are represented by primary colours on the coloured image of the second edition: red for material, blue for mental and yellow for relational processes. In turn, the intermediate 'semiotic spaces' are represented by intermediate secondary colours (green for verbal processes, purple for behavioural, orange for existential). A footnote comments that the minor process types appear to vary more across languages than the major types (Halliday 2004a, 171; 2014, 215).

Each core area has three semiotic regions, related areas of experiential meaning, written within the segments of the circle. For material processes these are choices of doing (to)/acting; creating, changing; for relational processes these are having attribute/having identity/symbolizing; for mental processes these are thinking/feeling/seeing. The intermediate minor processes label one segment of the circle only, for example verbal processes label the semiotic region of 'saying'.

In the following textual extract from Descartes' *Meditation II*, each clause has been placed on a separate line; the lexical verb of each clause is underlined and the process meaning it realizes is printed in small capitals.

> The Meditation of yesterday has <u>filled</u> my mind with so many doubts,
> MATERIAL
> that it <u>is</u> no longer in my power RELATIONAL
> to <u>forget</u> them. MENTAL
> Nor do I <u>see</u>, meanwhile, any principle MENTAL (= *understand*)
> on which they can be <u>resolved</u>; MENTAL
> and, just as if I had <u>fallen</u> all of a sudden into very deep water,
> MATERIAL
> I am so greatly <u>disconcerted</u> MENTAL
> as to be made unable either <u>to plant</u> my feet firmly on the bottom
> MATERIAL
> or <u>sustain</u> myself MATERIAL
> by <u>swimming</u> on the surface. MATERIAL (Descartes 1912, 85)

As already noted, the choice of experiential meaning in the process realizes the field of the context of situation. In Figure 5.1 we see in the centre of the circle, in the lozenge-shaped boxes, the three types of field realized by the three prototypical types of process: fields of *doing* by the Material processes, fields of *being* by the Relational processes and fields of *sensing* by the Mental processes. This brings us to what is most pertinent to a concern with narrative: the three worlds written adjacent to each of the three fields. Figure 5.1 models human experience as it can be interpreted through the system of transitivity, that is to say, a different world of human experience can be construed from each different prototypical process meaning: a physical world of doing from the choices of material processes, a world of abstract relations from choices of relational processes, a world of consciousness from choices of mental processes. We understand the different construal of these worlds of experience, and so we can recognize the figurative use of one world to explain another. In his 'Meditation', with a simple metaphor centred on the material process *fill*, Descartes can equate the nebulous spatialized entities of the world of consciousness – realized textually in the nouns *meditation, mind, doubts* – with concrete entities of the physical world ('vessel'? 'liquid'?). In a more extended and explicit translation in the final lines, Descartes explains his Mental process in the world of consciousness (*disconcert*) by choices of Material processes in the physical world (*fall, plant, sustain, swim*).

From the system of transitivity, with its choices of process meaning, we can trace the realization relation between language and human worlds of experience and, as Halliday points out, realization is a difficult concept. You could say that in language speakers can represent physical experience, culturally shared assumptions of relations – that is, social experience – and psychological experience. Or conversely, you could say (as Halliday and Matthiessen do in modelling the meaning base 'upwards' from the grammar), physical experience, social experience and psychological experience are the reality that we can construe for ourselves by means of language. The discussion in Chapter 2 (of Ellis' 'categorisation, of Whorf's 'configuration' of different languages) has already teased out some of the implications of this reading.

References

Abbott, H. Porter. 2008. *The Cambridge Introduction to Narrative*. 2nd ed. Cambridge: Cambridge University Press.

Descartes, René. 1912 [1637]. 'Meditation II'. In *A Discourse on Method*. London: J.M. Dent.

Genette, Gérard. 1980. *Narrative Discourse*. Ithaca, New York: Cornell University Press.

Halliday, M.A.K. and Ruqaiya Hasan. 1976. *Cohesion in English*. London: Longman.

Halliday, M.A.K. 1978. *Language as Social Semiotic*. London: Edward Arnold.

Halliday, M.A.K. 1994. *An Introduction to Functional Grammar*. 2nd ed. London, Melbourne and Auckland: Edward Arnold.

Halliday, M.A.K. 2002. *On Grammar*. Volume 1 in the Collected Works of M.A.K. Halliday, ed. Jonathan Webster. London and New York: Continuum.

Halliday, M.A.K. 2003. *On Language and Linguistics*. Volume 3 in the Collected Works of M.A.K. Halliday, ed. Jonathan J. Webster. London and New York: Continuum.

Halliday, M.A.K., revised by M.I.M. Matthiessen. 2004a. *An Introduction to Functional Grammar*. 3rd ed. London: Arnold.

Halliday, M.A.K. 2004b. *Language and Science*. Volume 5 in the Collected Works of M.A.K. Halliday, ed. Jonathan J. Webster. London and New York: Continuum.

Halliday, M.A.K. 2007. *Language and Society*. Volume 10 in the Collected Works of M.A.K. Halliday, ed. Jonathan Webster. London and New York: Continuum.

Halliday, M.A.K., revised by M.I.M. Matthiessen. 2014. *Halliday's Introduction to Functional Grammar*. 4th ed. London and New York: Routledge.

Halliday, M.A.K. and Christian M.I.M. Matthiessen. 1999. *Construing Experience Through Meaning, a Language-Based Approach to Cognition*. London and New York: Continuum.

Huisman, Rosemary. 1998; 2000. *The Written Poem, Semiotic Conventions from Old to Modern English*. London and New York: Cassell; Continuum.

Huisman, Rosemary. 2016. 'Talking about Poetry – Using the Model of Language in Systemic Functional Linguistics to Talk about Poetic Texts'. *English in Australia* 51 (2): pp. 7–19.

Huisman, Rosemary. 2019. 'The Discipline of English Literature from the Perspective of SFL Register'. *Language, Context and Text* 1 (1): pp. 102–120.

Maley, Yon. 1994. 'The Language of the Law'. In *Language and the Law*, edited by John Gibbons, pp. 11–50. London: Longman.

Matthiessen, Christian M.I.M. 2009. 'Ideas and New Directions'. In M.A.K. Halliday and Jonathan J. Webster (eds.), *Continuum Companion to Systemic Functional Lingusitics*. London and New York: Continuum.

Matthiessen, Christian M.I.M. 2015. 'Register in the Round: Registerial Cartography'. *Functional Linguistics* 2(9): pp. 1–48.

Martin, J.R. 2002. 'Meaning beyond the Clause: SFL Perspectives'. *Annual Review of Applied Linguistics* 22: pp. 52–74.

Silverman, Kaja. 1983. *The Subject of Semiotics*. New York and Oxford: Oxford University Press.

6 'Temporalization' and narrative texts, keeping time in language

Projection and narrative voice, expansion and narrative particularity

Chapter 6 continues the general discussion of SFL concepts, as developed in Chapters 2 and 5, but with an increasing focus on the register of narrative, the 'configuration of semantic resources' that users of English associate with a text identified as a narrative. These resources are strongly oriented to what I call 'particularity' and 'voice'. Keeping time in language, which I refer to as 'temporalization' – in contradistinction to the 'spatialization' of language discussed in Chapter 2 – is one consequence of 'particularity', and an important feature, given the central concern of narrative with temporal meanings. 'Voice' is also a central concern for its realization in language enables the complex generation of worlds within worlds, recognized in traditional concepts of narrator and character. Overall, the observations in this chapter, moving from generalizations about time in language to the detailed discussion of individual narrative texts, will contrast the particular and dynamic construal of experience in narrative with the general and static construal in 'scientific' discourse.

Temporalization of language in narrative discourse is not simply the opposite of spatialization in scientific discourse, but it does begin with the language of 'ordinary grammar', as described by Halliday (discussed in Chapter 2). In his account, 'ordinary grammar' is associated with phylogenesis and ontogenesis: that is, with the earlier stages of language development in the culture and in the individual. But with similar resources temporalization is also realized in the most advanced writing of narrative fiction in English. The education of primary and secondary teachers can, understandably, emphasize the teaching of 'extraordinary grammar' (such as that discussed in Chapter 2 on 'spatialization') to take school students from the language of early childhood into the technical language of secondary disciplines. (Most recently, in the interdisciplinary relation of systemic functional linguistics and 'legitimation code theory', the contribution of grammatical metaphor to 'semantic density' has been studied in various contexts of secondary teaching, Maton et al. 2016.) However, any assumption that such spatialized language is inherently 'better' (more impressive?) or necessarily more 'adult' is unfortunate. The mature language user varies language to suit its purpose, and the language of temporalization,

DOI: 10.4324/b23121-6

which restores time to the clause and expands the temporal meaning potential of the verb group, best realizes the demands of narrative.

The language of 'ordinary grammar' is fundamentally concerned with the dynamics of happenings and flows. In the context of discussing the utility of grammatical metaphor to scientific discourse, Halliday describes the nominal group as 'the grammar's most powerful resource for creating taxonomies'.

Paradigmatically, '*fruit* is a kind of *food*; *berry* is a kind of *fruit*; *raspberry* is a kind of *berry*' and the taxonomic power of this resource is extended by a grammatical structure which, syntagmatically, can accumulate lexical items within the one group: 'the *red-and-silver diesel-engined London Transport double-decker ninety-seven horsepower omnibus* celebrated in popular song' (Halliday 2004b, 123).

This contrasts with the grammar of the verbal group:

> It is not that processes cannot be construed as taxonomies; in a limited way they can, at least paradigmatically (*walk, run* ... are kinds of *move*; *stroll, sidle* ... are kinds of *walk*). But the verbal group typically contains only one lexical element; it expands, instead, in grammatical systems, such as tense and phase – moments of unfolding in time. In other words, what the grammar construes (congruently) as processes are precisely those phenomena that are not stable enough to accrue subclassifying features; whereas what the grammar construes (congruently) as entities are phenomena that are relatively stable, and hence accrue features which group them into classes.
>
> (Halliday 2004b, 124)

The verbal group 'expands'; it can realize 'moments of unfolding in time'. More generally, grammatical expansion, later discussed in detail, is a resource of narrative particularity.

As listed in Chapter 2, Halliday's six general terms for features of 'natural language' include Transitivity (i) (different types of process) and (ii) (two models of processes, transitive and ergative) and Tense and Aspect. The process meaning is realized in the lexical (final or only) verb of a verb group; the meanings of tense and aspect are also realized in the verbal group. These meanings variously refine the temporal meanings of the happening, the 'moments of unfolding in time', both in relation to other happenings and to the speaker. Matthiessen points out that Halliday's account of tense and aspect is different from earlier accounts (Halliday 2014, xviii): what others have labelled 'perfective' aspect and 'progressive/continuous' aspect Halliday describes as 'secondary tense'. For example, in the verbal group *had been swimming*, the primary tense is realized in 'had' and the overall tense (reading from right to left) is present in past in past (Halliday 2014, §6.3). Halliday reads tense meanings like this because the English tense system is recursive: it has three tense meanings (present, past and future), which can be repeated to orient different events to the here and now of the speaker/writer (the primary tense). The latter point makes it clear that this primary orientation is to the 'now' of bio-temporality in Fraser's model, the organic linear sequence from birth to death of the speaker/writer, at which natural level the meaning of 'the present' first evolves. Although, as discussed in Chapter 5, the system of transitivity enables the inference of three worlds in the human umwelt, it is specifically the time of the speaker's external physical world, inferred from material processes, that is realized in the tense system (this comment anticipates the comparison of Halliday and Fraser's worlds in Chapter 7).

So: Halliday does not use the term 'aspect' as it has been used else-where; instead he uses it to talk about *realis* and *irrealis* in language.

Halliday has suggested that natural languages typically embody two models of time (his bolding):

> a theory of linear, irreversible time, out of **past via present into future** (tense), and a theory of simultaneity, with the opposition between **being and becoming,** or **manifested and manifesting** (aspect). Languages have very different mixtures (English strongly foregrounds linear time[1]): but probably every language enacts both ...
> (Halliday 2003, 128)

This dual modelling is one of the 'extravagant' features of the semogenic power of language, that is its power as a meaning-making system (Halliday lists five types of features: comprehensive, extravagant, indeter-minate, non-autonomous and variable, 2003, 250). By 'extravagant' Halliday refers to complementary ways of construing experience: 'the systemic complementarities in the way language categorizes and "con-structs reality"' (2003, 252–254). One major complementarity, found, he says, in most languages, is that between the transitive and ergative con-strual of processes. Related to this construal is the complementarity of the two models of time:

> Another fundamental complementarity is between aspect and tense as construals of time: is time a linear flow, out of past through pres-ent and future, or is it an emerging movement between the virtual and the actual? ... Again, it seems it cannot be both; yet the grammar insists that it is, in some mixture or other according to the language.
> (Halliday 2003, 254)

In parentheses, Halliday notes that languages differ in their realization of this complementarity:

> (As you move across the Eurasian continent the balance tends to shift, with tense more highly systematized in languages at the western

end and aspect in those at the eastern – and perhaps a more even mix
in some languages in the middle, such as Russian and Hindi.)

(Halliday 2003, 254)

This complementarity of tense and aspect can be related to a familiar
debate in the philosophy of language: in the terminology of J.E.
McTaggart, time can be described in two different modes, the A series
(ordered as future, present and past) and the B series (earlier than and
later than) (Ingthorsson 2016). So English, which 'strongly foregrounds
linear time', favours the A series. Benjamin Whorf saw this linearity as a
general feature of SAE (Standard Average European), a feature resulting
from the reification/nominalization/objectification of temporal meaning.
Whorf writes:

[The three-tense system of SAE verbs] is amalgamated with that
larger scheme of objectification of the subjective experience of duration already noted in other patterns – in the binomial formula appli-
cable to nouns in general, in temporal nouns, in plurality and
numeration. This objectification enables us in imagination to 'stand
time units in a row'. Imagination of time as like a row harmonizes
with a system of THREE tenses; whereas a system of TWO, an earlier
and a later, would seem to correspond better to the feeling of duration as it is experienced.

(Whorf 2012, 184–185)

Thus – in contrast to the temporal configuration of Hopi as Whorf
records it – in SAE, the B-series experience of duration can be construed
as the A-series telling of sequence.

It is true Whorf writes that Hopi also has three tenses, but the temporal
meanings are very different from the three-tense system of SAE. Hopi has
'past (i.e., past up to and including present), future, and generalized (that
which is generally, universally, or timelessly true)' (Whorf 2012, 132). His
discussion of Hopi past and future suggests these meanings are more like
Halliday's discussion of aspect, a construal of time 'as an emerging movement between the virtual and the actual', that is as the virtual future
coming into being in the actually experienced past and present. Certainly,
these tense choices relate more to what a speaker subjectively knows, or
does not yet know, rather than to an objectified linear sequence (objectified in date and clock time, the public convergence of individual biotem-
poralities). Whorf writes (his small caps):

For if we inspect consciousness we find no past, present, future, but a
unity embracing complexity. EVERYTHING is in consciousness, and
everything in consciousness is, and is together. There is in it a sensuous
and a nonsensuous. We may call the sensuous – what we are seeing,

hearing, touching – the 'present' while in the nonsensuous the vast image-world of memory is being labelled 'the past' and another realm of belief, intuition, and uncertainty 'the future'; yet sensation, memory, foresight, all are in consciousness together – one is not 'yet to be' nor another 'once but no more'. Where real time comes in is that all this in consciousness is 'getting later', changing certain relations in an irreversible manner. In this 'latering' or 'durating' there seems to me to be a paramount contrast between the newest, latest instant at the focus of attention and the rest – the earlier. Languages by the score get along well with two tenselike forms answering to this paramount relation of 'later' to 'earlier'. We can of course CONSTRUCT AND CONTEMPLATE IN THOUGHT a system of past, present, future, in the objectified configuration of points on a line. This is what our general objectification tendency leads us to do and our tense system confirms.

(Whorf 2012, 185)

Whorf's description of time and consciousness was written in the late 1930s. Fifty-odd years later, in his account of the brain (as discussed in Chapter 1), Gerard Edelman makes not dissimilar comments.

In summary, Halliday sees most languages as having two models of time, both a B-series and an A-series, though different languages give greater emphasis to one or the other. The English language, I suggest, effectively developed these complementary models of time in the early period of Latin contact. In its morphology, Old English had two tenses, present and past. Literacy, as we understand it, came to English speakers with the Latin of Roman Christianity (the conversion dates from 597 CE on). Latin verbs realize SAE linear meanings of primary and secondary tense in their conjugations; written English, translating Latin, develops the construal of Latin-like temporal meanings with auxiliary verbs. Whorf, as already noted, associates the linear A-series with SAE objectification, the translating of the 'flux' of the world 'into things'. It is feasible that the development of English to a complementary modelling of time, both the B-series and the increasingly dominant linear A-series, is associated with the cultural transition from orality to literacy. Indeed, Halliday has commented that 'nominalization is not a necessary feature of systematic reality construction; Whorf remarked of Hopi, many years ago, that its technical terms were mainly verbs. But it is a feature of all **written** systems of knowledge ...' (Halliday 2004b, 44).

By the sixteenth century, in the post-printing era of European development, such literate pressures are telling (Eisenstein 1979, 1983). Halliday notes the comparable features of scientific languages and standard languages during this period:

In this historical context, new demands were being made on people's semiotic potential: in particular, much of the discourse of those having authority and status was now being addressed to strangers, or printed in books which would be read by persons unknown, so there were no longer the shared experiences and shared expectations which shaped the discourse of medieval societies.

(Halliday 2004b, 122)

Yet more or less parallel with the semiotic demands of the new science (from the seventeenth century on), another discursive development was taking place. In a hackneyed phrase, this is 'the rise of the novel', a literary genre also responding to the semiotic demands of cultural change, primarily in the economic system (in another phrase, 'the emergence of capitalism'). As narrative theorists, affirm, this is a genre centred on the telling of time.

How can we speak of time? The earlier discussion of the drift of grammatical metaphor has implied a negative and a positive answer to this question. First, negatively, to efface meanings of time we can choose the general end-point of drift: the lexically condensed single clause with relational process and nominalized participants, as in the discourse of science. But second, positively, to realize the meaning of temporal sequence we can choose from the different lexicogrammatical structures on the drift axis. Given that 'time is of the essence' in narrative, one can predict that narrative grammar will resist the drift to nominalization, that, in the extreme, it will favour the realization of temporal sequence in successive clauses. The next chapter, taking up Fraser's model of polyvalent time of different temporalities (as described in Chapter 3), extends the meaning of temporal sequence to different sequences, each associated with one temporality. This effectively extends the discussion of cohesion, the non-structural links between clause complexes in the texture of a text (as mentioned in Chapter 5). In this chapter, however, the focus is on temporal meaning within the one clause and on the meaningful links between clauses in the one clause complex.

Halliday and Matthiessen write:

> there are semantic domains that are construed in more than one place in the grammar, by more than one system local to one particular grammatical unit ... There are two fundamental semantic domains of this kind – expansion and projection,
>
> (Halliday 2004a, 593; 2014, 666)

Both these domains, it emerges are central to the register of narrative. I begin with projection.

For narrative, projection is the means by which the voice of one world of experience can be embedded within the world of another; the notion of 'one world' will be extended in Chapter 7. (The linguistic understanding is wider: projection is 'the logical-semantic relationship whereby a clause comes to function not as a direct representation of (non-linguistic) experience but as a representation of a (linguistic) representation', Halliday

2004a, 441; 2014, 508.) The traditional literary terms for this projection are direct speech or thought, indirect speech or thought, to which is sometimes added free indirect speech or thought. In narrative texts, logical projection is typically realized in the grammar of the clause complex, with a projecting clause and a projected clause. The projecting clause (the literary 'tag') has a verb realizing a verbal (e.g. 'she said') or mental (e.g. 'he thought') process; the projected clause realizes a quote (direct, in quotation marks) or a report (indirect, beginning with 'that …', sometimes elided). So-called free indirect speech is not tagged but the wording of the clause is understood to realize the voice of a character. But projection is strictly a semantic domain rather than a grammatical choice and authors can variously play with these conventions. In the following extract, from Margaret Atwood's *Hag-Seed* (2016), direct speech and thought are both tagged ('said Felix', 'he thought'/'admonished himself') but quote marks (double, as in the original punctuation) are reserved for speech. This removes any graphic difference between tagged thought and free indirect thought.

The principal protagonist, Felix Phillips, a (resentfully) retired 'famous director', is being interviewed by Estelle (a professor who oversees the course) for a position in the 'Literacy Through Literature' program at the Fletcher County Correctional Institute (the previous teacher had unexpectedly died):

> "I'd need to do things in my own way," said Felix, pushing his luck. "I'd want considerable latitude." It was the beginning of the semester and the dead teacher had barely got started, so Felix himself would have room to create. "What do they usually read for this course?"
>
> "Well, we've relied on *The Catcher in the Rye*," said Estelle. "Quite a lot. And some stories by Stephen King, they like those. *The Curious Incident of the Dog in the Night-Time*. Many of them identify with that, and it's simple to read. Short sentences."
>
> "I see," said Felix. Catcher in the bloody Rye, he thought. Pablum for prep school juveniles. It was a medium- to maximum-security facility; these were grown men, they'd lived lives that had driven them far beyond those parameters. "I'll be taking a somewhat different tack."
>
> "I hesitate to ask what tack," said Estelle, cocking her head archly. Now that she'd accepted him for the job, she was relaxed enough to flirt. Watch your trousers, Felix, he admonished himself. She doesn't have a wedding ring, so you're fair game. Don't start anything you can't finish.
>
> (Atwood 2016, 52)

As earlier noted, projection is the means by which the voice of one world of experience can be embedded within the world of another, but in this extract the voice of the narrator's world has, for the most part, been erased by the projection of a voice from the experience of the character Felix.

Some years ago, Boris Uspensky, from his close study of Tolstoy's novel, *War and Peace*, suggested different 'planes' on which different voices in narrative might be identified: the ideological plane, the spatio-temporal plane, the phraseological plane and the plane of psychology (1973); Seymour Chatman combined these planes with the speech categories of speech act theory (1978, 161–166). (The title of his study, *Story and Discourse*, situates it in the dualism of the structuralist tradition, discussed in Chapter 4.) Gérard Genette, from his close study of Proust's writing, devoted one of five chapters in *Narrative Discourse* to the category 'Voice', in which he differentiated the textual 'speaking' of narrators and characters (1980). Figure 6.1 represents my conflation of the work of these authors (an earlier version was published in Huisman 2005, 26).

The 'box' of Figure 6.1 encloses the visible wording of the text. To the left and outside of this box, I could have written 'Uspensky: ideological plane of the implied author'. However, in SFL terms, the conflation of four planes would be misleading. The context of situation, constituted by field, tenor and mode, is the sense that a reader makes of a text; it is understood **both** from the wording of that text (the SFL dimension of stratification) **and** from the potential of the reader's own context of culture and experience of language (the SFL dimension of instantiation). The ideological plane, on which the implied author is said to emerge, is the reading in which dual interpretations, such as those of satire or parody, may be construed – or not, according to the reader's encultured disposition. In SFL terms, this reading derives from the reader's construed tenor of the context of situation, by which the reader understands attitudes to the subject matter of the field. A compliant reader may align interpretation, singular or dual, with an 'implied author' (the stock example of compliant dual interpretation would be the usual response to Jonathan Swift's 'A Modest Proposal' of 1729). However, a resistant reader may introduce dual interpretations, as in the strong feminist re-readings of traditional fairy tales (Dworkin 1974). Overall, it is the compliance or otherwise of the reader, from the potential of their context of culture – rather than the mere presence of an implied author – which emerges from a focus on ideology. (For a ground-breaking empirical study, theorized within the SFL model, of the ideological power of language and its emergence in children's socialization, see Ruqaiya Hasan's papers in Volume 2 of her collected works, and especially her discussion in Section IV, 'The World and the World of Meanings', 2009, 355–454.)

In SFL terms, Uspenky's other three planes, spatio-temporal, phraseological and psychological, describe the reader's construal of field (subject matter), tenor (attitude) and mode (organization of the message) from the ideational, interpersonal and textual meanings of the narrative text. On

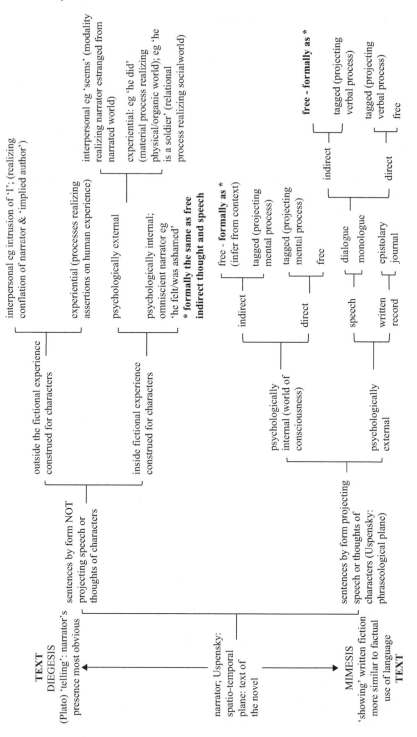

Figure 6.1 Narrative voice and grammatical projection: narrator and character.

the spatio-temporal plane, the mode varies between nodes of 'showing' and 'telling' as the fictional voice becomes more overtly present. Uspensky's phraseological plane distinguishes between language which is worded as the speech of characters and language which is not so worded; this is the contribution of logical projection to the field. From this point – Uspensky's psychological plane – the speech of characters branches into those literary and SFL concepts already mentioned: psychologically internal thoughts (projected by mental processes) and psychologically external speech/writing (projected by verbal processes), both of which can be projected directly or indirectly, and tagged or free. The branching of 'sentences by form not projecting speech or thoughts of characters' is also interesting: into 'inside the fictional experience construed for characters' and 'outside the fictional experience construed for characters'. Choices of both experiential and interpersonal meanings distinguish the various possibilities of these two branches.

Of particular interest to the discussion of projected speech/thought is the central area of Figure 6.1, where the wording of a narrator and the wording of an untagged indirect speech or thought of a character are indistinguishable. For example (from Alice Munro's short story, 'The Turkey Season', 1998, 289): in 'When we came out of the Turkey Barn it was snowing. Lily said it was like a Christmas card ...' the second sentence is tagged ('Lily said') indirect speech in the voice of the character Lily. Untagged ('It was like a Christmas card ...') it would have the same wording as the voice of the narrator. This feature, the conflated voices of character and narrator, is a familiar topic to those studying modernist prose fiction in the ongoing flow of so-called 'stream of consciousness' narrative.

In Figure 6.1, the vertical axis rises from characters' language which is most mimetic to language which is most overtly telling (diegetic in the Platonic sense, Huisman 2005, 18–19). Prose fiction is written text, composed by an author. Thus the 'most mimetic' text is composed as written/composed by a character. Maintained throughout a narrative, as in so-called epistolary novels, such text effaces the fictional projection of a narrator; a well-known early example is Samuel Richardson's novel *Pamela*, written in letters and journal entries and published in 1740; a modern example is Amanda Prantera's novel, *Capri File*, 2001, composed entirely in its characters' emails. The 'most diegetic' are realized in wording that steps outside the world of the characters, as in Henry Fielding's *The History of Tom Jones, A Foundling* (published in 1749), in which each of the 18 'Books' begins with an (implied) authorial chapter. (The title of subsequent chapters may also 'speak' to the reader directly, as for Chapter 14 of Book 7: 'A most dreadful chapter indeed; and which few readers ought to venture upon in an evening, especially when alone'.) Two centuries later, Paul Auster plays with the mimetic/diegetic axis in his metafiction: for example, in *City of Glass* (2006 [1985]) the first person narrator who turns up only in the last two pages of the novella, and who in the last paragraph tells us he is responsible for deciphering the story recorded in the notebook of a character, the vanished Quinn, criti-cizes his friend 'Paul Auster', who (the narrator feels) had not sufficiently helped Quinn in an earlier episode.

Questions of projection are returned to in the detailed study of specific texts in Chapter 9.

I turn now to the other semantic domain which Halliday described as 'construed in more than one place in the grammar', that of expansion. It is this resource that is central to narrative 'particularity', including the grammatical realization of 'temporalization' – keeping time in meaning.

Previously, I quoted from Halliday's contrast of nominal and verbal groups:

> But the verbal group typically contains only one lexical element; it expands, instead, in grammatical systems, such as tense and phase – 'moments' of unfolding in time.

(Halliday 2004b, 124)

This expansion of temporal meaning in '"moments" of unfolding in time' allows for the unfolding of temporal sequence (as already discussed in relation to tense and aspect) and the unfolding of temporal duration[2] (as in phase, later discussed). More generally, the analysis of strategies of expansion in different narrative texts suggests that expansion is more widely significant in the register of narrative, a significance that derives from narrative focus on the particularity of experience.

In Halliday's *Introduction to Functional Grammar*, a lengthy table headed 'Synoptic summary of expansion' itemizes the different 'places in the grammar' where meanings of expansion can be realized (Table 10(3) Halliday 2004a, 598–600; Table 10-3 Halliday 2014, 670–672; for fur-ther examples, see Martin 1992, 168–170). Logically, the simple verbal group can be expanded with choices of voice and tense; the verbal group complex can be expanded with the meanings of PHASE (of TIME: *start, keep*; of REALITY: *seem, turn out; begin by, end up (by), tend*) and the meanings of CONATION (*try, succeed; can, learn*). (The general SFL mean-ing of expansion includes meanings of elaboration, extension and enhancement; the meanings of TIME and REALITY *seem, turn out* are listed as elaborating, and the meanings of REALITY *begin by, end up (by), tend* as enhancing.) Given the wealth of detail in the 'Synoptic summary of expansion' and that temporal meanings are of particular interest in the study of narrative, Table 6.1 is selective; it illustrates the different grammatical realizations of expansion with choices of spatio-temporal meaning only (taken from the sub-category headings of expansion: enhancement: spatio-temporal: time). As already used in this paragraph, SFL system names are given in small capitals, category of meaning in bold, examples in italics.

Table 6.1 Temporal meaning realized in different grammatical structures of expansion

The cohesive tie of CONJUNCTION between clause complexes (non-structural link)	extent: *throughout*; point(s) *simultaneously*; prior: *previously*; subsequent: *next*; **various complex types:** *finally, at once, meanwhile*, etc.
INTERDEPENDENCY between clauses in the one clause complex (grammatical/ structural link)	point(s): paratactic: *now*; hypotactic: *when(ever)*; non-finite clause: *when, on*; prior: hypotactic: *before, until*; non-finite clause: *before, until*; **subsequent:** paratactic *then*; hypotactic & non-finite clause: *after, since*; **various complex types:** hypotactic: *as soon as*, etc
Embedding of DEFINING RELATIVE CLAUSE in the nominal group	extent: (a) *time (when/that)*; (b) *when/on which*
CIRCUMSTANTIATION in the clause	extent: DURATION *for*; point(s): TIME *at, on*; prior: *before*; subsequent: *after*; **various complex types:** *during*, etc.
ATTRIBUTION or IDENTIFICATION as relational process in the clause	extent: (a) *last, take up*; (b) *be throughout*; points: (b) *be at*; prior: (a) *precede*; (b) *be before*; **subsequent:** (a) *follow*; (b) *be after*; **various complex** types: (a) conclude, coincide with

For the detailed illustration of expansion, I now turn to three narrative texts. The texts differ in mode and context of culture. Text 1 is that of a spontaneous spoken 'narrative of personal experience' by an 11-year-old boy, recorded by William Labov in his collecting of oral narratives in Harlem, USA; Text 2 is extracted from a novel about nineteenth-century Iceland, *Burial Rites*, by Australian Hannah Kent, published in 2013; Text 3 is by the British author Anthony Trollope from his novel of ecclesiastical cupidity, *Barchester Towers*, first published in 1857. Sentence and clause(s) are numbered, thus 7.3 refers to the third clause within the seventh sentence; <<...>> signifies an interrupting clause; [[...]] signifies an embedded clause; <u>verb groups</u> are underlined; **conjunctions/link words** are bolded.

Text 1 (Labov 1972, 368–369)

1.1   **When** I <u>was</u> in fourth grade –
1.2   << **no**, it <u>was</u> in third grade –>>
1.3   this boy he <u>stole</u> my glove.
2.1   He <u>took</u> my glove

2.2   **and** <u>said</u>
2.3   **that** his father <u>found</u> it downtown on the ground.
3.1   I <u>told</u> him
3.2   **that** it <u>was</u> impossible [[for him <u>to find</u> downtown]]
3.3   'cause all those people <u>were walking</u> by
3.4   **and** just his father <u>was</u> the only one [[that <u>found</u> it]]?
4.   **So** he <u>got</u> all (mad).
5.   **Then** I <u>fought</u> him.
6.   I <u>knocked</u> him all out in the street.
7.1   **So** he <u>say</u>
7.2   he <u>give</u>
7.3   **and** I <u>kept on hitting</u> him.
8.1   **Then** he <u>started crying</u>
8.2   **and** <u>ran</u> home to his father
8.3   **and** the father <u>told</u> him
8.4   **that** he <u>ain't find</u> no glove.

Text 2 (Kent 2013, 122)

1.1   That morning we <u>started</u> on foot
1.2   **and** <u>returned</u> to the valley through an ill-tempered day full of spasms of snow.
2.1   I <u>thought</u>
2.2   I <u>would faint</u> from hunger.
3.1   We <u>stopped</u> in the yard of Kornsá
3.2   **and** << >> Mamma <u>whispered</u> in my ear,
3.3   <<before I <u>could finish</u> the whey [[<u>given</u> to me by the woman there]],>>
3.4   <u>pressed</u> a stone into my mitten
3.5   **and** <u>left</u> with Jóas on her back.
4.   I <u>tried to follow</u> her.
5.   I <u>screamed</u>.
6.   I <u>didn't want</u> [[to be left behind]]
7.1   **But** << >> I <u>tripped and fell</u>.
7.2   << as I <u>ran</u> >>
8.1   **When** I <u>got</u> back on my feet
8.2   my mother and brother <u>had vanished</u>,
8.3   **and** all I <u>could see</u> were two ravens, their black feathers poisonous against the snow.

Text 3 (Trollope 1857, 387)

1.1   At about nine the lower orders <u>began to congregate</u> in the paddock and park, under the surveillance of Mr. Plomacy and the head gardener and head groom,

1.2   who <u>were sworn in</u> as deputies,

1.3   and <u>were to assist</u> him

1.4   in <u>keeping</u> the peace

1.5   and <u>promoting</u> the sports.

2.1   Many of the younger inhabitants of the neighbourhood, <<...>> <u>had come</u> at a very early hour,

2.2   <<<u>thinking</u>

2.3   that they <u>could not have</u> too much of a good thing,>>

2.4   and the road between the house and the church <u>had been thronged</u> for some time

2.5   before the gates <u>were thrown</u> open.

3.   And then another difficulty of huge dimensions <u>arose</u>, a difficulty [[which Mr. Plomacy <u>had</u> indeed <u>foreseen</u> // and for which he <u>was</u> in some sort <u>provided</u>]].

4.   Some of those [[who <u>wished</u> [[to <u>share</u> Miss Thorne's hospitality]]]] <u>were</u> not so particular [[as they <u>should have been</u>]] as to the preliminary ceremony of an invitation.

5.1   They doubtless <u>conceived.</u>

5.2   that they <u>had been overlooked</u> by accident;

5.3   and instead of <u>taking</u> this in dudgeon,

5.4   as their betters <u>would have done</u>,

5.5   they good-naturedly <u>put up with</u> the slight

5.6   and <u>showed</u>

5.7   that they <u>did</u> so

5.8   by <u>presenting</u> themselves at the gate in their Sunday best.

The following examples of expanded meaning are described using the SFL terms listed in the left column of Table 6.1.

First, consider meaning in the simple verb group. In all three texts, the one-word realization of simple past tense as the primary tense is most frequent, as is typical in the register of narrative discourse, but all three texts also contain examples of verbal groups expanded by the realization of secondary tense: Text 1: 3.1 *were walking* (present in past time); Text 2: 2.2 *would faint* (future in past time) and *had vanished* (past in past time*)*; similarly, Text 3: 2.1 *had come* and, combined with the passive voice, 5.2 *had been overlooked.*

Second, consider meaning in the verb group complex. In contrast to the nominalized demands of scientific discourse as appropriate for the formulation of general laws, the expanded verbal group enables a narrative focus both on the unfolding process and on the particularity of on-going experience. Thus, even in the child's oral narrative, we find complex structures realizing the expansion of phase: Text 1: clause 7.3 *kept on hitting*; clause 8.1 *started crying*. Phase is also realized in Trollope's literate narrative: Text 3: clause 1.1: *began to congregate*, while in the short extract from Kent's novel, conation is realized in the verb group complex: Text 2: clause 4.1 *tried to follow*.

Third, consider expansion in the nominal group. It is here we begin to notice some differences between the oral narrative, Text 1, and the written literary narratives, Texts 2 and 3. In Text 1, most full nominal groups are just experiential Determiner plus Thing (*this boy, my glove*). In Text 2, though most 'things' are not elaborated, two notable exceptions, in clauses 1.2 and 8.3, frame the narrative sequence. In Text 2 clause 1.2, consider the nominal group *an ill-tempered day full of spasms of snow*. The noun *day* realizes a very dead grammatical metaphor, the experience of sequence construed as a thing (recall this was a characteristic of standard average European that Whorf contrasted with Hopi practice). However, both *ill-tempered* (that is, 'ill-made' – but potentially a pun of unhappy attitude) and *spasms* are contemporary lexical metaphors. Given the role of lexical relations in cohesive ties, lexical metaphor expands the collocational possibilities of textual realization. It is true that *spasms* is a grammatical metaphor, a noun realizing process meaning in the clause, but at the same time the word is now being used as a lexical metaphor, expanding the meaning potential in the text.

Now, consider clause 8.3 in Text 2: *and all I could see were two ravens, their black feathers poisonous against the snow*. Here the nominal group *their black feathers poisonous against the snow* loosely expands the experiential meaning of the nominal group *two ravens* – 'loosely', because a grammatical link is not explicitly realized. (Such expanding juxtapositions, increasing lexical density, often feature in the register of contemporary poetry.) *Poisonous* is another example of lexical metaphor, an incongruent lexical choice, but it is not a grammatical metaphor; it is rather an adjective formed from a noun by the usual morphology. (Halliday gives this explanation for 'transcategorization' in *venomous*: 'there is no semantic junction: *venomous* is not the name of an entity ... In metaphor, on the other hand, there is semantic junction ...; thus *venomousness* contains not only the feature 'entity' but that of quality as well' Halliday 2003, 100).

A brief *excursus* on lexical metaphor: lexical metaphor is certainly a way to expand the experiential meaning of a text. In an edited collection on grammatical metaphor, Anne-Marie Simon-Vandenbergen compares the similarities of and differences between lexical and grammatical metaphor and concludes that both should be grouped as lexicogrammatical metaphor (Simon-Vandenbergen et al. 2003, 223–255). Both types of metaphor exhibit the dislocation of congruent lexicogrammatical and semantic strata, what Martin has termed 'inter-stratal tension' (Martin 2020). However, grammatical metaphor retains the lexical item in an incongruent grammatical structure, whereas lexical metaphor uses an incongruent lexical item while retaining the congruent grammatical structure, or – to be more accurate – while retaining the grammatical context of the lexical item it displaces. (The latter *caveat* covers those examples where the lexical item displaced is already the result of grammatical metaphor – as with *spasms*.) Simon-Vandenbergen's examples of lexical metaphor from corpus data are frequently colloquial in tenor and, as she points out, variously 'fuzzy' – when is a metaphor conventional? dead? George Orwell laments the use of 'dying', 'stale', 'worn-out' and – even metaphorically – 'fly-blown' metaphors in English non-literary writing published in his time. (His first rule to those who write: 'Never use a metaphor, simile or other figure of speech which you are used to seeing in print', Orwell, 1968 [1946].) In contrast, in traditional literary criticism, especially of poetry but also of narrative, original or unusual lexical metaphor attracts comment, typically expanding the critic's interpretation of the text.

All three texts expand the experiential meaning of the nominal group by the embedding of defining relative clauses. In the following examples, such embedding is indicated by double square brackets: in Text 1: 3.4 *the only one [[that found it]]*; in Text 2: 3.3 *the whey [[given to me by the woman there]]*. In Text 3, the expansion is especially noticeable. Sentence 3. has an embedded clause complex: *a difficulty [[which Mr. Plomacy <u>had</u> indeed <u>foreseen</u> // and for which he <u>was</u> in some sort <u>provided</u>]]*. The next sentence, 4, has two examples of embedding: modifying a pronoun Head: *those [[who wished to share Miss Thorne's hospitality]]* and modifying an adjective Head: *so particular [[as they <u>should have been</u>]]*. The examples in Trollope's text are especially noticeable because, in these two sentences, 3 and 4, the author expands the nominal groups with embedding while at the same time contracting/condensing the clause structure of the sentence; in other words, each sentence is of one independent clause only (in sentence 3, the verb group of the independent clause is *arose*; in sentence 4 it is *were not*). These single clauses, with internal embedding, have a high lexical density; as with the grammar of scientific discourse, much meaning can be packed into one clause. Although Trollope was writing in 1857, he seems already to be aware of the stylistic dangers of such writing (Chapter 2 noted Halliday's warning against the inappropriate use of nominalization), and perhaps here is parodying that tendency. In context, the narrative meaning of this passage concerns those who 'crash the party', and so lack of social formality is described in language of high-written formality, some humour (potentially) emerging in the mis-match (as it does for this reader).

Expansion of the nominal group is also associated with spatialization (the subject of Chapter 2), but where narrative expansion is typically associated with a particular participant, as in *the Minister's decision*, the nominal expansion of spatialized language more typically realizes a generalized participant, as in *ministerial decision*. There 'ministerial' is functioning as a classifier: '[c]lassifiers are used in texts of all kinds of registers, but they are ... put to hard work in registers where space is at a premium [e.g. headlines] and in registers where classification is an important aspect of the field of discourse, as in scientific and technological registers' (Halliday 2014, 378). As discussed in Chapter 2, such registers are just those enabled by the development of grammatical metaphor, with that drift to nominalization which effaces the temporal meanings of 'happenings'. The general participants of these registers are typically brought together by relational processes, either intensive or circumstantial (for many examples: Halliday 2004b, 154; for 'circumstantial verbs': Halliday 2014, 294).

In contrast, in narrative texts, particular participants are associated with more varied realization of both experiential and interpersonal meaning in the verbal group, especially meanings construing the inner experience and attitudes of a particular participant.

Experientially, note the desiderative mental processes (Halliday 2014, 256–257) in Texts 2 and 3:

> Text 2: clause 6.1 *I didn't want [[to be left behind]]*
> Text 3: clause 4.1 (embedded) *who wished [[to share Miss Thorne's hospitality]]*

Interpersonally, note the modal meanings in Texts 2 and 3:

> Text 2: clause 3.3 *could finish*; clause 8.3 *could see*
> Text 3: clause 1.3 *were to assist him*; *could not have*; *should have been*

Modal assessment is a semantic domain variously realized (Table 10-6 in Halliday 2014, 680–685). Lest, from the examples above from the adult literate Texts 2 and 3, we are tempted to conclude that the child's oral Text 1 will be 'less complex', consider the following in Text 1: clause 3.2 *that it was impossible [[for him to find downtown]]*. This is an example of explicit objective modality (Halliday 2014, 181) in a clause of postposed Subject (Halliday 2014, 198). I read this as a determined effort by the 11-year old speaker to represent his proposition as indisputable fact, not opinion!

A caveat: 'particular participant', used above, when referring to a character in the narrative, does not necessarily mean 'individual person' – although the so-called 'rise of the novel' has been associated with this kind of individualized character, argued most emphatically by Ian Watt in his concept of 'formal realism':

> Formal realism ... is the narrative embodiment of a premise that Defoe and Richardson accepted very literally, but which is implicit in

the novel form in general: the premise, or primary convention, that the novel is a full and authentic report of human experience, and is therefore under an obligation to satisfy its reader with such details of the story as the individuality of the actors concerned, the particulars of the times and places of their actions, details which are presented through a more largely referential use of language than is common in other literary forms.

(Watt *The Rise of the Novel* 1957, 32,
quoted by Schwarz 1983, 63)

As Schwarz points out, in the 1950s Watt was reacting against the then dominant New Criticism, with its decontextualized study of literary text; by 1983 structuralist currents would re-evaluate the humanist assumptions of 'realism' and subsequently (in the Anglo-world) post-structuralist critique would undermine their semiotic certainties (Huisman 2005). The next chapters discuss the changing characteristics of English literary narratives in terms of different temporal worlds, including the construction of uncertain or inchoate worlds where the very understanding of 'particular' may be contested. At the other extreme, in earlier fictional narratives – fairy tales, religious homilies, Chaucer's *Canterbury Tales* – we have participants who are particular types, which are socially rather than individually identifiable or psychologically described, vivid though external details (of clothes, of behaviour) may be. Furthermore, an abstracted 'narrative role' is not necessarily realized by one particular participant; for example, the seven *dramatis personae* of Vladimir Propp's analysis of the Russian fairy tale are narrative roles that may be filled by one or more particular participants in the actual telling of a tale (Propp 1928).

This chapter set out to examine the register of narrative, the 'configuration of semantic resources' that users of English associate with a text identified as a narrative. Given the importance of time to narrative, the focus was on the 'temporalization of language', resources deployed to keep time in language. What in summary has been presented? First, the register of narrative, like Halliday's natural language, represents reality as what happens, rather than the existence of things. It resists the drift of grammatical metaphor that facilitates the nominalization of process meanings, that spatialisation of language that takes time out of language; in narrative, processes are typically realized in lexical verbs. The semantic role of Medium (and of Agent) associated with a process is typically filled by a particular participant (human or otherwise). Its 'configuration of semantic resources' also favours the logical resources of projection and expansion, projection for the complexities of narrative voice and expansion for the particularity of verbal and nominal meanings. Finally, experientially, the verbal group and the nominal group can both realize the systemic range of grammatical meanings congruently available to them, including incongruent lexical choice (lexical metaphor).

We humans live in spacetime – a dimension of sequential persistence or persistent sequentiality – and in natural language this experience is construed in the clause nucleus of Process and Medium as one happening. In the spatialization of Newtonian scientific discourse, reality is reconstrued as spatial, as a world of persistent Things, and Halliday described the mismatch of this language with the spacetime reality theorized by modern science. In the twentieth and twenty-first centuries, writers of narrative fiction have also tried to come to terms with the spatio-temporal demands of contemporary science. The following chapters will explore these efforts in the discussion of temporalities told in the sequence of modern and postmodern fiction. However, in this chapter, to exemplify narrative expansion, I end with an example of one sentence – and it is punctuated as one sentence – by the great postmodern American author, Thomas Pynchon, as he tells the space-time experience of one particular participant in his 1085-page-long novel, *Against the Day* (2006) (Table 6.2).

Table 6.2 Narrative particularity and grammatical expansion (an extreme example) (Pynchon 2006, 568)

Key:
verbal group is underlined; ^ indicates its omission
number is for one independent or dependent clause
[[...]] indicates an embedded clause
<<...>> indicates an interrupting clause
// separates clauses within the one clause complex (within embedded clauses)

Clause

1 Dally might have explained it
2 if somebody had insisted –
3 the Chicago Fair was a long time ago,
4 but she had kept a memory or two of silent boats on canals,
5 something began to stir
6 as the vaporetto made its way from the train station down the Grand Canal,
7 until, just at sunset, getting to the San Marco end,
8 and there was the pure Venetian evening, the blue-green shadows, the lavenders, ultramarines, siennas, and umbers of the sky and the light-bearing air [[she was breathing]], the astonishing momentum of the everyday twilight,
9 gas-lanterns coming on in the Piazzetta,
10 San Giorgio Maggiore across the water lit pale as angels,
11 ^ distant as heaven
12 and yet seeming only a step,
13 as if her breath, her yearning, could reach across to it
14 and touch –
15 she was certain for the first time in a life on the roll ₁[[that <<whatever 'home' had meant,>> this was older than memory, than the story ₂[[she thought // she knew.]]₂]]₁

Notes

1 In a comparison of English and Chinese, Halliday notes that '..."tense" (linear time) in Chinese is considerably less grammaticalized than in English, being construed through definite and indefinite time adverbs like "already", "soon", "yesterday", "last year", and there is no necessary representation of linear time in the clause' (Halliday & Matthiessen 1999: 300). On the other hand, 'phase' can be more grammaticalized in Chinese than in English, as in adding a 'postpositive verb', e.g. 'to break' becomes 'to break in two', 'to cut' becomes 'to cut in two' (1999, 299; also 307–308).

2 Bergson's use of the French term *durée* for the human experience of time, sometimes translated into English as 'duration', was discussed in Chapter 4 as related to nootemporality in Fraser's model of different temporalities. Genette was familiar with Bergson's writing but uses 'duration (*durée*)' as a term for the quantitative measurement of time: in his structuralist dualism of discursive telling and 'underlying' story, he conflates space and time in measuring the 'speed' of a narrative: the length of the text ('measured in lines and pages') and the duration of the story ('measured in second, minutes, hours, days, months, and years') (1980, 87–88).

References

Works of fiction

Atwood, Margaret. 2016. *Hag-Seed*. London: Hogarth.

Auster, Paul. 2006. *The New York Trilogy*. New York: Penguin. (1985 *City of Glass* first published; 1986 *Ghosts* and *The Locked Room* first published. Los Angeles: Sun & Moon Press).

Fielding, Henry. 2005 [1749]. *The History of Tom Jones, A Foundling*. London: Penguin.

Kent, Hannah. 2013. *Burial Rites*. Sydney: Picador Pan Macmillan.

Munro, Alice. 1998. *Selected Stories*. Toronto: Penguin.

Prantera, Amanda. 2001. *Capri File*. London: Bloomsbury.

Pynchon, Thomas. 2006. *Against the Day*. London: Jonathan Cape.

Richardson, Samuel. 1914 [1740]. *Pamela, or Virtue Rewarded*. London: J.M. Dent.

Trollope, Anthony. 2003 [1857]. *Barchester Towers*. London: Penguin.

General

Chatman, Seymour. 1978. *Story and Discourse, Narrative Structure in Fiction and Film*. Ithaca, NY and London: Cornell University Press.

Dworkin, Andrea. 1974. *Woman Hating, A Radical Look at Sexuality*. New York: Dutton.

Eisenstein, Elizabeth. 1979. *The Printing Press as an Agent of Change, Communication and Cultural Transformations in Early-Modern Europe*. Cambridge: Cambridge University Press.

Eisenstein, Elizabeth. 1983. *The Printing Revolution in Early Modern Europe*. Cambridge: Cambridge University Press.

Genette, Gérard. 1980. *Narrative Discourse, An Essay in Method*. Ithaca, New York: Cornell University Press.

Halliday, M.A.K. 2003. *On Language and Linguistics*. Volume 3 in the Collected Works of M.A.K. Halliday, ed. Jonathan J. Webster. London and New York: Continuum.

Halliday, M.A.K. 2004a. *An Introduction to Functional Grammar*, revised by Christian M.I.M. Matthiessen. 3rd ed. London: Arnold.

Halliday, M.A.K. 2004b. *The Language of Science*. Volume 5 in the Collected Works of M.A.K. Halliday, ed. Jonathan J. Webster. London and New York: Continuum.

Halliday, M.A.K. 2014. *Halliday's Introduction to Functional Grammar*, revised by Christian M.I.M. Matthiessen. 4th ed. London and New York: Routledge.

Halliday, M.A.K. and Christian M.I.M. Matthiessen. 1999. *Construing Experience Through Meaning, a Language-Based Approach to Cognition*. London and New York: Continuum.

Hasan, Ruqaiya. 2009. *Semantic Variation, Meaning in Society and Sociolinguistics*. Volume 2 in the Collected Works of Ruqaiya Hasan, ed. Jonathan J. Webster. London and Oakville: Equinox.

Huisman, Rosemary. 2005. 'The Basics of Narrative Theory'. In *Narrative and Media*, by Helen Fulton, Rosemary Huisman, Julian Murphet and Anne Dunn, pp. 11–44.

Ingthorsson, R.D. 2016. *McTaggart's Paradox*. London and New York: Routledge.

Labov, William. 1972. *Language in the Inner City, Studies in the Black English Vernacular*. Philadelphia: University of Pennsylvania Press.

Martin, J.R. 1992. *English Text, System and Structure*. Philadelphia and Amsterdam: John Benjamins.

Martin, J.R. 2020. 'Metaphors We Feel by: Stratal Tension'. *Journal of World Languages* 6 (1–2): pp. 8–26.

Maton, Karl, Sue Hood and Suellen Shay. 2016. *Knowledge Building, Educational Studies in Legitimation Code Theory*. London and New York: Routledge.

Orwell, George. 1968 [1946]. 'Politics and the English Language'. In *The Collected Essays, Journalism and Letters of George Orwell*, edited by Sonia Orwell and Ian Angus. London: Secker and Warburg.

Propp, Vladimir. 1968 [1928]. *Morphology of the Folktale*. 2nd ed. Austin: Texas University Press.

Schwarz, Daniel R. 1983. 'The Importance of Ian Watt's *The Rise of the Novel*.' *The Journal of Narrative Technique* 13 (2): pp. 59–73.

Simon-Vandenbergen, Anne-Marie, Miriam Taverniers and Louise Ravelli, editors. 2003. *Grammatical Metaphor, Views from Systemic Functional Linguistics*. Philadelphia and Amsterdam: John Benjamins.

Uspensky, Boris. 1973. *A Poetics of Composition: The Structure of the Artistic Text and Typology of a Compositional Form*. Berkeley: University of California Press.

Whorf, Benjamin Lee. 2012. *Language, Thought and Reality: Selected Writings of Benjamin Lee Whorf*, eds. John B. Carroll, Stephen C. Levinson, and Penny Lee. Cambridge, MA: M.I.T. Press.

7 Narrative worlds and their temporalities

Weaving the temporalities of different worlds with different modes of coherence in the texture of one narrative; dominant worlds in English literary texts, pre-printing to postmodern

The meaning of narrative is explored in many disciplinary contexts, serving many different purposes yet (as discussed in Chapter 4) one assumption runs through most disciplinary modelling: that narrative narrates time. This appears to be the fundamental assumption. However, a second persistent assumption is variously understood: that narrative projects 'a world'.

In film studies (Metz, 1974) and thence in studies of literary narrative (Genette, 1980), the world of the characters has been referred to as the *diegesis* of the film or novel. In *The Routledge Encyclopedia of Narrative Theory*, for the lemma **DIEGESIS**, this meaning is given as the first of the two senses of the word used in narrative theory (Herman et al. 2005, 107–108). (The second sense there given is relevant to the discussion of narrative voice in Chapter 6, Huisman, 2005, 18–19.) It is true that each character in that first diegesis may in turn become a narrator and tell of another literary world, a second diegesis, and so on, a potential narrative matryoshka:

> We will define this difference in level by saying that *any event a narrative recounts is at a diegetic level immediately higher than the level at which the narrating act producing this narrative is placed*. M. de Renoncourt's writing of his fictive *Mémoires* is a (literary) act carried out at a first level, which we will call *extradiegetic*; the events told in those *Memoires* (including Des Grieux's narrating act) are inside this first narrative, so we will describe them as *diegetic*, or *intradiegetic*; the events told in Des Grieux's narrative, a narrative in the second degree, we will call *metadiegetic*.
>
> (Genette 1980, 228, author's italics)

As discussed in the previous chapter, logically projection is the means by which the voice of one world of experience can be embedded within the

DOI: 10.4324/b23121-7

world of another (IFG2014 §7.5) and Genette's hierarchy of diegetic terms is effectively labelling different levels of projected worlds. This type of complexity is an old structure, as in Boccaccio's *Decameron* or Chaucer's *Canterbury Tales*. But, as outlined in Chapter 5, from considering the systemic model of language, and in particular from considering the meaning choices of the transitivity system and the worlds construed from them, we can identify another kind of complexity: at any one diegetic level, human semiosis simultaneously construes three overlapping worlds: the external and material world of physical action and events; the internal and psychological world of individual consciousness; the social world that is construed through human interaction and convention, including social identities and attributes. In short, at every level of narrative projection, another three overlapping worlds can be projected. Furthermore, the juxtaposition of the 'worlds' of Halliday's model of language (Chapter 5) and those of Fraser's model of time (Chapter 3) can augment even further the number of 'overlapping worlds' construable through narrative. However, before describing this juxtaposition. I want briefly to comment on other studies of narrative using the term 'world', specifically 'text-world' and 'storyworld'.

The 'text-world' is the central concept in 'Text-World Theory', developed from the work of Paul Werth in Amsterdam in the 1990s (Werth 1999) and continued by scholars in the United Kingdom. The theory incorporates insights from cognitive psychology and cognitive linguistics and is intended to apply to all uses of language, including fictional discourses:

> [Human beings] construct mental representations, or text-worlds, which enable us to conceptualise and understand every piece of language we encounter. How these text-worlds are formed, their conceptual configuration, and how we as human beings make use of them are the focus of Text World Theory.
> (Gavins 2007, 2. See Herman et al. 2005, 596–597)

These text-worlds are constructed from language in the context of each participant's 'discourse-world' – somewhat comparable, in terms of the SFL dimension of instantiation (Chapter 5), to the potential of cultural context and language previously experienced and now understood to be relevant to the particular context of situation. When linguistic terms are brought into text-world theory, the construction of that 'world' may collapse together categories that SFL would distinguish. Thus, in an article designed to be helpful to school-teachers in the teaching of poetry, the author explains:

> [Text-worlds] are built through word-building elements (aspects of time, place and entities) and developed through function-advancing

propositions (actions and events that propel the narrative forward and modify the contents of the initial text-world). In terms of grammar, word-builders are typically adverbs of time and place, noun phrases, preposition phrases and adjective phrases. Function-advancers are typically verbs.

(Cushing 2018)

In terms of SFL stratification, this account conflates the levels of semantics (function-advancers) and lexicogrammar (verbs); moreover, the function-advancing propositions seem comparable to Halliday's basic clause of everyday language (Medium + Process), though the account lists only grammatical units lower than the clause (the word and the phrase/group). When formulating text-world theory, Werth described his desire and intention to overcome the limits of formalist grammar (which he understood contemporary linguistics to be) by bringing context into the related study of discourse and text worlds (1999, 20). However, a functional grammar, like that of SFL, is axiomatically committed to analysing text in context. A recent study of comics 'as communication' (Davies 2019) does indeed bring text-world concepts within the compass of an SFL model of language.

'Storyworlds', a term used by several contemporary scholars of narrative, are also mental models; the Routledge Encyclopedia entry describes storyworlds as models of who did what to and with whom, when, where, why, and in what fashion in the world to which interpreters relocate as they work to comprehend a narrative (Herman et al. 2005, 570). On the face of it, this sounds like the experiential meanings of the SFL transitivity system – process: (who) *did* (what); participants: *who* (did) *what to* and *with whom*; circumstance: *when, where, why* and *in what fashion*. In the SFL model, transitivity meanings realize field; in the context of situation this is the world construed as experienced. However, the term 'storyworlds' appears also to include tenor, the SFL concept for those taking part in the context of situation (the roles played and the values that those interacting give to the field, as described in Chapter 5). Thus:

Interpreters do not merely reconstruct a sequence of events and a set of existents, but imaginatively (emotionally, viscerally) inhabit a world in which things matter, agitate, exalt, repulse, provide grounds for laughter and grief and so on – both for narrative participants and for interpreters of the story. More than reconstructed timelines and inventories of existents, then, storyworlds are mentally and emotionally projected environments in which interpreters are called upon to live out complex blends of cognitive and imaginative response.

(Herman et al. 2005, 570)

This is an admirably complex 'storyworld' but, from an SFL perspective, the conflation of field and tenor obscures their different realizations in language, and makes it more difficult to discern patterns of relation between text and context. (In Chapter 6, interpersonal meaning, the realization of tenor, was commented on in the discussion of particular extracts.) For SFL, as described in Chapter 5, the concept 'world' refers only to field, that element of the context of situation that is construed from ideational meanings (both experiential and logical), but it is a complexity of worlds: physical, mental and social. Paradoxically, the more complex SFL understanding – of three overlapping worlds at any one level of projection – actually simplifies the analysis of narrative worlds. One can focus on the realization of each world and then consider the narrative texture, how those different worlds are 'woven' together. Though my focus here remains on language in the comparison of narratives from different social and historical contexts, this modelling can be used to compare narratives realized in different semiotic modes, with different affordances/technical possibilities.

I turn now to the juxtaposition of 'worlds' in the work of Fraser and Halliday. For the five evolutionary levels of nature, Fraser describes six 'worlds' of different temporalities and causation. From the prototypical choices of process meaning in language, Halliday/SFL construes three worlds of human experience. The comparable areas of the two sets of worlds are displayed in Table 7.1.

From the two most recently evolved levels of nature, Fraser infers three worlds: human social life, human mental life, organic life. From the three prototypical choices of process meaning in the transitivity system (relational, mental and material processes), Halliday infers three semiotic worlds in the human construal of experience: a world of abstract relations (the very construal of social attributes and identities), an internal world of consciousness, an external physical world. Fraser's worlds 1, 2 and 3 are of course the worlds of the extended human

Table 7.1 Complementary modelling of 'worlds' through time and language

Fraser's worlds of temporalities	SFL worlds construed from the experiential functions of process meaning
6. A world/story of human social life	The world of abstract relations (being)
5. A world/story of human individual life	The world of consciousness (sensing)
4. A world/story of life	The physical world (doing)
3. A world/story of matter	Not realized as a process choice
2. A world/story of possibility	"
1. A world/story of becoming	"

umwelt – that understanding of reality augmented by modern science. In contrast, the semiotic 'space' of the transitivity system encompasses only the worlds construed as human experience in the pre-scientific umwelt, the environment in which human functional needs first emerged, and in which human language evolved. Juxtaposing the temporality (and causality) of Fraser's worlds with the meaning choices of the comparable worlds in Halliday's model enables us to tease out more fully the ideational texture of a narrative. Certainly, in the phylogenesis of natural language, as it evolved, one can tell at least of the physical world, the world of consciousness and the social world of abstract relations, but Fraser's model offers the potential of telling beyond those limitations, that is, telling, stories of the extended human umwelt.

The term 'story' is another constant in narrative studies, though theorized with different inflections. In Chapter 4, I referred to Gerald Prince's five entries for **story** in his *Dictionary of Narratology* (2003, 93), but here I quote from a brief mention under the lemma **narrative**:

> The story always involves temporal sequence (it consists of at least one modification of a state of affairs obtaining at time t_0 into another state of affairs obtaining at time t_n), and this is its most distinctive feature.
>
> (Prince 2003, 59)

Fraser's model of time associates each world with a different temporality. In line with Prince's words, I can assume that a story told of a particular world will be told in the temporality of that world, as set out in Table 7.2. For worlds 4, 5 and 6, the paraphrases for Fraser and Halliday's worlds are conflated.

Moreover, as 'the story always involves temporal sequence', a story of a particular world will involve the temporal sequence of that world, and what is understood as coherent sequence in one world is different from that understood in another. The study of many narratives has led me to identify the characteristic sequence by which the story told in a particular

Table 7.2 The six worlds of stories and associated temporalities

World of story	Temporality
6. A world/story of human social life; of being	Sociotemporality
5. A world/story of human individual life; of sensing	Nootemporality
4. A world/story of life; of doing, happening	Biotemporality
3. A world/story of matter	Eotemporality
2. A world/story of possibility	Prototemporality
1. A world/story of becoming	Atemporality

world can be understood as coherent. Table 7.3 gives the six different types of world of story, each with its own characteristic realization of coherent narrative sequence, associated with its different type of temporality.

A different kind of story can be told for each world: a story of human society, a story of the individual's mental world, a story of the lived world, a story of an existent but relative world, a story of possibility in an uncertain world, a story of becoming in a chaotic world. A first-world story of chaotic becoming (Fraser's world of 'Heraclitean flux') is one where 'everything happens at once' in incoherent sequence. A second-world story of uncertain possibility is one where the instant cannot be uniquely identified; you may know, or at least think, that something happened, but you can't make a confident identification; its sequence of events is indeterminate. A third-world story of material being has identity and determinable sequence, but the latter is reversible – what you see depends on where you stand. A fourth-world story is the familiar one of organic life, with the organism/character moving sequentially in chronological sequence from past birth to future death, and satisfying its organic needs in its biotemporal present. A fifth-world story is that of the mental life of the individual human; its principle of sequence is associative, so that its temporality accommodates memory and imagination, prediction and fantasy. Finally, a sixth-world story, that of human social life, is one in which social identities, attributes and socially symbolic relations generally are told. Its principle of sequence is equative, relating what is understood to be socially significant, and similar or dissimilar. Note that I am not equating any one narrative with just one type of story; the plurality of temporal worlds implies that, even at the initial level of projection, the one narrative may tell more than one kind of story.

As narrative is dependent on the symbolic organization of some semiotic medium, such as language or image or dance; it could not originate until the physical/physiological, mental and social levels of humans had

Table 7.3 The mode of coherence associated with the story of each world

Type of world	Story of ...	Temporality	Coherent narrative sequence
6. Social	Human social life	Sociotemporality	Equative sequence
5. Mental	Human individual life	Nootemporality	Associative sequence
4. Organic	Life	Biotemporality	Chronological sequence
3. Material	Being	Eotemporality	Reversible sequence
2. Uncertain	Possibility	Prototemporality	Indeterminate sequence
1. Chaotic	Becoming	Atemporality	Incoherent sequence

evolved – that is, until, in Edelman's terms, higher-order human consciousness had evolved. This consciousness is associated with the most recently developed level of nature (Fraser's 'human minding') so from the earliest oral narratives all the temporal levels had evolved. Yet until recently the human umwelt – the understanding of reality – was in terms of the most recent two levels only, those associated with the three worlds of human experience, biotemporal, nootemporal and sociotemporal, so stories were variously told within that understanding. From the late nineteenth century, however, the new epistemologies of worlds beyond sensible human experience have influenced aesthetic experimentation.

Given the pervasiveness of weaving metaphors when talking about language and sense – text, texture, the thread of an argument and so on – you could say that the ideational texture of the one narrative text is produced by the weaving together of stories (story as 'thread') of different worlds, in one way rather than another. Thus the narrative texture of an individual text may be characterized by such weaving; this enables us to compare the texture of different narratives, and to identify the emergence of new textures at different historical periods (in SFL terms: on the dimension of instantiation, to accumulate the potential of text-types from the instances of text). From such comparison/identification, we can find the balance or dominance of different worlds of story in different narratives. It becomes obvious that those studies of narrative that assume a monovalent time equivalent to the biotemporality of world 4 (as described in Chapter 4 for the 'scientific' orientation in narrative studies) have assumed the dominance of the world of physical experience, or even, albeit unintentionally, that narrative *is* the representation of the physical world of human experience. Chronological sequence is 'natural' to that organic world, the linear arrow from birth to death – in the everyday world of experience, you must walk up to a door before it is possible for you to walk through it – but other temporal worlds are characterized by different concepts of what constitutes coherent sequence.

The study of the ideational texture of narrative texts can be put to many uses. The particular focus of my work has been to compare the texture of narrative texts in English from different historical periods. Significantly, this comparison reveals a different emphasis or dominance, a general difference in texture, so that the weaving of different temporalities can be characterized as an historical phenomenon. As already intimated, the progressive inclusion of Fraser's evolutionary earlier levels in the human understanding of reality (the extended human umwelt) has come about comparatively recently. Such understanding, variously dispersed through a century of two world wars and the global communication of instability, feeds into a 'poetics of indeterminacy', to use the title of American critic Marjorie Perloff's 1981 publication. In recent literary history, this 'indeterminacy' may be referred to as postmodernism but from a more panoramic perspective there appears to be an inverse relation between natural evolution and literary narrative. Nature has evolved in a direction of apparent solidity and community, literary narrative has developed towards telling stories of becoming (for an ambitious descriptive overview, see Thomas Pavel's 'The Novel in Search of Itself: A Historical Morphology', in Volume 2 *Forms and Themes* of Moretti's *The Novel*, Moretti 2006, 3–31). This chapter now gives a summary account of the changes in temporal texture through such literary history, while subsequent chapters provide more detailed illustration from specific texts.

Given that, until the end of the nineteenth century, the last two evolutionary levels with their three associated worlds constituted the human umwelt, it is unsurprising that pre-twentieth century narratives weave together stories of these three worlds, though in different ways.

The earliest (pre-printing) narratives are dominated by stories of the social world. In a story of human social life, the mode of coherence is that of equative sequence. One makes coherent sense of the story not by knowing what event follows what (chronologically), but by knowing what is socially similar or dissimilar to what. (In the next chapter, I discuss the Old English poem *Beowulf*, in which the narrative frequently juxtaposes events and roles of similar social significance, rather than biologically sequential events.) The sociotemporality of such a world is concerned not with one event after another but with the comparability of experience. Social roles and social identities, socially defined good and bad attitudes and semiotic values, tie the text cohesively. In characters and plot such stories tell the equative sociotemporality of their production – stories of social identities rather than individual identities, of external social conflicts rather than internal personal torments. From the habitual construal of this world, its persistence, a people can understand their history, myths, social rituals and conventions of behaviour.

Examples of social-world stories, as in traditional folk and fairy tales, can lend themselves to the kind of reductive functional analysis made by the Russian formalist Vladimir Propp in 1928: a finite list of 'narrative units'/functions (31), a finite number of social roles (7 in Propp's *dramatis personae*). In contrast, the work of the Russian Mikhail Bakhtin locates the social-world stories of classical narratives in an historical context. In a paper on the development of the novel (more accurately, on the development of 'novelness', what Bakhtin understands as characteristic of the novel, Clark and Holquist 1984, 275–278), Bakhtin introduces the concept of 'the *chronotope* (literally, time space)' for 'the intrinsic connectedness of temporal and spatial relationships that are artistically expressed in literature' (Bakhtin 1981, 84), The varieties of chronotope he identifies in classical and mediaeval texts point to subtypes of texts with a dominance of sociotemporality. For example, in what he calls the adventure-time of Greek romances, there are only two moments of biotemporality in the life of its stereotyped characters: the lovers meet, the lovers marry.

In between there can be any number of adventures, any one of which can be equated with any other in significance, that is as exemplification of the unchanging attributes (fidelity, chastity) of the lovers (Bakhtin 1981: 85–110). A narrative primarily characterized by sociotemporality is not necessarily simple – though because of our later assumptions about narrative, the different complexity of such works does not always translate easily into modern tellings. (The translation from verbal to multimodal telling/showing introduces even more divergence: one might compare the 2004 film *Troy* with Alexander Pope's translation of the *Iliad*.)

I wrote earlier that there appeared to be 'an inverse relation between natural evolution and literary narrative'. Previous to Fraser's most recent natural level of 'human minding' is the organic level of 'life'. This level is associated with Halliday's human experience of 'doing' in the external physical world: a story of organic life is focused on the individual character, for whom one observable event follows another in chronological sequence, a narrative trajectory from birth to inevitable death. Inversely, this earlier level of natural evolution can be associated with the later period of literary development, post-mediaeval, with the invention of the printing press and the development of the book-trade. The growth of the English novel in the seventeenth and eighteenth centuries, together with the social context of that growth, has been well documented (for example, in Watt 1957; Mayer 1997; Keymer 2017). In the narratives of this period, we find an increased emphasis on the individual and the possibilities and causes of personal success or failure in society and, consequently, the organic/external and mental/internal worlds of the individual human being (worlds 4 and 5) receive more attention. The social world (or worlds) becomes a backdrop for this individual's experience. This is especially noticeable in the so-called 'picaresque' novel, where the protagonist, initially of a low social position, moves through different social settings. These earlier printed novels in English are the narratives most characterized by a chronological mode of coherence as the reader follows the life of the principal protagonist. Thus the novels are often focused on the personal history of a particular individual and titled by the name of that individual: Defoe's *Moll Flanders* (1722), Fielding's *Tom Jones* (1729).

Moving from the eighteenth century into and through the nineteenth, we find the texture of the novel becomes more complex, reaching its apotheosis in the so-called classic realist novel – what many people still think of as 'the novel', perhaps – whether with third person narration with an omniscient narrator (as with George Eliot's *Middlemarch*, 1871–1872) or with first person narration by a character (as with Charles Dickens' *David Copperfield*, 1850). In the classic realist text we read the densest and most coherent interweaving of stories from all three worlds, physical, social and mental, which natural language evolved to construe. The dense texture derives from a tight integration of the temporalities of the last three worlds, Fraser's three worlds of the natural human *umwelt*. The integration of the organic and mental temporalities gives the illusion of a psychologically 'real' character: with organic temporality the narrative tells a story which moves chronologically with its principal character; with mental temporality the narrative tells a psychological story of the character's thoughts and feelings about the organic present, with associated memories of the past and expectations of the future linked to the biotemporal present. Simultaneously the sequential narrative path of this character is situated in a particular and explicitly detailed social context, told in the historical temporality of a particular social positioning, with the equative coherence of explicit social values (as, for example, in the indexical social meanings of clothes and manners). Thus the narrative of the classic realist novel, for the attuned reader, coheres strongly through the modes of coherence of all three worlds of human experience: the equative coherence of the social world, the chronological coherence of the lived external world, and the associative coherence of the individual interior world. Paradoxically, the classic realist novel seems 'most real' not because it describes 'one world' most realistically but because it gives equal attention to describing the overlapping three worlds of everyday human experience, even though, at a given textual moment, one world may appear to dominate. Moreover, with a third person omniscient narrator, the reader may be given access to the mental worlds of different characters. Such a narrative is more accurately described as hyperreal, assuming a divine rather than human perspective on 'reality'.

Newtonian physics, operating as it does in the constant gravitational environment of the earth, seemed to confirm the integrated temporal coherence of the nineteenth-century classic realist novel. The technological advances driven by that physics and the sciences generally certainly contributed to what Ursula Heise calls, 'the mechanization and standardization of public time' (1997, 36). However, the revised scientific notions of space-time gaining currency at the beginning of the twentieth century began to extend the cultural umwelt. The experience construed by natural language, via the possible choices of the transitivity system, is that of the natural human umwelt, a reality of overlapping physical, mental and social worlds. How can natural language construe the experience of the extended umwelt, the realities of worlds of relativity, probability, even chaos? Yet – remembering H. Porter Abbott's dictum: 'Narrative is the way our species organizes its understanding of time' – one could predict that narrative would be further deployed to tell stories of these newly understood worlds, construing the experience of their unearthly temporalities in stories of counter-intuitive coherence.

In so-called modernist novels of the early twentieth century (such as by Marcel Proust in French, by James Joyce and Virginia Woolf in English), this extended human umwelt undermines the narrative confluence of subjective personal experience and 'objective' social reality: the Newtonian objective universe turns out to be an Einsteinian one of subjectively positioned observation. Moving earlier again through Fraser's evolutionary levels, we recognize the determinable, but reversible, eotemporality of the physicist's world 3, with its contingent relation of location in time and space. Whether from this scientific recognition of subjective perspective, or from the contemporary influence of Henri Bergson's teaching on *durée*, the internal personal experience of time, the narrative consequence was similar: the modernist novel of the early twentieth century is overtly concerned with the associative coherence of Fraser's world 5, that of the consciousness of an individual. In Chapter 3, I mentioned Fraser's account of the individual experience of conflict between the sociotemporal and nootemporal worlds (Fraser 1999, 39). Heise comments on 'the intense interest in the nature and working of private temporality' in the modernist novel and notes that 'the temporal operations of the human mind and its potential conflicts with the linerarity of public time became one of the most persistently recurring topics' (to literary examples, Heise adds the art of Salvador Dali in his 'melted clocks', Heise 1997, 36–37). As discussed in Chapter 4, this public time of co-ordinated clock time, co-ordinating and controlling the linear biotemporal lives of workers in the industrial cities of Europe, is explicitly what Bergson reacted against in his theorizing of *durée*.

The modernist novel still maintains an integration of the organic and mental worlds, the worlds of one human as living organism and thinking individual; in consequence, the integrity of the individual character in the novel is not under threat. As Brian McHale (1987) puts it, modernism is concerned with epistemology, the possibilities of knowing, rather than ontology, the possibilities of being (though in the extended umwelt principle Fraser describes the 'collapse of ontology into epistemology': what you think 'reality' 'is' depends on what you know). Stories of simple eotemporality may provide the basic plot of the science fiction story. The origins of the latter are contemporaneous with the extended umwelt provoking the modernist narrative (H.G. Wells published *The Time Machine* in 1895) and earlier science fiction typically conforms to the modernist convention of integrated character. Merely travelling forwards or backwards in space-time with only one timeline, as in the film *The Terminator* or in some of the Harry Potter stories/films, does not necessarily rupture the ontological expectations of modernism. In contrast, in the later part of the twentieth century into the twenty-first, so-called 'post-modernist' narratives, such as the prose fiction of Thomas Pynchon and Paul Auster, can bring disruption into every aspect identified as 'being' in the earlier fiction. Of course, a little goes a long way: quantitatively disruptive features may not be dominant, but any such disruption qualitatively attracts the concern of the reader as they try to 'make sense' of the story (as the next chapter will remark, Paul Auster's earlier fiction is more openly disruptive than his later).

Much has been written on the emergence of early twentieth-century modernist literature and its environment of influence; I am not suggesting a simple linear relation between science and literary innovation. Indeed Bergson, whose ideas are seen as so significant in the period, famously disagreed with Einstein, and displacements of space and time are more immediately seen in art, as in the multiple perspectives of Picasso or Braque, which in turn more directly influenced literary production. For example, in his autobiography (1951), William Carlos Williams describes the excitement of the poets, himself and others, after they visited the Armory Show, the 'International *Exhibition* of Modern Art', in New York in 1913. (On Bergson's contribution, see Gillies 1996; Douglass 1986. On science and modernism more generally see Vargish and Mook 1999; Schleifer 2000; Whitworth 2001.) However, most postmodernist literature appears self-consciously aware of the extended umwelt of contemporary science.

Just what is literary postmodernism? There is no necessary agreement on its distinction from modernism; for example Bran Nicol, editor of *Postmodernism and the Contemporary Novel*, writes,

> while [Alain] Robbe-Grillet is included in some classifications of the postmodern, [Leslie] Fiedler makes the point that the *nouveau roman* is too 'serious' and 'neo-neo-classical' to be called postmodern. I agree with this point – if ever there was an artist who required the label 'late modernist' Robbe-Grillet is the one – and this is why, as fascinating as I find Robbe-Grillet's pronouncements on the novel, his work is not included in this reader.
>
> (2002, 137)

Thus Brendan Martin accumulates and collates various European and American understandings of 'postmodernism' in order to examine any 'residual modernism' in Paul Auster's 'postmodernity' (2008, 1–11). However, in the context of this book, I argue that narratives that include stories of Fraser's worlds 1 and 2 can be so called – the chaotic world 1 of atemporality, where everything happens at once, the uncertain world 2 of prototemporality, where you can't point to the instant when something happens but only to a statistical possibility. The atemporal story, with an incoherent mode of coherence, undermines the very possibility of identity – of all the entities traditionally understood to constitute narrative: differentiated character, setting, event ... – while the prototemporal story undermines the certainty of identification. In a postmodern fiction these counter-intuitive stories are (or may be) woven together with stories from all four other worlds. As remarked earlier, although they are not necessarily dominant numerically in the words of the text, their ideational meaning is so noticeable – by the modes of coherence of other worlds, they just don't make sense – that even a little of them can earn the literary label 'postmodern'.

The postmodern narrative can bring 'becoming' into any aspect identified as 'being' in the classic realist or modernist narrative and the temporal fragmentation of character has been particularly noted. Ursula Heise writes:

> One of the most striking developments in the transition from the modernist to the postmodernist novel is the disintegration of narrator and character as recognizable and more or less stable entities, and their scattering or fragmentation across different temporal universes that can no longer be reconciled with each other, or justified by recurring to different psychological worlds. Whether it is the demise of identifiable characters that causes time to fracture, or the fragmentation of time that sets an end to character, is not easy to decide; what is clear, however, is that the time of the individual mind no longer functions as an alternative to social time [that is, as in modernist novels].
>
> (1997, 7)

Similarly, Heise sees 'divisions and fragmentations' in the 'social time' of the postmodern novel and continues, 'The weakening of individual as well as social and historical time as parameters for organizing narrative is the most crucial problem the postmodern novel articulates in its multiple formal experiments as well as many of its thematic concerns' (1997, 7). Overall, 'time' in postmodern novels has often been described, as above, in negative terms as being 'broken': it – and so the text telling it – is 'caused to fracture', is 'fragmented', is 'weakened'.

Different perspectives have been taken to this fracture. In the 'Epilogue' to my historical study of the poem as visual object I describe briefly the negative views of some critics, such as Fredric Jameson, who associate textual 'fragmentation' with cultural decline (Huisman 1998, 161–162). On the other hand, for example, Thomas Docherty sees the postmodern telling of characterization as ethically good, in that it 'allows us fully to appreciate the otherness of people, as we are prevented from reducing them to versions of the same (us)'. He writes:

> Postmodern characterisation gives us a view of subjectivity as always in process, endlessly deferred, 'about to be'. Its metaphysical portrayal of character both demystifies the process of characterisation and also makes the reader unable to impose a final definition on a particular character's identity.
>
> (Nicol 2002, 334)

This may or may not be seen as an advantage by those identifying themselves as politically less powerful (see Threadgold's critique of 'Butler and Discourse as Performativity', 1997, 82–84). Yet, perhaps surprisingly, stories of ontological disruption can have practical application. In 'Undoing' (a chapter in the edited collection, *Time and the Literary*), Catherine Gallagher discusses the limitations and usefulness of 'backwards moving' stories which involve travel back in the past and 'allow for a revision of the past ... gesture toward a different theoretical universe' (Newman et al. 2002, 11–29). The past is then given a quality similar to the future – that is, one of probability. From such a past, the present is virtual, rather than real, and the future is opened out to more than the possibilities of the 'real' present. Just such temporal play through narrative can be put to use outside the literary fiction: in torts cases in claims for damages, the plaintiff's lawyer can ask: what would the present and future for this claimant be if they had not suffered the damaging event?

It is obvious that a 'time' which, metaphorically, can be 'broken' is a time of unambiguous full presence and continuity and that such a time does not encompass all the temporalities of the extended umwelt. In contrast, in Fraser's model of multiple temporalities, the meanings of proto- and atemporal temporalities are included. Moreover, in this model the most recent is added to but does not replace the earlier; the worlds of the other natural levels, with their associated temporalities, have not disappeared. As earlier noted, Fraser has described the necessary conflicts of human life as it is lived through different worlds of experience: even at the one natural level of 'human minding', there are 'unresolvable' conflicts between sociotemporal and nootemporal experience. Aware of the extended umwelt, postmodern authors can envisage new plots, can add new conflicts to be reconciled as their characters negotiate the newly recognized worlds of experience along with the old.

Table 7.4 summarizes what has been discussed so far in this chapter: that, broadly speaking, there is an inverse relation between the evolutionary levels of nature and their associated worlds, as Fraser describes them, and the human telling of stories with the different temporalities of those worlds.

Fraser's model of temporalities is empirically based on the advancements of different disciplines so, as Fraser's dictum of the 'collapse of ontology into epistemology' implies, the topic of this chapter must remain open. Thus we can ask: what of the interrelation of narrative with one of the most recent scientific developments, the genetic stories in biology, where biological temporality extends beyond the life/death sequence of the individual organism? (Replication rather than sexual reproduction was the earliest form of life, and continues in the genetic code, that is Life began some millions of years before Death. The latter entered the biological story with sexual reproduction.) In 'Genome Time', in the edited collection *Time and the Literary* (Newman et al. 2002, 31–59), Jay Clayton uses his understanding of genome time ('where all the differences that matter to individuals are erased') to discuss Richard Powers' novel, *The Gold Bug Variations,* and the film *Gattaca* ('This is a society living fully

Table 7.4 Dominant worlds in English literary narratives, an historical summary

	Dominant worlds	Literary narratives	Story of	eg Texts/Authors
	6. external social world	pre-printing narratives	social attributes & roles; ritual, myth, classical & mediaeval 'chronotopes'	OE *Beowulf* [Bakhtin's examples: eg Classical Greek romances]
	4. external personal world	picaresque novel (17th & 18th C)	life as individual makes her/his way through changing social contexts (rise of capitalism)	Daniel Defoe Henry Fielding
	4, 5 & 6: integration of physical, mental and social worlds	classic realism (19th C)	life as individual & communal human experience	George Eliot
	3 & 5: epistemological uncertainty - relative and internal personal worlds	modernism (early 20th C)	relative being and human individual life	Virginia Woolf James Joyce
	1 & 2: ontological uncertainty - uncertain and chaotic worlds	post modernism (later 20th C on)	possibility & becoming	Thomas Pynchon

in genome time, a society that denies the openness of individual futures because of its belief in a destiny already written in the present', Newman et al. 2002, 49). So should Fraser's natural level 4 of organic being be subdivided into two worlds, like Fraser's level 5 of 'human minding', with one world limited to the individual organism, and another world persistent beyond the individual? Perhaps the most extraordinary narrative effort to tell in such biological time is the novel *Subscript* by Christine Brooke-Rose (1999). The first chapter tells the story of 'a pre-biotic chemical reaction some 4,500 million years ago'; subsequent chapters tell of different stages of life and the novel ends with the earliest human species 'some 8,000 years before writing'. The first person plural pronoun appears for the first time on page 73 (a tribe of creatures who have come down from the trees) – a world of earth-bound sociotemporality begins? – from which would evolve, as in Halliday's account of levels, the semiotic level of Edelman's higher-order consciousness and the possibility of narrative ...

References

Fictional works briefly referred to

Defoe's *Moll Flanders* (1722).
Fielding's *Tom Jones* (1729).
Charles Dickens' *David Copperfield* (1850).

George Eliot's *Middlemarch* (1871–1872).
Brooke-Rose, Christine. 1999. *Subscript*. Manchester: Carcanet.
Wells, H.G., *The Time Machine* (1895).

General

Bakhtin, M.M. 1981. *The Dialogic Imagination*, edited by Michaael Holquist, translated by Carol Emerson and Michael Holquist. Austin: University of Texas Press.

Clark, Katerina and Michael Holquist. 1984. *Mikhail Bakhtin*. Cambridge, MA and London: Belknap Press of Harvard University Press.

Cushing, Ian. 2018. '"Suddenly, I Am Part of the Poem": Texts as Worlds, Reader-response and Grammar in Teaching Poetry'. In *English in Education 52* (1). Accessed March 8 2021. https://doi.org/10.1080/04250494.2018.1414398

Davies, Paul Fisher. 2019. *Comics as Communication: A Functional Approach*. London: Palgrave Macmillan. https://doi.org/10.1007/978-3-030-29722-0

Douglass, Paul. 1986. *Bergson, Eliot and American Literature*. Lexington, KY: Kentucky University Press.

Fraser, J.T. 1999. *Time, Conflict, and Human Values*. Urbana and Chicago: Illinois University Press

Gavins, Joanna. 2007. *Text World Theory: An Introduction*. Edinburgh: Edinburgh University Press.

Genette, Gérard. 1980. *Narrative Discourse, An Essay in Method*. Ithaca, New York: Cornell University Press.

Gillies, Mary Ann. 1996. *Henri Bergson and British Modernism*. Montreal and Kingston: McGill-Queen's University Press.

Heise, Ursula K. 1997. *Chronoschisms – Time, Narrative and Postmodernism*. Cambridge: Cambridge University Press.

Herman, David, Manfred Jahn and Marie-Laure Ryan. 2005. *Routledge Encyclopedia of Narrative Theory*. London and New York: Routledge.

Huisman, Rosemary. 1998. *The Written Poem, Semiotic Conventions from Old to Modern English*. London and New York: Cassell.

Huisman, Rosemary. 2005. 'The Basics of Narrative Theory'. In *Narrative and Media*, by Helen Fulton, Rosemary Huisman, Julian Murphet and Anne Dunn, pp. 11–44.

Keymer, Thomas. 2017. *The Oxford History of the Novel in English*. Volume I: *Prose Fiction in English from the Origins of Print to 1750*. Oxford: Oxford University Press.

Martin, Brendan. 2008. *Paul Auster's Postmodernity*. New York and London, Routledge.

Mayer, Robert. 1997. *History and the Early English Novel, Matters of Fact from Bacon to Defoe*. Cambridge: Cambridge University Press.

McHale, Brian. 1987. *Postmodernist Fiction*. New York: Methuen.

Metz, Christian. 1974. *Film Language: A Semiotics of the Cinema*. New York: Oxford University Press.

Moretti, Franco, editor. 2006. *The Novel, Volume 2, Forms and Themes*. Princeton and Oxford: Princeton University Press.

Newman, Karen, Jay Clayton and Marianne Hirsch, editors. 2002. *Time and the Literary*. New York and London: Routledge.

Nicol, Bran, editor. 2002. *Postmodernism and the Contemporary Novel*. Edinburgh: Edinburgh University Press.

Perloff, Marjorie. 1981. *The Poetics of Indeterminacy*. Princeton: Princeton University Press.

Prince, Gerald. 2003. *Dictionary of Narratology*. Lincoln and London: University of Nebraska Press.

Propp, Vladimir. 1968 [1928]. *Morphology of the Folktale*. 2nd ed. Austin: Texas University Press.

Schleifer, Ronald. 2000. *Modernism and Time, The Logic of Abundance in Literature, Science, and Culture, 1880–1930*. Cambridge: Cambridge University Press.

Threadgold, Terry. 1997. *Feminist Poetics*, Poiesis, *performance, histories*. London and New York: Routledge.

Vargish, Thomas and Delo E. Mook. 1999. *Inside Modernism, Relativity Theory, Cubism, Narrative*. New Haven: Yale University Press.

Watt, Ian. 1987 [1957]. *The Rise of the Novel: Studies in Defoe, Richardson and Fielding*. London: Hogarth.

Werth, Paul. 1999. *Text Worlds: Representing Conceptual Space in Discourse*. London: Longman.

Whitworth, Michael. 2001. *Einstein's Wake: Relativity, Metaphor, and Modernist Literature*. Oxford: Oxford University Press.

Williams, William Carlos. 1951. *The Autobiography of William Carlos Williams*. New York: Random House.

8 The meaning of 'story'

The mode of coherence of each thread/ story telling the temporality of the one narrative world, with examples from different historical periods

As described in Chapter 7, from the juxtaposition of Halliday's model of language and Fraser's model of temporalities, six threads of narrative story can be inferred, each with its characteristic temporality and each associated with a particular world of experience. Furthermore, in one social context or another, a particular narrative texture, woven from stories of different temporalities, may be identified. To explore this contention, the next chapter, Chapter 9, offers a detailed study of extracts from three novels of different periods and conventional literary classification: classic realist, modernist and postmodernist. However, in this chapter, the concern is to clarify the recognition of each temporal thread individually, taking examples, where possible, from texts from different historical periods.

Sociotemporality of the social world

Sociotemporality is the time of a story of human social life, telling of a social world of abstract relations of being. It is associated with a world of symbolic relations and social attributes and identities; its sequence is that by which a social group understands its history, its social being. The meaning of this narrative sequence is equative, a sequence of similarity or dissimilarity, construed as similar or dissimilar in socially understood terms. This equation of narrative sequence is comparable to the meaning choices of relational processes, of being or not being, which are realized in the clause, although the clauses of a text dominated by this thread are not necessarily relational clauses. Remember Fraser's characterization of the causation of this world as that of 'collective intentionality' and 'historical causation'; it is a construed world of shared experience. Here is an extreme example from the novel *The Cookbook Collector* by Allegra Goodman, published in 2010 (reproduced with permission of the Licensor through PLSclear):

> Years later, they remembered where they had been. At their desks or in their beds, indoors or out. Driving, walking, working, alert, or

DOI: 10.4324/b23121-8

half asleep. Each recalled momentary confusion. An airplane hit the World Trade Center. Pilot error? Technical glitch? And then the shock. A second plane. No accident. No mistake. The flames were real, as everyone could see on television. The Twin Towers burning, again and again. Bodies falling, again and again. The same towers, and the same bodies, and the Pentagon in flames. The scenes played constantly, at once heartbreaking and titillating, their repetition necessary, but also cheapening. Who, after all, could believe such a catastrophe after just one viewing? And who, after viewing once, could look away?

(Goodman 2010, 329)

This telling assumes the shared values of a particular social group, those who understand their social being as Americans in the social culture of the United States of America. (See McHale's account of the significance given this traumatic event, its 'historical causation' – the end of postmodernism? – by some American scholars, 2015, 172–175.)

More typically, as in the classic realist novel of the nineteenth century, the thread/story of the social world will be woven through the threads/ stories of other worlds. Here is a passage from George Eliot's novel, *Middlemarch*, published in 1871–1872 (a different passage is looked at in more detail in the next chapter); the sociotemporal thread is underlined:

Perhaps if he had been strong enough to persist in his determination to be the more because she was less, that evening might have had a better issue. If his energy could have borne down that check, he might still have wrought on Rosamond's vision and will. <u>We cannot be sure that any natures, however inflexible or peculiar, will resist this effect from a more massive being than their own. They may be taken by storm and for the moment converted, becoming part of the soul which enwraps them in the ardour of its movement.</u> But poor Lydgate had a throbbing pain within him, and his energy had fallen short of its task.

(Eliot 1994, 758)

The shift from third person narration (of the possible particular experience of a character in the bio- and noo- temporalities of that 'individual') to the first person plural narration (of assumed generalization about human experience) is a clear step from the physical and mental worlds of the characters to the sociotemporality of the social world, which here is assumed to be shared by (implied) author and (implied) reader. Genette would call this telling 'extra-diegetic', outside the diegesis/world of the characters. In the structural analysis of narrative 'voices' outlined by Uspensky (as in Figure 6.1) – implied author, narrator, character – this is the voice of an 'objective' (that is, universally shared) telling of implied authorial ideology.

The sociotemporal thread may run variously through texts of any period. It is, however, in pre-printing texts (pre-1500) that it is typically dominant. In fact, it was my dissatisfaction with the relevance of many contemporary theories of narrative to the Old English (pre-1100 CE) narrative poem, *Beowulf*, which first led me to this area of study. In particular, I found inadequate the assumption of chronological sequence for 'making sense' of any narrative. Fraser's polyvalent modelling of temporalities obviously offers more discriminating criteria, and applying his categories to close study of the poem *Beowulf* led me to conclude that the temporal texture of its text is dominated by sociotemporality (Huisman 2008, 2017). This is the time of the dominant story, though others are also told/woven into the texture. Barbara Hernstein Smith has warned that the plot summary of a narrative is not objective, that it is motivated by the interpretative focus of the summarizer (1980). Thus the more usual focus of narrative studies on biotemporal story, the one of chronological sequence, would yield, for *Beowulf*, something like the following conventional plot summary, foregrounding the actions of the individual warrior (the eponymous title is a modern appellation), together with those of the individual monsters:

> The poem tells of Beowulf's three fights. In the first two thirds of the poem, the monster Grendel has been <u>attacking</u> Danish warriors in the hall of King Hrothgar; Beowulf <u>comes</u> to Denmark from Geatland, <u>kills</u> the monster; then Grendel's mother <u>attacks</u> the hall. Beowulf <u>kills</u> Grendel's mother. He <u>returns</u> home to Geatland. In the last third of the poem Beowulf, now old and King of the Geats, <u>kills</u> a dragon but is himself <u>killed</u>.

All the underlined verbs realize material processes, those which construe the physical world of life in Halliday's transitivity system. But such a summary introduces a simple chronology that is not followed simply in 'the first two thirds of the poem', and indeed ignores much of the text of 'the last third of the poem'. The social world (or complex of social worlds) construed from the text includes the past and present interactions of many groups of northern Germanic peoples – Danes, Geats, Heathobards, Frisians, Franks and Swedes – with their many complicated feuds, marriages and treacheries, that have happened or have been told of in the past or predicted in the future. The dominance of the sociotemporal story in the narrative texture of *Beowulf* implies that the dominant mode of coherence in the narrative is equative and indeed it was the textual succession of like (and unlike) events, not successive in chronological time, which led to an earlier scholarly focus on so-called 'digressions'. But, as J.D. Niles eloquently argues in his book-length study of the poem, it is the life of the social group, rather than that of the individual, which is at the heart of the *Beowulf* narrative:

> Throughout *Beowulf*, interest centres not on man as solitary hero but on people and what holds them together ... [The poet] gave us a document every part of which either stresses the joys of harmonious living among the group, or brings out the gloom of life lived apart from the group, or develops the way in which people can contribute to the stability of the group by leading lives free from arrogance and threats. The poet's ethical concerns surface constantly, not only in speeches and gnomic comments but in the main narrative as well. Thus *Beowulf* fulfills its author's purpose of illustrating, in manifold ways, how societies are held together and how they fall apart.
>
> (1983, 233)

As discussed in Chapter 7, Fraser's social world of sociotemporal relations is comparable to Halliday's world of abstract relations; the latter is construed from the relational process meanings realized in individual clauses: the meanings of having attribute, of having identity and of symbolizing (see Figure 5.1). Here is an extreme example of such meaning choices. The extract is taken from the fifteenth century telling of the Arthurian legends by Thomas Malory (first in manuscript circulation, but one of the first texts printed by Caxton, in 1495); it tells the threnody of Sir Hector over the body of the dead Sir Lancelot (lexical verbs realizing relational processes are underlined):

> A, Launcelot!' he sayd, 'thou <u>were</u> hede of al Crysten knyghtes! And now I dare say,' sayd syr Ector, 'thou sir Launcelot, there thou lyest, that thou were never matched of erthely knyghtes hande.* And thou <u>were</u> the curtest knyght that ever bare shelde! And thou <u>were</u> the truest frende to thy lovar that ever bestrade hors, and thou <u>were</u> the trewest lover, of a sinful man, that ever loved woman, and thou <u>were</u> the kyndest man that ever strake wyth swerde. And thou <u>were</u> the godelyest persone that ever cam emonge prees of knyghtes, and thou <u>was</u> the mekest man and the jentyllest that ever ete in halle emonge ladyes, and thou <u>were</u> the sternest knyght to thy mortal foo that ever put spere in the reeste.
>
> (*Malory* 1971, 725)

(* passive construction for 'erthely knyghtes hande never matched thee', i.e. 'was never equal to you.')

Abstract relations are exactly those relations that are socially constructed; the extract shows a catalogue of conflicting social codes, those of chivalry, romance, Christianity and more. The word for 'virtue' (being *trewe*) realizes a different meaning in each of these different social constructions, but in the identity of Lancelot these conflicting social relations co-exist (and thereby hangs a narrative of conflicting loyalties).

In the early modern period of English literature, texts in which biotemporality is more dominant began to emerge. Accordingly, these types of narrative are discussed next.

Biotemporality of the world of life

Understandably, personal stories, especially those orally told, are likely closely to follow the biotemporal time of the individual teller, that is to be told in chronological sequence. This was noticeable in the stories recorded by William Labov (as discussed in Chapter 4), from which Labov concluded that chronological sequence was a necessary attribute of narrative. The following text from Labov's study was discussed in Chapter 6; here clauses are numbered (Labov's sentence punctuation) with R(elational, M(aterial) and V(erbal) signifying the process type; the verb group is underlined,

1.1R When I was in fourth grade –
<< no, it was in third grade –>>
1.2M this boy he stole my glove.
2.1M He took my glove
2.2V and said
2.3M that his father found it downtown on the ground.
3.1V I told him
3.2R that it was impossible [[for him to find downtown]]
3.3M 'cause all those people were walking by
3.4R and just his father was the only one [[that found it]]?
4.R So he got all (mad).
5.M Then I fought him.
6.M I knocked him all out in the street.
7.1V So he say
7.2M he give
7.3M and I kept on hitting him.
8.1M Then he started crying
8.2M and ran home to his father
8.3V and the father told him
8.4M that he ain't find no glove

(Labov 1972, 367–368)

Of the 19 numbered clauses in the passage, 11 clauses realize material processes, 4 realize verbal processes, 4 realize relational processes. (Strictly speaking, 8.1 *crying* realizes a behavioural process; such processes are 'on the borderline between "material" and "mental" processes: those that represent the outer manifestations of inner workings, the acting out of processes of consciousness (e.g. *people are laughing*) and physiological states (e.g. *they were sleeping*)', Halliday 2014, 215.) In the dominance of material processes, the teller is patently recalling an experience in the external world of individual experience, one of physical actions and happenings. The relational clause 1.1 that begins the sequence locates the event in the chronological sequence of the teller's life, that biotemporal time from birth to death; the next clause (unnumbered), correcting the information of 1.1, shows that this linear sequence is important to the teller. The relational clause in 3.2, with postposed Subject (equivalent to '[[for him to find downtown]] was impossible') and grammatical metaphor of interpersonal meaning (comparable to a congruent 'he couldn't find [it] downtown'), realizes tenor with a meaning of strong negative modality, but this meaning is expressed objectively (*it was impossible*), rather than subjectively (*I don't think it was possible/I think it was impossible*) (Halliday 2014, 692–693). By such objectivity, the speaker is appealing to a general social rather than individually personal judgement. Finally, verbal processes – a secondary choice, which on Halliday's system of transitivity (Figure 5.1) lies between the prototypical realms of relational and mental processes – realize that inter-world where two participants can co-ordinate their nootemporal thoughts in a shared social world.

No doubt speakers – or writers on social media – informally still tell each other personal stories organized by their understanding of biotemporal time; more radically, so also did the early writers of narratives which would become 'the novel'. Daniel Defoe's *Robinson Crusoe* was published in 1719. In the words of its 2001 editor, John Richetti, it 'must be one of the most popular books ever written ..., reprinted and translated continuously' (Defoe 2001, ix).

I open the book at random and copy the following extract (Defoe 2001, 123):

> About the beginning of August, as I say, I had finish'd my bower, and began to enjoy my self. The third of August, I found the grapes I had hung up were perfectly dry'd, and indeed were excellent good raisins of the sun; so I began to take them down from the trees, and it was very happy that I did so; for the rains which follow'd would have spoil'd them, and I had lost the best part of my winter food; for I had above two hundred large bunches of them. No sooner had I taken them all down, and carry'd most of them home to my cave, but it began to rain, and from hence, which was the fourteenth of August, it rain'd more or less, every day, till the middle of October; and sometimes so violently that I could not stir out of my cave for several days.

I've underlined the careful dating by calendar months; the chronological sequence of events is explicit, a sequence in a physical world external to but personally experienced by its first person narrator. This is a narrative dominated by the thread of biotemporality, the time of individual organic life. For Richetti, its 'enduring and universal appeal' is that of 'an archetype of modern heroic individualism and self-reliance' (ix). Defoe himself insists on the individual authenticity of his work, carefully distinguishing *Robinson Crusoe* from the romances of 'popular credulity'. The title page gives Crusoe himself as the author ('Written by Himself') and Defoe's *Preface* (speaking of himself as editor) says, 'The editor believes the thing to be a just history of fact; neither is there any appearance of fiction in it' (2001, 1 and 3). Clive Probyn, writing on English fiction from 1700 to 1789, comments, 'As in all of Defoe's novels, the shape of this book [*Robinson Crusoe*] is determined by the shape of an individual life' (1987, 31). This developing taste for a narrative focus on the individual, superseding the dominance of sociotemporal stories, will transform the temporal texture of English literary narratives.

As suggested in Chapter 7, there is a generally inverse relation between the direction of natural change and organic evolution and the direction of literary production, and this early narrative transition moves from Fraser's level 5 to level 4. It is not a movement between the two worlds, social and mental, of the one level 5. This would imply an historical progression – from the medieval to the early modern period – of narratives dominated by the associative sequence of the mental world, but this is evidentially incorrect. In the worlds of the natural human umwelt associated with Fraser's model of natural levels, two worlds correspond to the individual human: the mental world of Fraser's level 5 and the organic world of Fraser's level 4. The representation of consciousness certainly becomes important as the English novel develops, post-printing, but initially it is a representation tied to the biotemporal progression of the individual in the chronological sequence of their lived experience, as, for example, in Samuel Richardson's novel, *Pamela*.

Richardson's *Pamela*, first published in 1740, has sometimes been described as 'the first English novel' because of its overt concern with the individual's inner life. For Clive Probyn, 'Richardson's undeniable contribution to the novel lay … in the literary process of creating personality through the writing of letters and the articulation of thought processes' (1987, 61). The title page of the second edition (1741) includes the following passage (my marking: / indicates lineation, // indicates paragraph end; my transcription does not reproduce the graphic emphasis conveyed by choice of character type in size, case and font):

> Pamela:/ or,/ Virtue Rewarded./ In a Series of/ Familiar Letters/ from a/ Beautiful Young Damsel,/ To her Parents./ Now first Published/ In order to cultivate the Principles of Virtue and Religion in the Minds of the Youth of both sexes.// A Narrative which has its Foundation in

Truth and Nature; and at the same time that it agreeably entertains, by a Variety of curious and affecting Incidents, is intirely [*sic*] divested of all those Images, which, in too many Pieces calculated for Amusement only, tend to inflame the Minds they should instruct//

(Keymer and Sabor 2001, Volume 1: 3)

Richardson makes his purpose explicit: 'to cultivate the Principles of Virtue and Religion', that is, to promote the conventional values of the established social world, but these principles are to be told (in SFL terms, instantiated) through the individual experience of a young woman, fictional but true-to-life ('its Foundation in Truth and Nature' – Defoe's 'just history of fact' has become Richardson's fiction grounded in 'truth'). Thus, Richardson's title page hopes, the mental worlds ('Minds') of young readers will be both 'agreeably entertain[ed]' and 'cultivate[d]'. (Richardson appears to assume a simple conduit model of communication, Reddy 1979.)

Pamela's experience, to be conveyed in 'Letters', naturally in the first person, in a 'familiar' context to recipients most interested in the girl's welfare, is realized in a complex narrative texture: a biotemporal story of external events as her employer attempts to seduce her is woven tightly with the nootemporal story of Pamela's internal emotions, fears and convictions in relation to these events. But though both stories are essential to the narrative and 'representations of consciousness' (construed from Mental processes) are noticeably told in this epistolary novel,[1] the very sequence of the first-person letters implies a dominant chronological sequence of the biological progression; the mode of coherence is that of the organic world (Fraser's world 4), as the narrative tells the succession of 'presents' that constitute the directional flow of biotemporality. Of this linking thought to action, Richardson's phrase 'to the moment' is much quoted:

The Nature of Familiar Letters, written, as it were, to the *Moment*, while the Heart is agitated by Hopes and Fears, on Events undecided, must plead an Excuse for the Bulk of a Collection of this Kind. Mere Facts and Characters might be comprised in a much smaller Compass: But, would they be equally interesting?

(Richardson 1972, 4)

Though each letter is written from memory (the world of consciousness) Richardson apparently wants his character to relive, rather than merely record, each experience and its associated emotions. Occasionally, Pamela does tell of both her mental state in the past of experience and her mental state in the present of writing: for example, she writes of a failed attempt to escape, and the temptation she then felt to die by her own hand, with the embodied emotion of the material process 'trembled': 'God forgive me! but a sad thought came just then into my head! – I tremble to think of it!' (Richardson 1914, 149).

The epistolary novel, even when so concerned with its character's consciousness, can enclose the internal story of thought within the external story of life lived. Other eighteenth-century novels, such as Henry Fielding's *Tom Jones*, are even more readily accommodated to this texture. The focus is on the character as individual, negotiating his or her progress in life through the vagaries of the new social contexts. Though a nootemporal identity affirms the individuality of the principal character through the narrative (occasionally) telling the thoughts of that character, these thoughts are typically linked to external action. Similarly, stories of the external social world – descriptions of dress, manner, etiquette and so on, as well as place – are occasionally vivid, but their telling is subsumed to the dominant biotemporal story, as the principal character moves from one social location to another.

Nootemporality of the world of consciousness

In novels written before the twentieth century, an omniscient narrator is usually assumed to tell narrative 'truth' – that is, a reader accepts the external and internal worlds told. The external worlds are the shared social and individual physical worlds of the characters. The internal worlds are the private individual worlds of the characters. In terms of grammatical projection and narrative voice (discussed in Chapter 6), verbal and mental processes have similar potential: a clause realizing the narrator's voice (the literary 'tag') can grammatically project a clause which realizes a character's speech or thought. However, verbal processes fall between the two prototypical processes, relational and mental (Figure 5.1). Thus, verbal processes bring together, on the one hand, the shared experience that construes the social world and, on the other hand, the private experience of the world of individual consciousness. Statistically (Halliday 2014, 510), speech is more usually projected paratactically (traditional 'direct speech') and thought is projected hypotactically ('indirect thought), as in these examples from Trollopes's novel *Barchester Towers* (the projecting clause is underlined, original punctuation):

> "Don't be too particular, Plomacy," <u>his mistress had said</u>: "especially with the children. If they live anywhere near, let them in."
> (Trollope 2003, 338)

and

> Mr Harding neither could nor would believe anything of the sort; <u>and he thought, moreover,</u> that Mr Slope was rather impertinent to call himself by such a name.
> (Trollope 2003, 96)

In practice, Trollope's novels are copiously realized in direct speech; the numerous exchanges of conversation between the many characters tell the different refraction of individual consciousness through the social world. On the other hand, projected thought is infrequent (I had to search to find the above example). What is more frequent is what has been called free indirect thought, that is the narrative is realized in language which can be construed as that of a character.

> She [Miss Thorne] sipped her tea in silent sorrow, and thought with painful regret of the glorious days when her great ancestor Ealfried had successfully held Ullathorne against a Norman invader. There was no such spirit now left in her family except that small useless spark which burnt in her own bosom. And she herself, was not she at this moment intent on entertaining a descendant of those very Normans, a vain, proud countess with a frenchified name, who would only think that she graced Ullathorne too highly by entering its portals? Was it likely that an Honourable John, the son of an Earl De Courcy, should ride at a quintain in company with Saxon yeomen? And why should she expect her brother to do that which her brother's guests would decline to do?
>
> (Trollope 2003, 335)

The language of the omniscient narrator – who can describe Miss Thorne's inner state (sorrow) as well her external action (sipped), and who can project ('she ... thought') the character's 'modal assessment' (Halliday 2014, 679) of her own thinking ('with painful regret'; 'glorious days', 'great ancestor') – continues in the third person but segues into the wording of the character, as in the colloquial word choice of dismissive attitude, 'frenchified', and in the asking of questions. Overall, in evaluative meaning throughout the extract and in choice of speech function, the language realizes the tenor of the situation as understood in the projected consciousness of the character. (The usual mood choice of the narrator is declarative, realizing the speech function of statement which gives information, Halliday 2014, 136–137; variations of mood are typically associated with the dialogue of characters as they interact with statements, questions, commands and offers.)

Twentieth century novels can tell similar stories. In the following extract, without explicit projection, we see a transition within the paragraph from omniscient narrator to the consciousness of a character, again marked by a changed realization of tenor (from *The Cookbook Collector* by Allegra Goodman, reproduced with permission of the Licensor through PLSclear):

> Twenty years old, Orion had gazed across the table at Molly's father with a mixture of resentment and misery. He was good at math, of

course, but he excelled at building little computer systems piece by piece. Orion had always loved to tinker. He was a puzzle solver, no deep-thinking puzzle maker. He had done well in his CS courses: programming, distributed systems, hardware, algorithms, and graphics, for which he'd rendered a faceted crystal vase filled with water and a single red rose so that it cast an accurate shadow on a wood-grain tabletop. Were these exercises at all important? In Carl's presence, he'd felt acutely that computer science lacked a certain – he would never say the word aloud – but, yes, the field lacked a certain majesty.

(Goodman 2010, 134)

Eotemporality of the world of matter

William James' phrase 'stream of consciousness' is often used to describe the associative sequence through which the so-called modernist authors, such as Virginia Woolf (1882–1941) and James Joyce (1882–1941), realized the internal world of an individual character, the mental life of that individual with its own nootemporality. In James' words, already quoted in Chapter 4:

> Consciousness ... is nothing jointed; it flows. A 'river' or a 'stream' are the metaphors by which it is most naturally described. In talking of it hereafter, let us call it the stream of thought, of consciousness, or of subjective life ...

(James 1892)

However, the narrative texture of these authors may be more complex than the one 'flowing' association of one individual's nootemporality (as discussed in the previous section on nootemporality). In such complexity, the external world is touched through an inflecting sequence of internal and external perspectives between different characters and narrator. As the experiences of different characters, in their differing nootemporalities, intersect or diverge, the story of this world resembles the movement of large matter in the space-time of Fraser's level 3, where events can be determined in space-time but can be differently measured from different locations. Thus the modernist narrative can tell a story inclusive of eotemporality, the temporality of Fraser's level 3 – a story that is characterized by a reversible mode of coherence.

In the following extract from Virginia Woolf's *To the Lighthouse*, we are variously told: the thoughts and the speech of Mrs Ramsay; the inner state of Mr Tansley (the young man 'feeling himself out of things') and Mrs Ramsay's consciousness of that state; Tansley's (or the non-omniscient narrator's?) thoughts of Mrs Ramsay ('giving out a sense of being ready'); the narrator's description of Mr Carmichael's physical appearance in the less dominant story of the physical world ... This is a narrative of rapidly shifting epistemology, where there is not one unambiguous site of human knowledge, of construed interpretation of experience, which the reader can confidently assume (McHale 1987) (original punctuation):

> Insoluble questions they were, it seemed to her, standing there, holding James by the hand. He had followed her into the drawing-room, that young man they laughed at; he was standing by the table, fidgeting with something, awkwardly, feeling himself out of things, as she knew without looking round. They had all gone – the children; Minta Doyle and Paul Rayley; Augustus Carmichael; her husband – they had all gone. So she turned with a sigh and said, "Would it bore you to come with me, Mr. Tansley?"

> She had a dull errand in the town; she had a letter or two to write; she would be ten minutes perhaps; she would put on her hat. And, with her basket and her parasol, there she was again, ten minute later, giving out a sense of being ready, of being equipped for a jaunt, which, however, she must interrupt for a moment, as they passed the tennis lawn, to ask Mr. Carmichael, who was basking with his yellow cat's eyes ajar, so that like a cat's they seemed to reflect the branches moving or the clouds, passing, but to give no inkling of any inner thoughts or emotion whatsoever, if he wanted anything.
>
> (Woolf 1994, 20–21)

This writing is a master class in grammatical projection: tagged indirect thought ('insoluble questions they were, it seemed to her'; tagged direct speech (… and said, "Would it bore you to come with me, Mr Tansley?") combined with clauses which, variously, may be interpreted as untagged thought or speech of character or telling of narrator. This is the central area of conflation (depicted in Figure 6.1) of language ambiguously attributable both to the narrator and to the untagged thoughts and speech of characters.

The external physical world of the characters' experience, with verbs realizing material process meanings, is still told chronologically (perhaps with external descriptions internal to a narrator, such as the modal assessment, 'garish', in the following). For example, a paragraph from Woolf's novel *Mrs Dalloway* begins in the physical world: *Buses swooped, settled, were off – garish caravans, glistening with red and yellow varnish.* The next paragraph begins with Elizabeth (Mrs Clarissa Dalloway's daughter) getting on a bus. But in the first paragraph, biotemporal time is suspended as the text continues: first in the nootemporal time of Elizabeth, thinking about the buses (*But which should she get on to? She had no preferences. Of course, she would not push her way.*), then into another's nootemporality, making an external judgment – (*She inclined to be passive.*), which then segues into the register of spoken gossip by the other – a friend of her mother? – moving through remembered and repeated past experience into – finally – the wording of her mother

(*It was expression she needed, but her eyes were fine, Chinese, oriental, and, as her mother said, with such nice shoulders and holding herself so straight, she was always charming to look at; and lately, in the evening especially, when she was interested, for she never seemed excited, she looked almost beautiful, very stately, very serene. What could she be thinking?* ...). From the wording of Mrs Dalloway's opinion of her daughter, the paragraph ends with her explicitly tagged thought, returning the narrative to an omniscient narrator (*Well, thought Clarissa about three o'clock in the morning, reading Baron Marbot for she could not sleep, it proves she has a heart.*) This thought is located in Mrs Dalloway's biotemporal time of material processes in the physical world: it is a specific clock-time, she is reading; she could not sleep. But it is not located in the chronology of Elizabeth's experience – to which, as already noted, the story returns at the beginning of the next paragraph as Elizabeth gets on a bus (Woolf 1991, 148).

In Virginia Woolf's novels, the complexity of the nootemporal texture is extreme, especially through the polysemous use of projection (who speaks/thinks), weaving different threads/stories in the associative sequence of the consciousness of different characters. However the 'stream of consciousness' can also flow intensely with a particular character through focalization, 'who sees', rather than voice (Genette 1980, 185–186). I suggest 'seeing' can be understood more widely as 'sensing', using Halliday's gloss on the general meaning of mental processes (Figure 5.1). A notable example of focalization through sensing is the narrative of the novel *The Member of the Wedding*, by Carson McCullers (1917–1967). (McCullers, like William Faulkner, is often described as a writer of Southern Gothic literature.)

The novel begins:

> It happened that green and. crazy summer when Frankie was twelve years old. This was a summer when for a long time she had not been a member. She belonged to no club and was a member of nothing in the world. Frankie had become an unjoined person who hung around in doorways, and she was afraid.
>
> (McCullers 1962, 7)

After the visit of her brother and his bride-to-be, 'Frankie knew that everything was changed; but why this was so, and what would happen to her next, she did not know' (1962, 34). The third person narration closely follows the thread of Frankie's nootemporality, even as it is woven with the biotemporality of her physical world.

> Frankie sat on the bottom step of the stairs to her room, staring into the kitchen. But although it gave her a kind of a pain, she had to think about the wedding. She remembered the way her brother and

the bride had looked when she walked into the living room, that morning at eleven o'clock. There had been in the house a sudden silence, for Jarvis had turned off the radio when they came in; after the long summer, when the radio had gone on day and night, so that no one heard it any more, the curious silence had startled Frankie. She stood in the doorway, coming from the hall, and the first sight of her brother and the bride had shocked her heart. Together they made in her this feeling that she could not name. But it was like the feeling of the spring, only more sudden and more sharp. There was the same tightness and in the same queer way she was afraid. Frankie thought until her mind was dizzy and her foot had gone to sleep.

(1962, 35)

The SFL field of a narrative (as described in Chapter 5) has at least one social action of telling and a subject-matter told. When what is told by a narrator is what is seen/sensed by a character, the eotemporal misalignment may encourage more freedom of interpretation. In *The Member of the Wedding* the third person narration is consistently and intensely focalized through the character Frankie – on whose perspective the experienced adult reader will often cast a wry eye, a different position of observation/ interpretation. This is the modernist turn in the reversible sequence of Fraser's world 3, though McCuller's novel was published in 1946, a considerable time after the critical modernist year of 1922 (Goldstein 2017).

The last extract in this section illustrates a displaced perspective on consciousness even in the experience of one individual character. It is taken from the novel *Burial Rites*, set in early nineteenth-century Iceland (a short extract from this novel also appeared in Chapter 6). The narrative is told by the interleaving of different genres (including letters, reports), voiced by narrator and various characters, telling in the third and first person. The following extract is told in the first person by the character Agnes, who has been condemned to die for murder (upper case and italics are the author's).

WHEN I COME INTO THE badstofa I see that the officer who was sleeping is gone. He must have joined his friends; I can hear men talking in a mixture of Danish and Icelandic outside the window. They must not have seen the farm mistress push me back inside. The two sleeping daughters have gone also. I'm alone.

I am alone.

There is no watchful eye, no guard at the door, no rope, no fetters, no locks, and I am all by myself, unbound. I am paralysed by the thought of it. Surely someone has an eye to a keyhole? Surely someone has pressed his body to a crack in the wall, is waiting to see what I will do, waiting to storm the room with a finger pointing like a knife to my throat.

But there is no one. *Not a soul.*

I stand in the centre of the room, and let my eyes adjust to the gloom. Yes, I am quite alone, and a tremble of exhilaration passes along my skin, like the tremor on the surface of a pot of water about to boil. In this minute I can do anything: I can examine the cottage, or lie down, or talk aloud, or sing. I can dance, or swear, or laugh and no one will know.

I could escape.

A bubble of fear passes up my spine. It's the feeling of standing on ice and suddenly hearing it crack under your weight – both thrilling and terrifying together. At Stóra-Borg I dreamt of escape. Of finding the key to my fetters and fleeing – I never thought of where I might go. There was never a chance. Yet here, now, I could slip out of the yard and run down the far end of the valley, away from the farms, to wait and escape under night into the highlands, where the sky will cover me with her rough grey hand. I could flee to the heath. Show them that they cannot keep me locked up, that I am a thief of time and will steal the hours denied to me!

(Kent 2013, 69)

In the first paragraph, the first two sentences establish the conflated external (biotemporal) and internal (nootemporal) temporalities of the character: when I *come* … (material process) I *see.*. I *can hear.*. (mental processes). The linear biotemporality of the character is told in the tense choices: present for events in the character's present (*is gone*); primary or secondary past for events before her present (*was sleeping, must have joined; must not have seen, have gone*). At the same time, the mental world of the character dominates the text – not so much in realization of the field in mental processes but in realization of the tenor in choices of modality, modal meanings of attitude and judgment: probability (*must have*), ability (*can hear*). Relational processes – those meanings of 'being' which I have linked to the equative narrative sequence of sociotemporality – then tell an attribute of this character, *I am alone*; at a certain moment in her physical world, this is her status in the social world. But immediately, in the repetition of 'I am alone', and graphically marked by the author's italics, the narrative moves into the associative sequence of the character's consciousness. The following paragraphs touch lightly on the physical world (*I stand in the centre of the room,*) but material processes are told with internal modality (*and let my eyes adjust to the gloom*) as the character moves nootemporally into a possible biotemporal future (*I could slip out of the yard and run down the far end of the valley, …*). Perhaps irrelevantly, I am reminded of the permeability of early modernist poems (T.S. Eliot's before the twenties?), where the boundaries between external and internal worlds are impressionistically dissolved.

Prototemporality and atemporality, the worlds of possibility and chaos

The temporalities of Fraser's two earliest worlds are the very signs of postmodern narrative. I group them together here as writing of chance and writing of disordered identity typically co-occur, as in the writing of the American author Thomas Pynchon.

Much of Pynchon's writing has been called 'postmodern', including his 2006 *magnum opus* of 1085 pages, *Against the Day*. In the very subject matter of the novel, Pynchon appears to have embraced the universal, all-things-coexisting atemporality of Fraser's world 1. A misleading plot summary might be the high school history topic: 'the causes (and after-effects) of the first world war', and the historical period covered is indeed from 1893 to about 1920. However, the innumerable characters, geographical locations and social preoccupations defeat any attempt at informative plot summary. (Compare this postmodern excess with that of the modernist James Joyce in his novel *Ulysses*, which traces the minutiae of the one day of an individual rather than that of the many days of the multitude.)

Two extracts from *Against the Day* follow. In the first, characters dispute the temporal meaning of the word 'yet':

In Venice, the artist Hunter talks with Dally, a young woman – apparently in a shared context of situation before World War I (original punctuation):

> Hunter had somehow fetched up here, demobilized from a war that nobody knew about, obscurely damaged, seeking refuge from time, safety behind the cloaks and masks and thousand-named mists of Venezia.
>
> "There was a war? Where?"
>
> "Europe. Everywhere. But no one seems to know of it … here …" he hesitated, with a wary look – "yet".
>
> "Why not? It's so far away the news hasn't reached here 'yet'?" She let a breath go by, then – "Or it hasn't *happened* 'yet'?"
>
> He gazed back, not in distress so much as a queer forgiveness, as if reluctant to blame her for not knowing. How could any of them know?
>
> "Then I guess you're a time-traveler from the future?" Not mocking, really, nor much surprised either. *(text omitted)*
>
> (Hunter) "I wish I could remember. Anything. Whatever the time-reversal of 'remembering' is …"
>
> (Pynchon 2006, 577)

Here, the very mental processes of Halliday's transitivity system are probabilistic (the prototemporality of Fraser's world 2): 'remember' can mean to think from past to present, or from future to present.

In the second extract from *Against the Day*, the character Renfrew recommends an atemporal perspective (that of Fraser's world 1) for making sense of history:

> "Best procedure when considering the Balkans," instructed Renfrew, "is not to look at components singly – one begins to run about the room screaming after a while – but all together, everything in a single timeless snapshot, the way master chess players are said to regard the board."
>
> (Pynchon 2006, 689)

Paradoxically, suggests Renfrew, in a chaotic situation, individual identity impedes 'making sense'. Renfrew is one of two professors, he in Britain and Werfner in Germany, whose 'dangerous machinations' are much talked of – for example, by the Grand Cohen leader of a British order that explains history by reference to the Tarot pack (see his humorous construction of an alternative history of the Victorian era, Pynchon 2006, 230–231). It is not irrelevant to the narrative that Renfrew and Werfner are identical but reversed spellings (they are in fact the one person? or not?) and (prototemporally) other characters are never sure if they have seen one or the other. The concept of 'bi-location' (the name of one section of the novel) is used variously to describe doubling in physical matter, in history, in human individuality – for example, with doubled identity in the stories of actual doppelgangers, the one character in the novel who participates in situations at different places at the same chronological time …

Pynchon's *Against the Day* is postmodernism 'in your face', but the postmodernist narrative can lead the reader more quietly into the worlds of probability and chaos. In an historical study by different authors of 'representations of consciousness in narrative discourse in English', Alan Palmer, discussing narratives after 1945, describes the Epilogue of Ian McEwan's novel *Atonement* as unsettling. It displaces the reader's previous identification of story and character (Herman 2011, 273–297; also see James Phelan, 'Narrative Judgments and the Rhetorical Theory of Narrative: Ian McEwan's *Atonement*', Chapter 21 of Phelan and Rabinowitz 2005). I have made similar comments about Paul Auster's novel *Invisible,* published in 2009 (Huisman 2013).

In the 1980s, Auster wrote uncompromisingly postmodernist narratives in the three novellas of *The New York Trilogy*, dominated as they are by chance and the erasure of identity (Martin 2008, 103–144). Teresa Bridgeman, discussing 'Time and Space' in *The Cambridge Companion to Narrative*, cites Auster's *City of Glass* (first novella in the *Trilogy*) as an example of the 'non-realist' text, in which the 'traversing of spatiotemporal barriers is possible, and is indeed a feature of postmodern narratives where the reader's recognition of the trangression is part of the reading experience' (Herman 2007, 52). Bridgeman's article describes time in the biotemporal dualism of what I have called, in Chapter 4, the 'scientific' orientation in narratology: the chronological sequence of events as story, the chronological reading of the text as discourse. However, from the perspective of Fraser's model, Auster's postmodern narrative is weaving together stories of different temporalities – including a story with the atemporality and chaotic causation of Fraser's world 1.

In contrast, Auster's later novel *Invisible* could, for the most part, be read as modernist – through a proliferation of perspectives taken by different narrators, who tell in first, second and third person narration – ... until, in retrospect, the reader's confidence in the modernist ontology of person and event is taken away. At the end of the novel, the character (and first person narrator at that stage) Cécile (utterly confused about past events) sees and hears a strange sight: 50 or 60 men and women, breaking large stones into smaller stones, 'each one moving at its own speed, each one locked in its own cadence, and together they formed a fractious stately harmony ...' (Auster 2009, 307). Cécile records, 'That sound will always be with me. For the rest of my life, no matter where I am, no matter what I am doing, it will always be with me' (2009, 308). For the character, that perceptual experience in a moment of linear biotemporalty is translated into an ongoing nootemporality of association (the next chapter discusses similar translations in texts of different periods). For the reader too, each character has been 'moving at its own speed, each one locked in its own cadence'. Yet, the overlaying of these different tellings scarcely forms a 'fractious stately harmony' as the characters dispute and contradict each other. In the physical world of biotemporal coherence and identifiable causation, what did happen? What, in traditional terms, is the plot? In this novel, the 'large stone' of a single physical world (the chronologically coherent world of structuralist narrative theory), has been broken down into smaller and smaller stones of conflicting storytelling; the large stone is not recoverable. Overall, the juxtaposition of these different tellings gives a narrative dominated by a story of possibility, of the uncertain world of story comparable to Fraser's natural level 2. Thus the modernist storytelling of the different perspectives of individuals is contextualized and reinterpretable as a postmodern storytelling of uncertainty and indeterminacy.

In the novel *Sunset Park*, published (2010) the year after *Invisible*, Auster most explicitly writes of the absence of meaning. In an article comparing Auster's 1987 novel *In the Country of Last Things* with the 23 years later *Sunset Park*, I comment on the author's refining focus on identity (Huisman 2015). The titles of both novels signify a concern with 'end-times' – explicitly in 'last things' and metaphorically in 'sunset' – but whereas the earlier novel depicts a postmodern chaotic fictional world, the later novel represents chaotic features of the actually experienced world in the USA – the 2001 destruction of the World Trade Centre in

New York, the collapse of the housing market during the global financial crisis of 2007–2008. Yet, in the fictional incoherence of *Last Things*, the protagonist, Anna, is a modernist integrated fictional character, strongly present to the reader, 'as an individual who tells, even when much of what she tells is of absence' (Huisman 2015, 277). In contrast, in *Sunset Park*, the principal protagonist Miles is burdened by his human consciousness of time. At the beginning of the novel, he resolves to live only in the bio-temporality of the bodily 'now' (he is emptying houses abandoned by those who can't pay their mortgages) and so to repress the human pain of 'time understood'. By the last words of the novel, thinking about the destroyed towers, unable to bear even the trace of hope, Miles abandons himself to an atemporal sequence without human meaning – to achieve not a 'postmodern identity' but, as Fraser warned, to become an 'unthinking zombie'.

Note

1 In *The Epistolary Novel, Representations of Consciousness*, Joe Bray argues for the sophistication of Richardson's examination of consciousness, objecting to the modernists being credited with the 'inward turn' to subjectivity (Bray 2003, 40). I can agree with Bray that the representation of consciousness is important in *Pamela*, yet still argue that the dominant mode of coherence is the chronological sequence of biotemporality, the individual lived life, not the associative sequence of nootemporality.

References

Works of Fiction

Auster, Paul. 2006 [1985, 1986]. *The New York Trilogy*. New York: Penguin.
Auster, Paul. 1987 [1988]. *In the Country of Last Things*. New York: Penguin.
Auster, Paul. 2009. *Invisible*. New York: Picador.
Auster, Paul. 2010. *Sunset Park*. New York: Faber.
Beowulf and the Fight at Finnsburg. 1950 [c. 1000?]. 3rd ed. Edited by Fr. Klaeber. Boston: D.C. Heath & Company.
Defoe, Daniel. 2001 [1719]. *Robinson Crusoe*. Edited by John Richett. London: Penguin.
Eliot, George. 1994 [1871–1872]. *Middlemarch*. London: Penguin Books.
Goodman, Allegra. 2010. *The Cookbook Collector*. New York: The Dial Press.
Kent, Hannah. 2013. *Burial Rites*. Sydney: Picador, Pan Macmillan Australia.
Malory, Works. 1971 [1469–1470?]. 2nd ed. Edited by Eugene Vinaver. Oxford: Oxford University Press.
McCullers, Carson. 1962 [1946]. *The Member of the Wedding*. London and New York: Penguin Books.
Pynchon, Thomas. 2006. *Against the Day*. London: Jonathan Cape.
Richardson, Samuel. 1914 [1740]. *Pamela*. London: J.M. Dent.
Richardson, Samuel. 1972 [1753–54]. *The History of Sir Charles Grandison*. London: Oxford University Press.

Trollope, Anthony. 2003 [1857]. *Barchester Towers*. London: Penguin.

Woolf, Virginia. 1991 [1925]. *Mrs Dalloway*. London: Penguin Books.

Woolf, Virginia. 1994 [1927]. *To the Lighthouse*. London: Routledge.

General

Bray, Joe. 2003. *The Epistolary Novel, Representations of Consciousness*. London: Routledge.

Genette, Gérard. 1980. *Narrative Discourse, An Essay in Method*. Ithaca, New York: Cornell University Press.

Goldstein, Bill. 2017. *The World Broke in Two: Virginia Woolf, T.S. Eliot, D.H. Lawrence, E.M. Forster and the Year That Changed Literature*. London: Bloomsbury.

Halliday, M.A.K., revised by M.I.M. Matthiessen. 2014. *Halliday's Introduction to Functional Grammar*. 4th ed. London and New York: Routledge.

Herman, David, editor. 2007. *The Cambridge Companion to Narrative*. Cambridge: Cambridge University Press.

Herman, David, editor. 2011. *The Emergence of Mind, Representations of Consciousness in Narrative Discourse in English*. Lincoln and London: University of Nebraska Press.

Huisman, Rosemary. 2008. 'Narrative Sociotemporality and Complementary Gender Roles in Anglo-Saxon Society: The Relevance of *Wifmann* and *Wæpnedmann* to a Plot Summary of the Old English Poem *Beowulf*'. *Journal of the Australian Early Medieval Association* 4: pp. 125–137.

Huisman, Rosemary. 2013. 'Paul Auster's Storytelling in *Invisible*: The Pleasures of Postmodernity'. In *Storytelling: Critical and Creative Approaches*, edited by Jan Shaw, Liam Semler and Philippa Kelly, pp. 261–276. Houndmills, Basingstoke, Hampshire UK: Palgrave Macmillan.

Huisman, Rosemary. 2015. 'How Do You Write about What Is not There? How Do You Record What Is Absent? Scraping the Temporal Palimpsest in Auster's Fiction'. In *Time, Narrative, and Imagination: Essays on Paul Auster*, edited by Arkadiusz Misztal, pp. 271–291. Gdansk: Gdansk University Press.

Huisman, Rosemary. 2017. 'Facing the Eternal Desert: Sociotemporal Values in Old English Poetry'. *Kronoscope* 17: pp. 231–253.

Hernstein Smith, Barbara. 1980. 'Narrative Versions, Narrative Theory.' *Critical Enquiry* 7: pp. 209–218.

James, William. 1892. 'The Stream of Consciousness', Chapter 11 in *Psychology: Briefer Course*. London: Macmillan & Co. Reproduced by The Project Gutenberg, released 4 August 2017. www.gutenberg.org/files/55262/55262-h/55262-h.htm

Keymer, Thomas and Peter Sabor, editors. 2001. *The Pamela Controversy, Criticisms and Adaptions of Samuel Richardson's* Pamela *1740–1750*. London: Pickering and Chatto.

Labov, William. 1972. *Language in the Inner City, Studies in the Black English Vernacular*. Philadelphia: University of Pennsylvania Press.

Martin, Brendan. 2008. *Paul Auster's Postmodernity*. New York and London: Routledge.

McHale, Brian. 1987. *Postmodernist Fiction*. New York: Methuen.

McHale, Brian. 2015. *The Cambridge Introduction to Postmodernism*. Cambridge: Cambridge University Press.

Niles, John D. 1983. *Beowulf, The Poem and Its Tradition*. Cambridge, MA and London: Harvard University Press.

Phelan, James and Peter J. Rabinowitz, editors. 2005. *A Companion to Narrative Theory*. Malden, MA and Oxford: Blackwell.

Probyn, Clive T. 1987. *English Fiction of the Eighteenth Century, 1700–1789*. London: Longman.

Reddy, Michael. 1979. 'The Conduit Metaphor – A Case of Frame Conflict in Our Language about Language'. In *Metaphor and Thought*, edited by Andrew Ortony. Cambridge: Cambridge University Press.

9 Prose fiction and the texture of time

Detailed study and comparison of extracts from three 'canonical' novels of classic realism, modernism and postmodernism

In this chapter, extracts from three very different novels are analysed using the temporal concepts previously described. One consequence of having terms for different temporalities, and different kinds of narrative sequence, is that the analyst does not need an arsenal of terms, such as prolepsis, to describe a non-linear chronology. (For the dualism of his structuralist model of narrative with its assumption of 'time' as chronological sequence, Genette names *prolepsis*, telling before, and *analepsis*, telling after, as the two major forms of *anachrony*, his general term 'to designate all forms of discordance between the two temporal orders of story and narrative', 1980, 40.) Rather, the analyst can study the narrative texture of a text as the story threads of different worlds are woven together. The texture of an individual text is interesting in itself, but the method of analysis also facilitates the comparison of one narrative text with another for many different purposes, at different levels of generality – the study of author, period, culture and so on. In the following I study the narrative texture of three texts produced in different historical and social contexts, each context already (sociotemporally) identified in literary studies as a literary period.

The three passages are chosen from canonically different texts: the 'classic realist' novel, George Eliot's *Middlemarch* (published 1871–1872), the 'modernist' novel, Virginia Woolf's *To the Lighthouse* (published 1927), and the 'postmodern' novel, Thomas Pynchon's *The Crying of Lot 49* (published 1965). In each case, I have chosen a passage with some similarity of field, one in which the narrator tells us of a character's association of an event with an emotion. My comments on the first two novels are more discursive, while on the last, Pynchon's *The Crying of Lot 49*, I also offer some detailed grammatical analysis.

As mentioned in Chapters 7 and 8, the narrative of *Middlemarch* is one where the three worlds construed from the systemic transitivity system, those corresponding to Fraser's worlds 4, 5 and 6, are most fully instantiated and integrated within the one text. This is the environment of the earlier human *umwelt*, accessible to the human senses during the evolution of language: the overlapping experience of the physical world

DOI: 10.4324/b23121-9

of doing (material) processes, the world of consciousness of sensing (mental) processes, the social world of abstract relations, of being (relational) processes. In the classic realist novel, the narrative interweaves these three worlds into a text of distinctively close texture, although intermittently one world or another may appear to dominate. Given that we human beings, in our everyday language, can speak of the overlapping constraints and possibilities of all three worlds, it is this close inter-weaving of three stories, physical, mental and social, that gives the classic realist novel its characteristic feature of experiential density. However, the term 'realist' in the labelling of such narrative is misleading. In 'nootemporal reality', each of us lives only in our own psychological world. Told as in *Middlemarch*, the narrative has a verisimilitude that is patently denser than the 'reality' it is labelled as representing – that is, an omniscient narrator can tell of the inner world of every character.

The following extract comes some three hundred pages into the novel. Dorothea, wife of the scholarly Mr Casaubon, is visited in her home by Mrs Cadwallader, wife of the Rector (who had been asked to conduct a funeral), Sir James and Lady Chettam (who is Celia, Dorothea's sister), so they can watch the funeral from an upper window; the latter is in a room Casaubon occupied when he was 'forbidden to work' after illness, but now he is back in the library, where Dorothea too would have been except ...

> But for her visitors Dorothea too might have been shut up in the library, and would not have witnessed this scene of old Featherstone's funeral, which, aloof as it seemed to be from the tenor of her life, always afterwards came back to her at the touch of certain sensitive points in memory, just as the vision of St Peter's at Rome was interwoven with despondency. Scenes which make vital changes in our neighbours' lot are but the background of our own, yet, like a particular aspect of the fields and trees, they become associated for us with the epochs of our own history, and make a part of that unity which lies in the selection of our keenest consciousness.
>
> (Eliot 1994, 326)

The physiological, physically external world of chronological sequence (Fraser's world 4) governs the larger structure of the novel; the chapter from which this extract comes is sequentially chronological to the events of the previous chapter, in which the troubled death of the old man Peter Featherstone is narrated. At a less panoramic level within the one chapter, the psychological or social worlds (Fraser's 5 and 6) of associative or equative sequence can structure the narrative development of the text – in *Middlemarch*, even within the grammatical structure of a single sentence. In the first sentence of the extract, the narrator tells us that the character Dorothea witnesses (here a mental process) the funeral of 'old

Featherstone'. However, the choice of verb *witness* rather than the more general *see* is judicious. The semantic field of this lexical item includes the more specific 'see and remember', most explicitly in the legal use of the noun: a 'witness' is one who can tell what s/he has personally seen/ experienced in her/his biotemporal past and can now (nootemporally) 'bear witness' to that past event in the biotemporal present of the court-room. From the sensing (in Dorothea's consciousness) of this specific event (in Dorothea's physical world), the narrator segues seamlessly into Dorothea's biotemporal future, to tell that the event is one the character associates, in future (present as past in future) memory, with 'certain sensitive points'. Rather than an anomalous association, the narrator then suggests this to be a 'habit of mind' for this character. Still in the same sentence, with the linking conjunctive phrase 'just as', the narrator tells of the present association of event and emotion to an event already in Dorothea's biotemporal past (past as present in present): her visit to St Peter's in Rome, and its association in her memory with an emotional state, 'despondency'. The narrator even uses the word 'interwoven' to describe how the two threads/stories (of physical and mental worlds) are brought together. The narrative texture is analogously construing the texture of human experience: in this one sentence, the omniscient narrator has collapsed the chronological sequence of the character's biotemporal experience into the associative sequence of memory in the character's nootemporal present. It is the subjective association of events in the character's internal consciousness, not the objective occurring of them in the external physical world, which is dominant at this point of the narrative sequence.

However, in the following sentence the narrator immediately tells outside the character Dorothea's consciousness and indeed outside the world of the novels' characters altogether (extra-diegetic narrative, in Genette's terms, 1980, 228–231):

> Scenes which make vital changes in our neighbours' lot are but the background of our own, yet, like a particular aspect of the fields and trees, they become associated for us with the epochs of our own history, and make a part of that unity which lies in the selection of our keenest consciousness.
>
> (Eliot 1994, 326)

Here, the narrator of *Middlemarch* emphatically includes the 'implied reader' in the text with first person plural pronouns *our and us*, the former used four times. A sympathetic identity of subjectivity, or ideological reading position (in Uspensky's terms and as depicted in Figure 6.1), is assumed between narrator and reader. (So invoked by the words of the narrator, the actual reader may in turn construe the ideological values of an 'implied author'.) In the previous sentence, the narrator's omniscience extended internally and externally over a character. Now, in this sentence, that omniscience appears to extend over all readers: as in the mediaeval homily, the narrative experience of a particular character is 'explained' as exemplum of all human experience. Paradoxically, such universality writes in a particular view of the social world – that these individual histories are written within the experience of a more general history. This equative conflating of individual traits to social attributes is characteristic of a story of sociotemporality.

In Fraser's account of the different integrative levels of nature, as introduced in Chapter 3, it was noted that each level not only determines a 'qualitatively different temporality' but also 'adds new, unresolvable conflicts to those of the level or levels below it'. Fraser's highest natural level of 'human minding', the evolutionary level of Edelman's higher-order consciousness, enables the co-emergence of two human worlds – of internal individual consciousness and external social relations – but the 'qualitatively different temporalities' of these two human worlds also add new, unresolvable conflicts. The next paragraph, immediately following those quoted above, explicitly tells of the disjunction between Dorothea's psychological world and social world:

> The dream-like association of something alien and ill-understood with the deepest secrets of her experience seemed to mirror that sense of loneliness which was due to the very ardour of Dorothea's nature. The country gentry of old time lived in a rarefied social air: dotted apart on their stations up the mountain they looked down with imperfect discrimination on the belts of thicker life below. And Dorothea was not at ease in the perspective and chilliness of that height.
>
> (Eliot 1994, 326)

Thereafter, the chapter returns to the detailed chronological sequence of the novel, narrating the direct conversational exchange of the 'visitors' and Dorothea – with brief incursions into the psychological worlds of both Dorothea and her husband, as Dorothea reacts to her husband's entrance, and both react to unexpected news from the visitors. These reactions are internal: part of the reaction is not to let others know what they are thinking or how they feel. In the classic realist novel, the detailed narrative co-presence of social, mental and physical stories/threads in the depiction of characters enables these personal unravellings in the context of 'unresolvable conflict' to be explicitly realized in the text.

As discussed in Chapter 7, the term 'modernism' has been used to label new developments in narrative writing in the early twentieth century and Virginia Woolf's novels *Mrs Dalloway* (1925) and *To the Lighthouse* (1927) are quintessentially modernist texts. Both begin in the middle of a conversation: in *Mrs Dalloway* narrated as indirect speech (*Mrs Dalloway said she would buy the flowers herself.*); in *To the Lighthouse*, as direct speech, in answer to a pretextual question (*"Yes, of course, if it's fine tomorrow," said Mrs Ramsay. "But you'll have to be up with the lark," she added.*). The reader will later understand why Mrs Dalloway is buying flowers (for her party that evening), and that Mrs Ramsay's young son, James Ramsay, wants the family to make an expedition 'to the Lighthouse', but in Woolf's writing such knowledge about the physical world of her characters can be postponed, is mundane. The significant story is that of her characters' mental worlds, what they associate with what, not what they do after what:

> To her son these words conveyed an extraordinary joy, as if it were settled the expedition were bound to take place, and the wonder to which he had looked forward, for years and years, it seemed, was, after a night's darkness and a day's sail, within touch.
>
> (Woolf 1994, 4)

The text continues with a passage that, in field, can be compared with that just discussed from *Middlemarch*, as the narrator tells how emotions can become attached to events:

> Since he belonged, even at the age of six, to that great clan which cannot keep this feeling separate from that, must let future prospects, with their joys and sorrows, cloud what is actually at hand, since to such people even in earliest childhood any turn in the wheel of sensation has the power to crystallise and transfix the moment upon which its gloom or radiance rests, James Ramsay, sitting on the floor cutting out pictures from the illustrated catalogue of the Army and Navy Stories, endowed the picture of a refrigerator as his mother spoke with heavenly bliss.
>
> (Woolf 1994, 4)

In the physical world of chronological sequence, the narrator tells a story of the little boy's actions: over a period of his biotemporality he is sitting on the floor, cutting out pictures. Then, at the particular moment of his biotemporal present in which his mother speaks, he is cutting out a picture of a refrigerator. In that moment, the 'thing' of the physical world and the emotion of the mental world, are co-joined, and – like Dorothea's despondency 'interwoven' with 'the vision of St Peter's at Rome' – this conjunction can now be present, in the mind, in any future moment. As in *Middlemarch*, the narrator here is describing the inter-relation of two worlds, how the individual's biotemporal experience of the physical world can be translated into the nootemporality of her/his individual world. Indeed, the narrator explicitly describes James as an instance of 'that great clan', those many human beings, for whom this translation is a characteristic experience.

How do the two novels differ? Essentially, because, in *To the Lighthouse*, the psychological world remains dominant. In *Middlemarch*, immediately after the passage cited, the narrative returns to the chronological sequence of shared physical reality and the conventional exchange of conversation (inter-subjective reality) among several characters. In *To the Lighthouse*, however, after the extract above, the text segues seamlessly within the one sentence from the internal world of the child to the internal world of his mother, passing on the way through an external but not omniscient narrative gaze:

> (internal to the child)
> *The wheelbarrow, the lawn-mower, the sound of poplar trees, leaves whitening before rain, rooks cawing, rooms knocking, dresses rustling – all these were so coloured and distinguished in his mind that he had already his private code, his secret language,*

> (external transition – note 'appeared')
> *though he appeared the image of stark and uncompromising severity, with his high forehead and his fierce blue eyes, impeccably candid and pure, frowning slightly*

> (internal to the observer's judgement of his appearance, rather than internal to the child)
> *at the sight of human frailty,*

> (a judgement which accords with that of his mother)
> *so that ...*

> (internal to the mother)
> *... his mother,* [her biotemporality] *watching him guide the scissors neatly round the refrigerator,* [her nootemporality] *imagined him all red and ermine on the Bench or directing a stern and momentous enterprise in some crisis of public affairs.*
>
> (Woolf 1994, 4)

The narrative shifts from the nootemporality of the child's psychological world, populated with the idiosyncratic associations of his physiological experience, to the nootemporality of the adult's psychological world, in which imagination can superimpose the chronological future on the present. This narrative shift from the mental world 5 of one character to the mental world 5 of another effaces a single position of narrative objectivity. As discussed in Chapters 7 and 8, this modernist effacement suggests a story of the extended human umwelt, Fraser's world 3, in which sequence is not fixed but dependent on an observer's positioning.

One narrative consequence of the awareness of such a textual dominance, one of subjective telling, is the disruption of sociotemporality, the consensus of social or tribal agreement. That shared social perspective, seen in George Eliott's *Middlemarch*, is not possible, except perhaps for momentary and evanescent moments. Woolf's novel *To the Lighthouse* is written in three parts. In the third and last section Lily, an artist, steps back from her canvas and muses:

> What is the meaning of life? That was all – a simple question; one that tended to close in on one with years. The great revelation had never come. The great revelation perhaps never did come. Instead there were little daily miracles, illuminations, matches struck unexpectedly in the dark; here was one. This, that, and the other; herself and Charles Tansley and the breaking wave; Mrs Ramsay bringing them together; Mrs Ramsay saying 'Life stand still here'; Mrs Ramsay making of the moment something permanent (as in another sphere Lily herself tried to make of the moment something permanent) – this was of the nature of a revelation. In the midst of chaos there was shape; this eternal passing and flowing (she looked at the clouds going and the leaves shaking) was struck into stability. Life stand still here, Mrs Ramsay said. 'Mrs Ramsay! Mrs Ramsay!' she repeated. She owed this revelation to her.
>
> (Woolf 1994, 156–157)

But, in the remorseless experienced sequence of human physical time, of biotemporality, Mrs Ramsay is already dead. Only in the nootemporality of her own mind can Lily bring together, as Mrs Ramsay had brought together, recognized shape and permanence to the moment, that recognition of stability which is basic to the socially similar or dissimilar. The three parts of *To the Lighthouse* are sub-titled, 'The Window', 'Time Passes', and 'The Lighthouse'. The central part, 'Time Passes', rapidly summarizes the biotemporal life of the characters between parts one and three; there is no apparent moral to be drawn from the various random outcomes, as characters die or suffer, irrespective of their narrative importance or social virtue. The world-view of the narrator, as much as that of any character, is just one possible perspective. In effacing the interpretative consensus of sociotemporality, the omniscient authority of the narrator is also effaced.

Thomas Pynchon published his short novel, *The Crying of Lot 49*, in 1966. Pynchon's writing is often cited as an example of postmodern fiction (and sometimes as a parody of postmodern fiction!); in the anthology *Postmodernism and the Contemporary Novel* (Nicol 2002), Pynchon has more references in the Names index than any other author. In Chapter 6, for an extreme example of narrative expansion I quoted a lengthy sentence from Pynchon's 2006 novel, *Against the Day* (itself a narrative of extreme length, at over a thousand pages). Here's a quote from the inside front flap of the dust jacket on that publication:

> Meanwhile, Thomas Pynchon is up to his usual business. Characters stop what they're doing to sing what are for the most part stupid songs. Strange and weird sexual practices take place. Obscure languages are spoken, not always idiomatically. Contrary-to-fact occurrences occur. Maybe it's not the world, but with a minor adjustment or two it's what the world might be.

This adjustment is not always minor! Readers can find the modernist narrative difficult, as it tells what is idiomatically associated in one character's consciousness, or as it moves in and out of one mind or another, but the postmodern narrative can be not so much difficult as impermeable, from the construal of everyday human experience. The postmodern novel can have narrative sequences according with any of Fraser's six worlds and six temporalities, though still being told in human language that evolved to assume the experience of worlds 4, 5 and 6. The impermeability of postmodern fiction can be traced at the formal level, that is, the choices of the lexicogrammar may inhibit our easy interpretation. To exemplify this assertion, I now look in detail at an extract from *The Crying of Lot 49*, with a close grammatical analysis of one segment of the extract.

At the beginning of the novel, the young woman Oedipa Maas receives a letter, telling her she has been named executor of the estate of her ex-lover, Pierce Inverarity. Her husband advises her to visit their lawyer, Roseman. Oedipa, hearing the complex duties of the executor, asks if she can get someone else to do the job for her and Roseman answers (original punctuation):

> "Me ... some of it, sure. But aren't you even interested?"
> "In what?"
> "In what you might find out."

> (Pynchon 1965, 20)

This could be a question to us, the reader. As readers of a novel, our expectations of 'finding out' run in fairly predictable channels: we'll find out who are important characters, we'll find out more about them, including significant events those characters experience, and the sequence of those events will be interwoven into a plot and finally we'll find out the outcome of those events for those characters, and understand, even solve, any mysteries or complications developed along the way. For popular fiction, these 'predictable channels' are the conventional structures of literary genre and bookshop shelving: the love story, the detective story, the spy thriller and so on. More literary – that is, writing that is more highly valued by the literary establishment (Huisman 2019) – fiction, whether classic realist or modernist, typically encourages the reader to pursue more complex or subtle understandings of the social and psychological worlds of the narrative, but still to reach a sense of finality, of something completed. But for the character Oedipa, and for the reader of this novel, things are very different.

The following long extract immediately follows the lawyer Roseman's comment, 'In what you might find out'. It's a long single paragraph, closing the chapter. (Verb groups realizing mental processes are **underlined**; the expressions '(=a)' etc. cross-refer to the relevant grammatical analyses that follow.)

As things developed, she was to have all manner of revelations. Hardly about Pierce Inverarity, or herself; but about what remained yet had somehow, before this, stayed away. There had hung the sense of buffering, insulation, she had **noticed** the absence of an intensity, as if watching a movie, just perceptibly out of focus, that the projectionist refused to fix. And had also gently conned herself into the curious, Rapunzel-like role of a pensive girl somehow, magically, prisoner among the pines and salt fogs of Kinnaret, looking for somebody to say hey, let down your hair. When it turned out to be Pierce she'd happily pulled out the pins and curlers and down it tumbled in its whispering, dainty avalanche, only when Pierce had got maybe halfway up, her lovely hair turned, through some sinister sorcery, into a great unanchored wig, and down he fell, on his ass. But dauntless, perhaps using one of his many credit cards for a shim, he'd slipped the lock on her tower door and come up the conchlike stairs, which, had true guile come more naturally to him, he'd have done to begin with. But all that had then gone on between them had really never escaped the confinement of that tower. In Mexico City they somehow wandered into an exhibition of paintings by the beautiful Spanish exile Remedios Varo: in the central painting of a triptych, titled "Bordando el Manto Terrestre," were a number of frail girls with heart-shaped faces, huge eyes, spun-gold hair, prisoners in the top room of a circular tower, embroidering a kind of tapestry which spilled out the slit windows and into a void, seeking hopelessly to fill the void: for all the other buildings and creatures, all the waves, ships and forests of the earth were contained in their tapestry, and the tapestry was the world. Oedipa, perverse, had stood in front of the painting and cried. No one had **noticed**; she wore dark green bubble shades. For a moment she'd **wondered** if the seal around her sockets were tight enough to allow the tears simply to go on and fill up the entire lens space and never dry (=a). She could carry the sadness of the moment with her that way forever, **see** the world refracted through those tears, those specific tears, as if indices as yet unfound varied in important ways from cry to cry (=b). She had looked down at her feet and **known**, then, because of a painting, that what she stood on had only been woven together a couple thousand miles away in her own tower, was only by accident known as Mexico, and so Pierce had taken her away from nothing, there'd been no escape (=c). What did she so **desire** escape from? (=d). Such a captive maiden, having plenty of time to **think**, soon **realizes** that her tower, its height and architecture, are like her ego only incidental: that what really keeps her where she is is magic, anonymous and malignant, visited on her from outside and for no reason at all (=e). Having no apparatus except gut fear and female cunning **to examine** this formless magic, **to understand** how it works, how to measure its field strength, count its lines of force, she may fall back on superstition, or take up a useful hobby like embroidery, or go mad, or marry a disk jockey (=g). If the tower is everywhere, and the knight of deliverance no proof against its magic, what else? (=f)

(Pynchon 1965, 20–22)

In the first half of the extract, there is only one mental process (*noticed*), though the third person narrator focalizes through the character's consciousness, with nominalization of a mental process (*the sense of buffering*), with the psychological association of a comparative simile (*as if watching a movie*) and the attitude (modality, realizing tenor) of uncertainty (*somehow* repeated). In the latter half of the extract, from sentence (=a), Oedipa is explicitly the one who senses (in SFL, the semantic role of 'Senser') and mental processes accumulate. These are typically realized in the verbs of projecting clauses. Thus many of the clauses realizing material processes (meanings of action in the physical world) together with clauses realizing relational processes (meanings of symbolic relations in the social world) are in dependent projected clauses. In this grammatical way, external experience is construed through the character's internal mental world. Is this a narrative, like those of modernist fiction, told primarily in the world of consciousness of one character or another? It is true that the distinction between 'modernism' and 'postmodernism' can be a varying – or at least postponed – response of interpretation (as suggested in the Chapter 8 discussion of Paul Auster's novel, *Invisible*). However, in this extract the narrative sequence progressively undermines the modernist focus; rather than the associative sequence of modernism, the narrative becomes increasingly chaotic, with the (oxymoronic) coherence of world 1, where 'everything happens at once'.

Sentence (=f) is the second-last sentence in the chapter; its grammatical structure, analysed below, realizes a semantic scattering of experience. (See the appendix to this chapter for a key to the analysis following and also for an analysis of all sentences in the extract numbered (=a) to (=g).) All unidentified process choices are material or behavioural. Sentence (=f):

C1 / C2 **Having** no apparatus except gut fear and female cunning
C2 RELATIONAL
C3 **to examine** this formless magic, C3 MENTAL? *hypotactic enhancement: cause, purpose*
C4 **to understand** MENTAL [[how it **works** // how **to measure** its field strength, MENTAL? // **count** its lines of force, MENTAL?]] C4 *paratactic extension*
C1 *hypotactic enhancement: cause, reason*
C5 she **may fall back** on superstition, C5 independent *(metaphor)*
C6 or **take up** a useful hobby like embroidery, C6 *paratactic extension*
C7 or **go** mad, C7 RELATIONAL *paratactic extension*
C8 or **marry** a disk jockey. C8 *paratactic extension*

In clause C3 and clause complex C4, only one verb, 'understand', unambiguously realizes a mental process. In certain contexts, 'examine', 'measure' and 'count' might all be interpreted as material processes, something the character does in the external world. However, in context all three verbs can be read as realizing mental processes, that is as referring to the intellectual attention the character can bring to bear on the situation. This attention reveals that the character has four possible courses of action: two a negative retreat from action (*fall back on superstition, go mad*), two a positive taking up of action (*take up a useful hobby like embroidery, marry a disk jockey*). The first action – exemplified by the mediaeval, even mythological, female occupation of embroidery, as shown in the painting 'Bordando el Mano Terrestre' described earlier in the extract – is undermined by the opposition of 'useful' and 'hobby': this is action to fill spare time, rather than necessary purposeful activity. The second action is one of which the narrator has already told: in her biotemporal future from the situation in Mexico, the character Oedipa is married to Mucho, a disk jockey. This future course of action is told here to be the result of intellectual powerlessness; lacking ('masculine'?) rationality with her instinctive powers of 'gut fear' and 'female cunning', the woman is unable to examine, understand, measure, count the means of her captivity – and 'marries a disk jockey'.

In the final sentence (=g) of this paragraph, also the final sentence of the chapter, the impossibility of successful interpretation is made clear (another oxymoron!). Oedipa the character – and the reader, who, as suggested previously, is following a similar interpretative trajectory to

Oedipa – cannot reach a conclusive understanding of human experience. Sentence (=g):

C1 **If** the tower <u>is</u> everywhere, C1 RELATIONAL *hypotactic enhancement: condition, positive,*
C2 **and** [if] the knight of deliverance [<u>is</u>] no proof against its magic,
C2 RELATIONAL *paratactic extension*
C3 what else? C3 independent

To construe sense from the truncated structure of (=g) C3, the reader may infer a complete clause, such as 'what else can she do?' (realizing a material process) or 'what else is there?' or 'what else can there be?' (realizing an existential process, that intermediate between the material and the relational process in Figure 5.1) – but the narrator withholds any explicit wording. The narrative has moved through Oedipa's mental world to a physical world with no differentiated processes for her to act and a social world with no differentiated existents to be. For Oedipa, and the reader, there is no escape into specific meaningfulness.

Originally, I chose particular extracts from the three novels – *Middlemarch*, *To the Lighthouse*, *The Crying of Lot 49* – because they appeared to have something in common: each told how an event was associated with a character's emotion. However, the association in each is very differently inflected. *Middlemarch* describes how a particular emotion becomes permanently associated with a particular event: Dorothea, when despondent, will think of St Peter's, at Rome. *To the Lighthouse* describes how a particular event or object becomes permanently associated with a particular emotion; for the child James, 'refrigerator' has come to signify joy so that the child is developing his own code of subjective symbols. But *The Crying of Lot 49* describes a lack of association: Oedipa tries to hold on to a specific emotion, so that in future she can interpret all experience through it, as in sentences (=a) and (=b):

> For a moment she'd **wondered** if the seal around her sockets were tight enough to allow the tears simply to go on and fill up the entire lens space and never dry. She could carry the sadness of the moment with her that way forever, see the world refracted through those tears, those specific tears, as if indices as yet unfound varied in important ways from cry to cry.

Oedipa's desire is self-contradictory, a desire to collapse the distinction between the three worlds of everyday human experience, the human umwelt, in a present moment that lasts 'forever'. Sadness is of the individual's consciousness, tears are of the individual's bodily experience, the world is external to the individual. This is the character's desire for interpretative coherence, just as the reader tries to construe coherent meaning, but in the chaotic and unpredictable worlds of 'indices as yet unfound', experience/stories can be understood only with the causations and temporalities of the extended human umwelt.

The model of narrative presented in this book has shown how the word 'time' is misleading: time is plural, 'temporalities'. Moreover, despite being a grammatical noun, 'time' is not a thing but a sequence, and so not just one 'chronological' sequence but a different sequence for each temporality and for the telling of different stories. In this chapter, the comparison of texts from (sociotemporally) recognized different literary traditions for the English novel, classic realism, modernism and postmodernism, shows an historical progression as each narrative weaves a different texture with stories of different temporalities. Thus stories of the human umwelt become encompassed by stories of the extended human umwelt and, using Fraser's words, narrative ontology is equated with narrative epistemology. Or with Halliday's terms, we can study narrative as social semiotic.

Appendix

Key:

Cx....Cx delimits one clause or clause complex.
[[...]] delimits an embedded clause/clause complex, not numbered;
// separates clauses in an embedded clause complex.
<<...>> delimits an interrupting clause.
Verbal groups are <u>underlined</u> and the lexical verb **bolded.**
The process type is in SMALL CAPITALS; all unidentified process choices are Material or Behavioural.
Conjunctions are **bolded.**
Dependency (taxis) and logico-semantic relations are *italicized.*

Sentence (=a)

C1 For a moment she'<u>d</u> **wondered** C1 MENTAL independent *projecting*
C2 **if** the seal around her sockets <u>were</u> tight enough RELATIONAL [[<u>to allow</u> the tears simply <u>to **go on**</u> // **and** <u>**fill up**</u> the entire lens // **and** never <u>**dry**</u>]]. C2 *hypotactic projected clause*

Sentence (=b)

C1 She <u>could</u> **carry** the sadness of the moment with her that way forever, C1 independent *(metaphor: 'carry an emotion')*

C2 <u>see</u> the world MENTAL [[<u>**refracted**</u> through those tears, those specific tears,]]

or C3 <u>**refracted**</u> through those tears, those specific tears C3 *hypotactic enhancement: manner, means*

C4 **as if** indices [[as yet <u>**unfound**</u>]] <u>**varied**</u> in important ways from cry to cry C4 RELATIONAL *hypotactic enhancement: manner, comparison*

C2 *paratactic extension*

Sentence (=c)

C1 She <u>had</u> **looked** down at her feet C1 independent

C2/C3 **and** <u>**known**</u>, then, because of a painting, C3 MENTAL *paratactic projecting*

C4/C5 **that** [[what she <u>**stood**</u> on]] <u>had</u> only <u>been</u> **woven** together a couple thousand miles away in her own tower, C5 *hypotactic projected clause*

C6 <u>was</u> only by accident **known** as Mexico, C6 MENTAL *paratactic extension*

C7 **and so** Pierce <u>had</u> **taken** her away from nothing, C7 *paratactic enhancement: result*

C8 there'<u>d</u> **been** no escape. C8 RELATIONAL *paratactic elaboration*

C4 *hypotactic projected clause complex*

C2 *paratactic extension*

Sentence (=d)

What <u>did</u> she so <u>**desire**</u> escape from? MENTAL independent

---

Sentence (=e)

C1 Such a captive maiden,
C2 <<<u>having</u> plenty of time [[to <u>think</u> MENTAL]]>> C2 RELATIONAL
hypotactic elaboration or *enhancement: cause, reason*
soon <u>realizes</u> C1 MENTAL independent *projecting*
C3 /C4 <u>that</u> her tower, its height and architecture, <u>are</u> like her ego
only incidental: C4 RELATIONAL *hypotactic projected clause*
C5 that [[what really <u>keeps</u> her // where she <u>is</u> RELATIONAL]] <u>is</u>
magic, anonymous and malignant, [[<u>visited</u> on her from outside
and for no reason at all.]] C5 RELATIONAL *paratactic extension*
C3 *hypotactic projected clause complex*

Sentence (=f)

C1 / C2 <u>Having</u> no apparatus except gut fear and female cunning
C2 RELATIONAL
C3 <u>to examine</u> this formless magic, C3 MENTAL? *hypotactic
enhancement: cause, purpose*
C4 <u>to understand</u> MENTAL [[how it <u>works</u> // how <u>to measure</u> its field
strength, MENTAL? // <u>count</u> its lines of force, MENTAL?]] C4 *paratactic extension*
C1 *hypotactic enhancement: cause, reason*
C5 she <u>may fall back</u> on superstition, C5 independent
(metaphor)
C6 or <u>take up</u> a useful hobby like embroidery, C6 *paratactic
extension*
C7 or <u>go</u> mad, C7 RELATIONAL *paratactic extension*
C8 or <u>marry</u> a disk jockey. C8 *paratactic extension*

Sentence (=g)

C1 If the tower <u>is</u> everywhere, C1 RELATIONAL *hypotactic enhancement: condition, positive,*
C2 and [if] the knight of deliverance [<u>is</u>] no proof against its magic,
C2 RELATIONAL *paratactic extension*
C3 what else? C3 independent

References

Works of fiction

Eliot, George. 1994 [1871–1872]. *Middlemarch*. London: Penguin Books.
Pynchon, Thomas. 1965. *The Crying of Lot 49*. New York: Harper and Row.
Pynchon, Thomas. 2006. *Against the Day*. London: Jonathan Cape.
Woolf, Virginia. 1991 [1925]. *Mrs Dalloway*. London: Penguin Books.
Woolf, Virginia. 1994 [1927]. *To the Lighthouse*. London: Routledge.

General

Genette, Gérard. 1980. *Narrative Discourse, An Essay in Method*. Ithaca, New York: Cornell University Press.
Huisman, Rosemary. 2019. 'The Discipline of English Literature from the Perspective of SFL Register'. *Language, Context and Text* 1 (1): pp. 102–120.
Nicol, Bran, editor. 2002. *Postmodernism and the Contemporary Novel*. Edinburgh: Edinburgh University Press.

10 Poetry and the texture of time

Extending the model of temporalities to the traditional, modernist and postmodern poem, and the complex poetic 'weaving' of temporal meanings

Time is of the essence for narrative, and the temporal texture of a narrative is woven from the threads of different temporalities, If narrative is relevant to poetry, then such poetry will be organized with a temporal texture (to recall Porter Abbott's original response to 'what does narrative do for us?': *narrative is the principal way in which our species organizes its understanding of time*, 2008, 3). What then has been said of so-called 'narrative poetry'?

The *Routledge Encyclopedia of Narrative Theory* has an entry **Narrative Poetry** but begins with the statement, 'poetry has been relatively neglected in recent narrative theory, apart from the Homeric poems and a few other exceptions, and even these tend to be treated as though they were essentially prose fictions' (Herman et al. 2005, 357). This is said to be 'doubly surprising', as many poems possess a narrative aspect and conversely, many 'of the worlds most valued literary narratives', especially in oral cultures, are poems.

Narrative poetry has been a lemma in the second (Preminger et al. 1974), third (Preminger and Brogan 1993) and fourth (Greene et al. 2012) editions of *The New Princeton Encyclopedia of Poetry and Poetics* (I have not been able to consult the first edition). In her 1982 article, 'From Image to Action: The Return of Story in Postmodern Poetry', Marjorie Perloff quotes from the second edition entry in the context of arguing that poetry (lyric) and the novel (narrative) have 'increasingly played to separate audiences', and that 'the equation of poetry with the lyric is almost axiomatic in contemporary criticism'. (I return to this article.)

The entry for the third edition begins with a definition of 'narrative': 'a verbal presentation of a sequence of events or facts (as in *narratio* in rhetoric and law) whose disposition in time implies causal connection and plot'. Although, it adds, further definition of narrative poetry is elusive: 'we can, at least practically, talk about literary narrative as a subtype of narrative in general, and further, talk of sub types of literary narrative: prose fiction and narrative poetry' (Preminger and Brogan 1993, 814).

DOI: 10.4324/b23121-10

After some brief discussion of narrative theory, the entry finds it difficult to classify such poems further:

> The variety of narrative poetry is such that it must defeat any attempt to sort it into a manageable taxonomy. Evidence to suggest the futility of classification: in 1819, Wordsworth published 'The Waggoner' and Byron the first cantos of *Don Juan,* while Shelley composed 'The Mask of Anarchy' and Keats 'Lamia'. What besides verse measure and the fact that they are in English brings these poems within the compass of a definition more specific?
>
> (Preminger & Brogan 1993, 817)

In the final paragraph of the entry, the entry's author encourages textual study that is not constrained by classical notions of genre:

> If modern theorists of narrative have mostly concentrated their efforts on prose, it is perhaps because analysis of prosody, as of figures, schemes, and tropes, has customarily been applied to the lyric. If it is understood that narrative poems are susceptible of the same kind of analysis, with the difference that prosodic effects feed into the general effect produced by a particular narration, then we can approach individual texts unworried by classificatory anxieties, reasonably confident that we are looking at real similarities and equally real differences.
>
> (Preminger and Brogan 1993, 817)

Eleven years later (2004), when asked to write on narrative poetry in Australia, I was unsurprised to find little critical work on the topic (my piece discusses long narrative poems by Les Murray, Dorothy Porter and John Tranter, Huisman 2004). However, as noted in Chapter 4, the first decade of the twenty-first century showed an upsurge in narrative studies and by the fourth edition of the *Princeton Encyclopedia* in 2012, the entry on narrative poetry is more expansive:

> Narrative turns the raw material of story – the 'telling' of a concatenation of events unfolding in linear time – into a (more or less) artful organization of those events that may complicate their chronology, suggest their significance, emphasize their affect, or invite their interpretation. Narrative *poetry* heightens this process by framing the act of telling in the rhythmically and sonically constructed language of verse.
>
> (Greene et al. 2012, 914)

Yet, in terms of my methods, this definition is more limiting than the previous. The third edition talked of 'sequence of events' and 'disposition in time' – which, on reflection, could be expanded to include the different types of sequence characteristic of the different temporalities. But 'linear time' and organization that 'complicate[s] chronology' unambiguously imply a structuralist dichotomy, the ordering and disordering in story and discourse of the one time, Fraser's biotemporality of the physical/organic world.

The fourth edition entry also includes a discussion of 'Criticism', reinforcing Perloff's earlier opinion on the 'almost axiomatic' equation of poetry with the lyric in critical attention:

> Little critical work has focused specifically on narrative poetry, although the critical taxonomies and terminologies developed by narrative theorists such as Chatman, Genette, and Ricoeur may be usefully applied to narrative in verse. This is, to a large extent, the result of a critical tendency to rely on a poetry/prose binary that reduces poetry to lyric and elides the presence and work of poetic narrative; the influential stylistic poetics of Jakobson, e.g. associates epic with the 'metonymical' capacity of prose fiction as opposed to the 'metaphoric nature of lyric'.
>
> (Greene et al. 2012, 915)

The paragraph above mentions Chatman, Genette, Ricoeur and Jakobson but the divergence of their theoretical approaches to narrative complicates their application (to prose as well as to poetry). This divergence is described in Chapter 4. Genette's work was discussed within the 'scientific' orientation of structuralist theory, with its assumption of a dichotomy based on a monovalent time, that of biotemporality; similarly, the approach of Chatman (mentioned in Chapter 6) assumes a structuralist dualism. In contrast, the work of Ricoeur is included in the 'philosophical' orientation, that with a recognition of nootemporal meaning. Finally, Jakobson continues a Saussurean structuralism but – unlike Barthes, whose early assumption of formalist linguistics when formulating his 'narrative grammar' is also discussed in Chapter 4 – within a functional modelling of language (*viz.* Jakobson's famous *dictum* of the 'poetic function': it 'projects the principle of equivalence from the axis of selection into the axis of combination' [Jakobson 1960, 358], as, for example, in the choice of rhyming words in the linear sequence of a poetic text).

While the fourth edition entry offers less clarity on narrative theory, it makes several insightful observations about poetry and time (grist for my translation into temporalities):

> the boundaries between narrative and lyric verse are always fungible: poems usually classified as lyric may supply a significant amount of narrative context for an act of reflection unfolding in arrested time (as in the work of Elizabeth Bishop, Robert Lowell, and Seamus Heaney).

... The epic narrative of John Milton's *Paradise Lost* elaborately reorders linear chronology and interrupts narrative sequence with prolepsis and flashback.

... The heightened ordered language of pre-20th century narrative poetry does mean ... that the illusion of experience so valued in the realist novel will be adumbrated by the visible and sometimes elaborate artifice of poetic form,

... Poetic fictions can ... draw on the dynamics of lyric to interrupt linear narrative drive, sometimes offering pauses, reflection, and dilation by way of a shift in the genre of represented utterance....

(Greene et al. 2012, 915)

An example of the last is given as the 'elegiac digressions within the later stages of *Beowulf*'; this is a topic on which I have written elsewhere (Huisman 2017), disputing a traditional use of the term 'digression'. As discussed briefly in Chapter 8, I contend that the meaning of sociotemporality, with its coherent sequence of equative events, is the dominant temporal thread in this Old English poem.

In the first observation ('the boundaries between narrative and lyric verse are always fungible: poems usually classified as lyric may supply a significant amount of narrative context for an act of reflection unfolding in arrested time'), a distinction appears to be being made between a 'lyric time' and a 'narrative time'. 'Lyric time', as an 'act of reflection', is time because it is 'unfolding', sequential, and the word 'time', as Chapter 2 argues, is the nominalization of sequence. 'Reflection', the nominalization of the mental process from the lexical verb 'to reflect', implies this 'lyric time' is that of nootemporality, the time of experience in the world of individual consciousness. 'Narrative time', as 'arrested time', suggests a monovalent understanding of time as that of the physical world with the one temporal sequence of chronology arrested, stopped. In contrast, a polyvalent understanding of time implies alternation, not arrest, a change from one time to another. In narrative terms, the story of the biotemporal experience of the chronological sequence of events in the individual's physical world is overwoven with a story of the nootemporal experience of associations in the individual's world of consciousness.

To exemplify these general claims I turn to a sensitively close reading of Samuel Coleridge's poem, 'Frost at Midnight', by Katherine Robinson (2016). Robinson explores the text under the sub-heading 'The poet shows how reality and imagination can become one'. 'Reality', it will emerge, refers to the physical world of the poet's experience; 'imagination' (another nominalization of a mental process, 'imagine') refers unambiguously to the poet's experience of his own world of consciousness. Fraser – as earlier discussed – points out the potential conflict between these different worlds of experience for the one individual, but in this poem the narrative weaves a reconciliation of biotemporal and nootemporal stories. At the same time, Robinson's reading illumines how the poem is dominated (as I would put it) by nootemporality, with its characteristic coherence of association.

In the first lines, the poetic persona describes the lack of disturbance in his physical and social worlds – with the consequence that his world of consciousness ('meditation', another nominalized mental process) can be 'disturbed and vexed', brought to present attention ('vex' from Latin *vexare*, to disturb or shake):

> The frost performs its secret ministry,
> Unhelped by any wind. The owlet's cry
> Came loud—and hark, again! loud as before.
> The inmates of my cottage, all at rest,
> Have left me to that solitude, which suits
> Abstruser musings: save that at my side
> My cradled infant slumbers peacefully.
> 'Tis calm indeed! so calm, that it disturbs
> And vexes meditation with its strange
> And extreme silentness.

In this absence of external stimulation, the poet's attention focuses on the one small physical detail which is still active …:

> the thin blue flame
> Lies on my low-burnt fire, and quivers not;
> Only that film, which fluttered on the grate,
> Still flutters there, the sole unquiet thing.

and 'Methinks" – the old 'it seems to me' rather than 'I think' – explicitly records the transition of the poet's attention from the external physical world to the internal world of consciousness …

> Methinks, its motion in this hush of nature
> Gives it dim sympathies with me who live, …

within which the present 'unquiet thing' is associated with previous experience:

> But O! how oft,
> How oft, at school, with most believing mind,
> Presageful, have I gazed upon the bars,
> To watch that fluttering stranger!

From here, the poetic persona first remembers his past, his school days, is then recalled to the physical present by his sleeping child ('Dear babe, that sleepest cradled by my side …'), and then imagines the future he wishes for the child. As Robinson writes, 'Coleridge forges poetic patterns to represent the workings of memory and imagination' (2016). Robinson recognizes that a simple understanding of time is not adequate to describe this sequence:

> The word *extreme* [Coleridge's 'extreme silentness'] derives from a Latin adjective meaning far away or foreign – outside the boundaries of a given territory. This 'extreme' silence dissolves the boundaries of the self and draws the poet toward something distant. In this case, the distance is temporal; watching the 'stranger', [colloquial term for the ash from the fire 'fluttering' on the grate] the poet recalls old memories and also vividly imagines his son's future. In the imagination, multiple time frames coexist at once; time is no longer simply a linear progression.
>
> (2016)

A 'linear progression' is the chronological sequence of biotemporality, the time of the space through which the body ages. But in the metaphorical space of the mind, events of biotemporal experience can be brought together in nootemporal sequence; for the poet here, as Robinson puts it, 'Silence turns the self into a wanderer' (2016). I respect this subtle reading but with some translation. Rather than the silence dissolving the boundaries of the self, it has allowed the poet to enter more fully into the individual human self, its internal world of higher-order consciousness, where the long perspectives of memory and imagination can be conjoined in the experienced present.

I alluded earlier to Perloff's 1982 article, 'From Image to Action: The Return of Story in Postmodern Poetry'. Perloff is a subtle reader of poetry, paying close attention to the particular text rather than to general criticalisms ('Theory … usually lags behind practice', 1982, 416), and she begins by linking the poetry of literary 'modernism' to earlier preoccupations: 'the dominant poetic mode of early modernism remains the lyric'. She lists features of such a poem: it is one characterized by an isolated speaker, who is located in a specific landscape, who meditates or ruminates on some aspect of his or her relationship to the external world, and who finally comes to some sort of epiphany, a moment of insight or vision, with which the poem closes. 'Meditates', 'ruminates': these are mental processes of the world of consciousness; it is clear Perloff is describing a poetic persona telling noetically. As Fraser put it (quoted in Chapter 3), 'the noetic umwelt is created by our capacity to produce symbolic transformations of experience and manipulate them as part and parcel of reality' (Fraser 1982, 29). At the same time, Perloff's account emphasizes the singular perspective (an individual 'epiphany') already described as characteristic of the eotemporal world of modernist prose (see Table 7.4). Perloff does note that 'Pound and the early Eliot are … exceptions to this rule [of the early modernist lyric]' and the dichotomy of lyric and narrative is ripe for deconstruction: the fourth edition of the *Princeton Encyclopedia*, commenting that 'poetic narrative is a capacious category', allows it to include 'albeit in fragmented or subverted form, the modernist lyric sequences of Hart Crane, T.S. Eliot, Ezra Pound, and W.C. Williams' (Greene et al. 2012, 911).

Perloff then turns to poems by Frank O'Hara ('Poem', beginning 'Lana Turner has collapsed!'), John Ashbery ('They Dream Only of America') and Edward Dorn (*Slinger*, a 'four-book epic of the Wild West') in order to demonstrate that these poems 'allude to story' or 'keep us guessing' as to what the story is about, or tell of the death of 'I' in a story where the 'real hero … is language itself' (1982, 424). In modernist poetry, she writes, '[d]ifficult as it may be to express his [*sic*] particular emotions except in terms of images and metaphors, the poet never doubts their validity, their ability to signify'. In contrast, in 'the longer narrative poems of the past decade', just such doubt exists. This is the disruptive move from epistemology to ontology, as Brian McHale put it, when describing the literary move from modernism to postmodernism (1987). Perloff's detailed discussion of the three postmodern poems identifies several features comparable to those identified in the prose fiction of Thomas Pynchon and Paul Auster, as discussed in Chapters 8 and 9. In short, so-called 'postmodern' poetry, like prose, invokes the temporalities of Fraser's worlds 2 and 1, where nothing is confidently known (prototemporality) or even identifiable (atemporality). It was sometimes said of so-called 'language poetry', emerging from the early 1970s in the United States, that it impeded the construal of a world of experience, denying the transparency of language through which 'meaning' could be directly understood – and so it could serve the political purpose of drawing attention to the constructive nature of language systems/social systems (George Hartley gives a critical account in *Textual Politics and the Language Poets*, 1989). But this is an understanding of meaning as limited to that of the human umwelt, that world of social, mental and physical experience in which language first emerged. In contrast, in the extended human umwelt, worlds of probability and chaos can be experienced through the imaginative projections of human fictions, in prose and poetry, to which both Fraser (2007) and Edelman (1994) alluded.

Some 20 years later, Perloff provides back-cover blurb for an anthology of Australian poetry, *Calyx, 30 Contemporary Australian Poets* (Brennan and Minter, 2000). She writes that the poets 'represent the cutting edge of Australian practice' in poetry that US and UK readers may not know about but cannot 'afford to ignore' and continues:

> Highly varied as these poets are with respect to national origin, ethnicity and gender, they share an energy, a graphic, often racy vocabulary, a theoretical sophistication and a willingness to derail the very lyric forms that, paradoxically, they know and love.

The back-cover blurb of *Calyx* also includes an endorsement by John Kinsella, an Australian poet. Although Perloff observed (1982) that literary theory usually lags behind practice, practice may be stimulated by theory. The symbiotic relation between literary theory and literary practice was particularly noticeable in the 1990s, as English translations of earlier French works became more readily available and their conceptual vocabulary was taken up to provide a critical discourse for talking about postmodern fiction or poetry. In Chapter 4, I mentioned that Bergson's early twentieth-century work on 'becoming' influenced the French philosopher Gilles Deleuze and psychoanalyst Félix Guattari. In a strange echo of Whorf's comments on the 'spatialization' of time in SAE (Standard Average European, as in Chapter 2), Deleuze and Guattari describe 'becoming' as a rhizome, an object with a multiplicity of connections (Deleuze and Guattari 1988, 239). Taking up this discourse, Kinsella writes in the *Calyx* blurb:

> [This] new anthology of contemporary Australian poetry is unique: a space in which poetry is organic, rhizomic, molecular, and alive.

So this is one solution to the inadequacy of simple chronology for describing such literary practice: reconceptualize temporal succession as spatial links, the mapping of multiplicities. I agree that an insistence on time as biotemporality of chronological succession is as unhelpful for the study of postmodern texts as it is for the study of the Old English *Beowulf*. However, as Fraser's work has clearly established, time itself is multiple, nested as different temporalities with different properties. Further, as different temporalities are recognized, the multiple possibilities of 'space' also become apparent, with each temporality characteristic of a different world of experience.

What does it mean to derail the modernist lyric? 'Derailment' is a disaster in the physical world, but in the nootemporal world of the individual poet it may be a stimulant to creative production, and in that of the individual reader, a stimulant to more creative interpretation. Such derailment may take place, I suggest, as the poet moves further back through the evolutionary worlds and levels of temporality. Modernism had taken literature into the eotemporal world of situated point of view; postmodernism takes the text into the prototemporal world of possibility, and, finally, the atemporal world of becoming. When Douglas Barbour reviews *Calyx* in the online journal *Jacket* (2001), he takes 'identity' as a kind of cline for postmodernism, distinguishing between

> poets who use the 'I' in what appear to be fairly lyric or narrative ways, poets who seem to hold the 'I' in their poems up to question, and poets who almost seem to ignore the 'I' at least as a sign of identity assumed or dropped.

Those in Barbour's less problematic first group, with a poetic persona
that appears to have ontological consistency, may nonetheless derail a
reader's modernist expectations through a recalibration of temporalities
(as in, for example, 'Everything Holy' by M.T.C. Cronin, Brennan
and Minter 2000, 121–123). At the other extreme of those who 'almost
seem to ignore' the 'I' in their poems, the very complexity of temporality
may emerge as the poetic 'subject', as it does in my reading of the
poem 'Psychopathologies of the Commonplace' by Louis Armand (his
punctuation):

> inchoate & always coming back to a point of starting out
> "before the air mirrored us"
> the zero of endless (re)birth in conjunctions of "to be"
> & other non-places? times square,
> for example, or caught mid-flight above the date line
> like an embryonic consciousness
> but what does it matter to have been here or there? the same
> narrative of disappointment in the eyes of everyone
> or alone crossing an intersection "somewhere"
> was it strange that the scene never appeared to be questioned
> by our passing it? that the intimacy of streetlights
> was nothing more than a wished-for recognition
> of ourselves in the embrace of the inanimate (at dusk
> in a half-familiar suburb, or menaced by the distant
> barking of a dog, cerberus-like, guarding each avenue
> of escape) ... & being lost
> always in the unspecific "as though" & "as though"
> with our motives no longer returning
> in the disguise of ordinary things, even when it seemed
> they were all written down (the testimonials, the witnessed
> accounts of mundane fact) ... but when in time
> we are left to the dumb-show of our shadows' diminishing
> how will we know which of those meanings
> ever concerned us? "today" or "tomorrow" or "today"
> as if there were a difference
> in the way it would end (that stupid blinking of an eye
> exhausted of perception) and afterwards
> to remember, to name it at last, even as the words break off
>   and no longer resemble us (did they ever?)
>   (2000 Brennan and Minter, 25–26)

Lexical items can summon up past texts; is it the reference to 'street-
lights' (street lamp?), or the 'stupid blinking of an eye' (though not
twisted), which resonates (for me) with T.S. Eliot's *Rhapsody on a Windy
Night*, that early modernist poem written (1910–1911) when Eliot was

at the Sorbonne, attending Henri Bergson's lectures on time? Armand's rewriting of 'time' is not as thorough-going as Thomas Pynchon's; here 'remember' still comes 'afterwards' in the biotemporal directional arrow of the physical world: in an extract from Pynchon's *Against the Day*, quoted in Chapter 8, 'remember' can be from the future as well as the past. Nonetheless, Armand's poetic questioning of the very possibility of narrative 'truth' in the inconstancy of temporal interpretation ensures his 'postmodern' reception. His 'inchoate' time is the time not yet fully formed – the no-time of atemporality or, at most, the possibility of time in prototemporality. And the 'words which resemble us' are the words of the human umwelt, the context of the evolution of language and these 'inchoate' temporalities are of the extended human umwelt. Although, in his review of *Calyx*, Barbour placed this poem in the 'poets who almost seem to ignore the "I"' category, in first person plural pronouns ('us', 'our', 'we') the poetic persona appears to be the human race. If the story of the first 'Fall' is the human emergence into Edelman's 'higher-order consciousness', with language developed to talk about the experience of the human umwelt, Armand's poem effectively (for me) tells the story of a second 'Fall' – another experience of exclusion from what has 'made sense' and of new conflicting demands – into the unearthly context of the extended human umwelt. I would call it a 'postmodern narrative poem'.

I turn now to two very short poems that would scarcely be called 'narrative poetry' but in which the temporal weaving is strikingly complex. Poetry is that art for which the medium of expression is speech and/or writing, the two modes of what traditionally has been called 'language' (Jewitt et al. 2016, 15). One of the characteristics frequently attributed to poetry is that of intensifying, augmenting, the resources of meaning-making afforded by these modes (technically, 'affordance': 'different modes offer different potentials for making meaning', Jewitt et al. 2016, 155). Thus my book *The Written Poem* studies the evolving meaningful-ness of graphic realization in English poetry from the unlineated manuscript pages of Old English to contemporary visual display (Huisman 1998). Here I'm exploring the question: how can a poetic text intensify, augment, the meanings of temporality? In these two poems, two of the human worlds of experience are crucial to interpretation: the biotemporality of the body, in the sequence of individual chronology, and the noo-temporality of the mind, in the sequence of individual association. (For reference, Table 10.1 shows just Fraser's 'nested integrative levels of nature' as they are experienced in the worlds of the human umwelt, with the relevant stories of human experience and their characteristic temporalities and coherent sequence.)

Antigone Kefala's collection of poetry, published in Australia in 2016, is called *Fragments*. A fragment is a piece broken off or detached; an incomplete piece; a portion; a scrap, a morsel, a bit. The word entered

Table 10.1 Temporalities and modes of sequence for stories of the human umwelt

Nested integrative levels of nature	Worlds of the human umwelt	Story of ...	Temporality	Coherent narrative sequence
5. 'Human minding'	6. Social	External: human social life	Sociotemporality	Equative sequence
	5. Mental	Internal: human individual life	Nootemporality	Associative sequence
4. Living matter	4. Organic	External: human individual life	Biotemporality	Chronological sequence

English in the fifteenth century from Latin *fragmentum*, from the verb *frangere* 'to break'. Moving up the levels of stratification (as described in Chapter 5), from this lexical choice the reader construes a meaning and from that meaning this reader construes a context: that this collection makes modest claims for its texts – they will always imply an absent larger whole, from which these small pieces have been broken off. This contextual modesty is realized even at the material level of graphic expression: it is no surprise that the poems are often very short.

Consider 'The Voice' (Kefala 2016, 3):

The Voice

At the sound
I turned
my veins full of ice
that travelled
at high speed
releasing fire.

This return
the past attacking
unexpectedly
in the familiar streets.

Again, at the lexical and semantic levels of this poem there is reduction: the title gives just the fragment of another human presence, *the voice*; in the text of the poem, even the human quality implicit in the word *voice* is lost – it is just *the sound*. But this fragment of a human presence, the poem tells us, activates an intense physiological response in the hearer. The first stanza tells of a moment of stimulus and response, a fragment of time in the sequence of biotemporality.

Yet in the chronological sequence of biotemporality which, for an individual, advances sequentially from birth to death, this moment is not in the 'now' of the poem. The English tense system gives us some choices for ordering a chronological sequence and the poet uses the simple past tense 'I turned' to mean the action is completed before the biotemporal time of poetic speaking. ('The now' of the poem is the moment of feigned dialogue in the biotemporal time of the reader, construing meaning in the physical act of reading the linear text.)

So in the first stanza, the poet gives a narrative report on an event experienced in the poet's biotemporal past, and the physical/physiological sensations that accompanied that experience.

However, the second stanza begins with 'this return', the deictic 'this' of proximity immediately locating the experience of the first stanza in the nootemporal 'now' of the poet, that is, what the speaker is thinking about. Biotemporal and nootemporal time are now sequentially different: in the phenomenon we call memory, in the act of remembering, the first stanza event in the biotemporal past is brought into the nootemporal present. On the biotemporal timeline, using the English tense system to order the chronology of events, it is possible to refer to an event earlier than a past event by the use of the so-called pluperfect tense, the past in past meaning choice. But in the second stanza the poet is not ordering events chronologically by using the tense forms of verbs. Rather, the past which was past, which preceded the events of the first stanza, is what returns to memory, and grammatically that event is brought into the nootemporal 'now' as a participant, realized by the nominal group 'the past'. In the nootemporal moment of the remembered event, this past, as a participant, is able to take up a semantic role available to participants, that of agency, in relation to the process 'attack'.

Similarly, the experiences of the physical and mental worlds have been conflated through language. 'Attack' is a material or action process; in non-metaphoric use such processes construe the physical world. Yet the action here is in the mental world of the 'I'. The biotemporal past in past is now a nootemporal 'thing' which attacks. The participant that suffers that attack is not explicit; implicitly it is the 'I' of the first stanza, whose extreme bodily response has been described. Finally, the adverb 'unexpectedly' describes a relation of biotemporal future to nootemporal present: expectation, like imagination, is a noetic projection. Before the past biotemporal time of the event in stanza 1, the 'I' had not projected a future with this event.

Overall in this little poem, there is a concentration of biotemporal past, past in past, nootemporal future in past in past, all packed into one nootemporal moment, a fragment of individual human experience.

For the second poem by Kefala, recall the earlier discussion of Augustine's confusion, of Edelman's account of different stages of development of the human brain, of Fraser's discrimination between time felt (in the earlier brain of remembered present) and time understood (in the later brain of extended temporalities). As Augustine acknowledged, time felt and time understood cannot be simply reconciled, while for Fraser, 'the human experience of time, in its everyday sense, is a balancing act between these two extremes...' (2007, 264). Biotemporality, spoken of, is a temporality of the human umwelt, a 'time understood' by the individual, but the biotemporal 'now' corresponds to 'time felt', that of the unspeakable experience of the self.

Consider the conflict of time felt and time understood in this poem by Kefala (2016, 4):

Letter II

The light today
clean as if made of bones
dried by a desert wind
fell in the distance on the roofs
and I remembered you.

Nothing will bring you back
only this light
falling so innocently
yet so self-contained
in an unbearable indifference.

In the biotemporality of the body's external world, the poem tells the time (today, but in the past tense 'fell', chronologically earlier than the time of 'now'), tells what event it saw 'the light fell'. and where the event took place 'in the distance on the roofs'.

In the nootemporality of the mind, the poem judges the quality of the light ('clean'), which is then associated with the comparison ('as if ...'), and in the associative sequence for this individual (bones > skeleton > death?), nootemporality is dominant ('I remembered you').

The second stanza confirms the reader's hypothesis of loss, perhaps of death – 'nothing will bring you back' – and of conflict that cannot be reconciled. That conflict is between the nootemporal memory of the world understood, in which 'you' is brought back in the world of the mind, and the biotemporal experience of a 'self-contained' and 'indifferent' felt world which cannot bring 'you' back to the world of the body – a situation that is, nootemporally, unbearable.

A critic of Kefala's earlier work wrote, 'Kefala can render the music of the moment so perfectly, she leaves one almost singing with the pleasure of it' (2016, back cover blurb). Both the short poems quoted seem to offer no more than 'a moment' – a biotemporal fragment of time felt, which is none the less augmented, intensified in significance, with the meaning of time understood.

The work of Marc Wittmann, based on insights from psychology and neuroscience, may help to explain how, paradoxically, the apparent linearity of language – heard or read – can be construed with such complexity, such concentration, in the temporal moment. In Chapter 2 of his book *Felt Time, The Psychology of How We Perceive Time*, Wittmann discusses the concept of *temporal order threshold of perception*. Research demonstrates that, even though we take our conscious experience to be continuous, it actually occurs in small discrete steps. The temporal order is that of two stimuli (for any sense); the threshold describes the basic interval required for an individual to correctly identify their sequence. The more precise a person's temporal perception, the smaller the interval between the stimuli can be, and so the lower the *temporal order threshold*. All that is processed within a duration less than the threshold will be experienced as simultaneous.

Again, in Chapter 3, Wittmann elaborates: 'what I am aware of right now is a dynamic image of the world; all that occurs in the moment has a duration' (2016, 45). It appears that 'individual events' result from 'a mechanism of temporal integration in perception and motor operations that lasts from two to three seconds' (2016, 48), as in the behaviour of handshakes and the rhythm of verbal communication (2016, 50), or the period of a single relaxed breath (2016, 58). The successive 'now's of this 'feeling of presence' are linked together by short-term or working memory; it is this duration which 'gives rise to the feeling that one's own ego exists continuously in the world' (2016, 51).

So the research described by Wittmann undermines our intuitive confidence in the present moment, the 'now', as instantaneous, a single step in a sequence of steps. Rather we live in a sequence of integrated durations. In such a context of integrated duration, the poetic moment can be filled more fully; the poet can concentrate the ordinary affordance of language.

This chapter has taken us in a potentially circular argument. If narrative is the way in which our species organizes its understanding of time, then, yes, a postmodern narrative text can be organized in such a way as to tell us the temporality of the extended human umwelt; we can understand probability and chaos are parts of experience and necessarily do not 'make sense' in the coherence expected of our bodily, mental and social worlds. By those criteria I've called Armand's poem 'a postmodern narrative poem'. But what of Kefala's? In 1982, Perloff describes 'the late modernist lyric' as having 'the solitary "I" in the timeless moment' and predicts that 'these hall-marks ... will become less prevalent'. Instead 'a narrative that is not primarily autobiographical will once again be with us, but it will be a narrative fragmented, dislocated and often quite literally non-sensical' (Perloff 1982, 425). By these criteria Kefala's poems are basically modernist – a solitary I and a moment – and yet not modernist at all; far from being 'timeless', the moment is burdened with temporalities, and this weight of time fragments the 'I', dislocates its mental self from its bodily self of 'now'. I would call these poems postmodern narratives of the self, but however labelled, these poems are bijoux of temporal texture.

References

Poetry

Brennan, Michael and Peter Minter, editors. 2000. *Calyx, Contemporary Australian Poets*. Sydney: Paper Bark Press.
Kefala, Antigone. 2016. *Fragments*. Artarmon, NSW: Giramondo Publishing.

General

Abbott, H. Porter. 2008. *The Cambridge Introduction to Narrative*. 2nd ed. Cambridge: Cambridge University Press.
Barbour, Douglas. 2001. 'An Alphabetical Appreciation of the Latest Australian Anthology: Review of *Calyx: 30 Contemporary Australian Poets* by Michael Brennan and Peter Minter (eds)'. *Jacket* 15 (December). Accessed 11 May 2021. http://jacketmagazine.com/15/barb-r-calyx.html
Deleuze, Gilles and Felix Guattari. 1988 [in French 1980]. *A Thousand Plateaus, Capital and Schizophrenia*. London: The Athlone Press.
Edelman, Gerald. 1994 [1992]. *Bright Air, Brilliant Fire: On the Matter of the Mind*. London: Penguin Books.
Fraser, J. T. 1982. *The Genesis and Evolution of Time, a Critique of Interpretation in Physics*. Amherst: Massachusetts University Press.
Fraser, J. T. 2007. *Time and Time Again, Reports from a Boundary of the Universe*. Leiden and Boston: Brill.
Greene, Roland, Stephen Cushman, Clare Cavanagh, Jahan Ramazani, Paul F. Rouzer, Harris Feinsod, David Marno, and Alexandra Slessarev, editors. 2012. *The Princeton Encyclopedia of Poetry and Poetics*. 4th ed. Princeton: Princeton University Press
Hartley, George. 1989. *Textual Politics and the Language Poets*. Bloomington: Indiana University Press.
Herman, David, Manfred Jahn and Marie-Laure Ryan, editors. 2005. *The Routledge Encyclopedia of Narrative Theory*. London and New York: Routledge.
Huisman, 1998; 2000. *The Written Poem, Semiotic Conventions from Old to Modern English*. London and New York: Cassell; Continuum.
Huisman, Rosemary. 2004. 'Narrative Poetry'. *Five Bells* 11 (4): pp. 15–18.
Huisman, Rosemary. 2017. 'Facing the Eternal Desert: Sociotemporal Values in Old English Poetry'. *Kronoscope* 17: pp. 231–253.

Jakobson, Roman. 1960. 'Concluding Statement: Linguistics and Poetics'. In *Style in Language*, edited by Thomas A. Sebeok, pp. 350–377. Cambridge, Massachusetts: Massachusetts Institute of Technology.

Jewitt, Carey, Jeff Bezemer and Kay O'Halloran. 2016. *Introducing Multimodality*. London and New York: Routledge.

McHale, Brian. 1987. *Postmodernist Fiction*. New York: Methuen.

Perloff, Marjorie. 1982. 'From Image to Action: The Return of Story in Postmodern Poetry'. *Contemporary Literature* 23 (4): pp. 411–427.

Preminger, Alex, Frank J. Warnke, O.B. Hardison, editors. 1974. *Princeton Encyclopedia of Poetry and Poetics*. 2nd ed. London: Macmillan Education UK.

Preminger, Alex and T.V.F. Brogan, editors; Frank J. Warnke, O.B. Hardison, Jr., and Earl Miner, associate editors. 1993. *The New Princeton Encyclopedia of Poetry and Poetics*. 3rd ed. Princeton: Princeton University Press.

Robinson, Katherine. 2016. 'Samuel Taylor Coleridge: "Frost at Midnight"'. Poem Guide by the Poetry Foundation. www.poetryfoundation.org/articles/70316/samuel-taylor-coleridge-frost-at-midnight

Wittmann, Marc. 2016 [in German 2014]. *Felt Time, the Psychology of How We Perceive Time*. Cambridge, Massachusetts, and London: Massachusetts Institute of Technology.

11 Digital culture and the texture of time

Post postmodernism or ...

In 1998 I published the book *The Written Poem, Semiotic Conventions from Old to Modern English*, on the graphic expression of poetry. Part One, 'Contemporary Poetry', discussed various understandings of visual display by late nineteenth- and twentieth-century poets. Part Two described the historical evolution of the 'seen poem' and the subjectivity of its reading from manuscript to and through print culture and included chapters headed 'The Transition to a Literate Subject, 1500–1800' and 'The Reading Subject and the Writing Subject, 1800–1990'. However, by the time of publication I felt compelled to add an 'Epilogue', with the title, 'The Postmodern Subject and the New Media Poem'.

The 'new media poem', so-called, had been the particular focus of a 1996 issue of the journal *Visible Language*; in its editors' words,

> the work of [these] poets takes language beyond the confines of the printed page and explores a new syntax made of linear and non-linear animation, hyper-links, interactivity, real-time text generation, spatiotemporal discontinuities, self-similarity, synthetic spaces, immateriality, diagrammatic relations, visual tempo, multiple simultaneities, and many other innovative procedures.
>
> (1996, 98)

This is poetry of digital, not print, culture, computer generated since the 1960s but now accelerated by the public advent of the World Wide Web in 1993. Thus, in 2007, 11 years after this issue of *Visible Language*, Christopher Funkhouser publishes his study of the earlier poetry under the title, *Prehistoric Digital Poetry: An Archaeology of Forms, 1959–1995* (he credits a German computer scientist, Theo Lutz, with creating the first examples in 1959).

In the 1996 issue of *Visual Poetry*, the new media poets described their poetic practices and the changing relations of writer and reader (the very terms are misleading); in positive terms as I wrote, they showed that they 'are acutely conscious of what they are doing and why, because the new poetics in which they are writing foregrounds the practices of

DOI: 10.4324/b23121-11

production', not the product of 'a text'. My discussion focused on two aspects of their work: the 'essential quality of immateriality' and 'their positive affirmation of the postmodern subject'. Yet more relevant now, to the matter of this chapter, is the parenthesis I added to the latter: 'their positive affirmation of the postmodern subject (though I think post post-modern is more accurate – or let us say twenty-first-century subject)' (Huisman 1998, 161).

I would scarcely be surprised then, a few years later, to read Alan Kirby's article entitled 'The Death of Postmodernism and Beyond' (Kirby 2006), with, under the subheading 'What's Post Postmodernism?', assertions such as 'somewhere in the late 1990s or early 2000s, the emergence of new technologies re-structured, violently and forever, the nature of the author, the reader and the text, and the relationship between them'. Yet what is different, negative, in Kirby's account is captured in those adverbs of extreme meaning, 'violently' and 'forever'. Similarly, in an earlier sentence he had written: 'the terms by which authority, knowledge, selfhood, reality and time are conceived have been altered, suddenly and forever'. I cannot resist seeing the mead benches upended, the warriors (writers?) scattered. What presented new opportunities for innovation to the new media poets is now, to Kirby, a Grendel ending the traditions of Heorot and the peace of Hrothgar's (the editor's?) authority.

Kirby goes on to call this monstrous post post-modernism 'pseudo-modernism':

> Let me explain. Postmodernism conceived of contemporary culture as a spectacle before which the individual sat powerless, and within which the questions of the real were problematised. It therefore emphasised the television or the cinema screen. Its successor, which I will call *pseudo-modernism*, makes the individual's action the necessary condition of the cultural product.
>
> (2006)

He describes the television show 'Big Brother' as a 'typical pseudo-modern cultural text' because 'it would not exist materially if nobody phoned up to vote its contestants off'. Again, the internet is 'the pseudo-modern cultural phenomenon *par excellence*' because 'its central act is that of the individual ... [moving] through pages in a way which cannot be duplicated' and 'you can easily make up pages yourself (eg blogs)'. In 2009, Kirby elaborates his 'challenge to postmodern theory' in the book *Digimodernism: How New Technologies Dismantle the Postmodern and Reconfigure Our Culture*; his new term *digimodernism*, replacing 'pseudomodernism', points nicely toward both digital technology and the individual's finger actions, clicking, scrolling and swiping. Meanwhile, the contemporaneous development of social media was making Kirby's remarks even more prescient: Facebook was founded in 2004;

Jack Dorsey sent the first 'tweet' on Twitter in 2006; Steve Jobs 'unveiled' the first iPhone in 2007 (though so-called 'smartphones' had been around since the mid-1990s); Instagram was launched in 2010 and so on …

The collection, *Supplanting the Postmodern: An Anthology of Writings on the Arts and Culture of the Early 21st Century* (Rudrum and Stavris, 2015), includes both Kirby's 2006 article and extracts from his 2009 book, *Digimodernism*. The 2006 article is placed in Part One, 'The sense of an ending', one of six pieces by different scholars which the editors describe as giving 'a range of positions in the debate around the demise of the postmodern'. The selected passages from Kirby's 2009 book are in Part Two, 'Coming to Terms with the New', which includes eight pieces by various authors. Each piece is titled by the particular new '-ism' (introduced in Part One) that its writing represents, and preceded by the editors' comments on its positioning within the 'new' paradigm. (The eight titles are *Remodernism, Performatism, Hypermodernism, Automodernism, Renewalism, Altermodernism, Digimodernism, Metamodernism*. For an account of more efforts at naming what 'comes after' postmodernism, see McHale 2015, 175–177. McHale finds 'post-postmodernism' the 'ugliest coinage', but the 'most useful and least inadequate term' 'for the time being'.) In some ways, Kirby refutes the labels of the editors. By the time he publishes *Digimodernism* in 2009, Kirby has refined his analysis. He now sees 'pseudomodernity' as 'a dimension of one aspect of digimodernism' (Rudrum and Stavris 2015, 275) and 'digimodernism' as a continuation of 'modernity' rather than a cultural 'new phase of history' (so not a 'digimodernity'). In fact he finds the lexis of 'endings' and 'rupture' – the very repetition of 'post' as temporal interruption – to be typical of late twentieth century postmodern discourse (Rudrum and Stavris 2015, 274). Moreover, his interest is now in the 'cultural landscape', rather than the 'far-reaching philosophical implications' he introduced in his 2006 article, which, in 2009, he lists as having been 'selfhood, truth, meaning, representation and time' (Rudrum and Stavris 2015, 275); in the 2006 article itself, the list reads 'authority, knowledge, selfhood, reality and time'. But given the focus of this book, it is these 'implications', to which I will return, which particularly interest me.

In Chapter 5, I quoted Halliday and Hasan's 1976 answer to the question, 'what is a text?':

> The concept of texture is entirely appropriate to express the property of 'being a text'. … a text derives this texture from the fact that it functions as a unit with respect to its environment …
>
> (Halliday and Hasan 1976, 2)

Three years later (1979), Michael Reddy, in critiquing the 'conduit metaphor' (of meaning transferred directly from speaker/writer to listener/reader) pointed out the confusion of the one word, such as text or poem, being used to refer both to wording/graphic display and meaning: objectively, this poem has 14 lines, the lexical item 'sand' appears twice, grammatically once singular, once plural; subjectively, (I think) this poem is about *hubris* ... Here the objectivity is that of the text in print culture, a visually available finite physical object and this generalization applies equally to Eliot's classic realist *Middlemarch* or Pynchon's postmodern *Against the Day*. In detailed study of the texture of the finite text in print culture, SFL, as outlined in Chapter 5, can investigate the individual text alone (theme and information, cohesion) and in the context of similar text-types (register). But with digital culture, what does it mean to say '[a text] functions as a unit with respect to its environment'? (Kirby puts forward an 'antilexicon'– a list of words whose meanings need to be rethought for 'digimodernism': author, interactive, listener, nonlinear, passive/active, publishing, reading, text, typing, user, viewer, Rudrum and Stavris 2015, 280–294.) In Chapter 10, Antigone Kefala's poems were presented as 'fragments', but they are still, in print, the complete text of the author. And even in the hyperlinks of the earlier 'new media poems' there was still some authorial control of potential pathways of reading. But when Neil Sadler uses 'fragmented' in the title of his book *Fragmented Narrative: Telling and Interpreting Stories in the Twitter Age* (mentioned at the end of Chapter 4), he points to textual practice without unity in terms of individual authorship (2022, 49–50) and this will have temporal consequences. Sadler discriminates between three kinds of storytelling to which the 'fragments' on social media may contribute: vertical storytelling (narratives which are built up through sequentially posted fragments); horizontal storytelling (a single fragment implies a larger whole without a sequential accumulation); ambient storytelling (where 'shared stories form a constellation of evaluations') (2022, 51–74). He comments that the second type is least studied, while the third type 'has received more attention in the digital media literature' (for example, Michelle Zappavigna's publication, with a chapter on 'Ambient Affiliation', 2013). Perhaps this greater attention looks for a positive potential in the diversity of communal construction, stories that are sociotemporally generated from the many rather than nootemporally composed by the one, but Sadler's analysis shows that the trajectories of ambient storytelling are the most unpredictable – susceptible, in Fraser's terms, to atemporal construction.

In his article of 2006, writing on 'fragments' that proliferate before the explosion of social media, Kirby focuses on the temporal absence, the lack of sequential continuity, in digital culture, a lack that is a negative from the ideological perspective of print culture:

> A pseudo-modern text lasts an exceptionally brief time. Unlike, say, *Fawlty Towers*, reality TV programmes cannot be repeated in their original form, since the phone-ins cannot be reproduced, and without

the possibility of phoning in they become a different and far less attractive entity. Ceefax* text dies after a few hours. If scholars give the date they referenced an internet page, it is because the pages disappear or get radically re-cast so quickly. Text messages and emails are extremely difficult to keep in their original form: printing out emails does convert them into something more stable, like a letter, but only by destroying their essential, electronic state. Radio phone-ins, computer games – their shelf-life is short, they are very soon obsolete. A culture based on these things can have no memory – certainly not the burdensome sense of a preceding cultural inheritance which informed modernism and postmodernism. Non-reproductive and evanescent pseudo-modernism is thus also amnesiac: these are cultural actions in the present moment with no sense of either past or future.

(2006)

* Ceefax, used by the BBC, was 'the world's first teletext information service'. Being analogue rather than digital, it was discontinued in 2012, an appropriate footnote to Kirby's remarks.

In the temporalities discussed in this book, where has a not dissimilar description of 'time experienced' been given? Not, I think, in the temporalities of Fraser's levels 4 (organic) and 5 (human minding) of human experience in the traditional umwelt, though Kirby is describing an experience of human beings. It is not a kind of sociotemporality; Kirby has rejected the concept of a 'digimodernity' but, more significantly, this time must involve the direct participation of the human body (clicking, speaking …). Yet it is not the biotemporality of the organic level as humans understand it, an inevitable progress from one bodily state to another. Further, this time is non-replicable and non-recoverable so it is not comparable to Fraser's nootemporality with its associative capacities of memory and prediction. Finally, the extended human umwelt, as its description implies, may be extended further by the discoveries of science and the developments of technology – but these temporalities do not depend on human intervention. However, when we return to Chapter 1 of this book we do find something that appears similar.

Edelman's theory of human consciousness is of two kinds: primary consciousness and higher-order consciousness. Edelman explains the difference between the two states in temporal terms: he refers to primary consciousness as 'the remembered present', one lacking the temporal sense that gives rise to the higher order:

[Primary consciousness] is limited to a small memorial interval around a time that I call the present. It lacks an explicit *notion* or a concept of a personal self, and it does not afford the ability to model the past or the future as part of a correlated scene.

(Edelman 1994, 122)

I suggest Kirby's depiction of 'pseudomodernism' echoes Edelman's observations on primary consciousness, when he (Kirby) writes, 'Non-reproductive and evanescent pseudo-modernism is thus also amnesiac: these are cultural actions in the present moment with no sense of either past or future' (2006).

To distinguish a basic difference of 'digimodernism' from postmodernism, Kirby introduces the phrase 'apparently real', describing it as 'one of digimodernism's recurrent aesthetic traits' (2015, 295). The apparently real 'proffers what seems to be real … and that is all there is to it' (2015, 296); he gives examples from reality TV, from docusoaps. In contrast, for postmodernism, there was *nothing real* 'out there'. Kirby's examples of postmodern texts include Pynchon's *The Crying of Lot 49*, discussed here in Chapter 9, with its multi-layered possibilities of meaning. 'Pynchon,' he writes, 'doesn't resolve these multiple and incompatible versions of the "real"' (Rudrum and Stavris 2015, 296). Kirby concludes that the apparently real of digimodernism has three associated textual functions: its deployment of a (pseudo) scientific discourse; the engulfing of the self (addictiveness), and its 'immersion in the present' (Rudrum and Stavris 2015, 298). His discussion of these three functions aims particularly to draw out their difference from the texts and assumptions of postmodernism; my focus again is on the temporal attributes he discerns in these textual functions.

'It is commonly reported', Kirby writes,

> that such digimodernist forms as text messaging, e-mail, chat rooms, video-games, reality and participatory TV, and the Internet in general have addictive properties [he queries the appropriateness of 'addicted'] … However, the keyboard trance is a recognizable phenomenon … The digimodernist text does seem to possess the property of overwhelming the individual's sense of temporal proportion or boundaries … This derives from their apparent or experiential reality: combining manual action with optical and auditory perception, such a text overpowers all competing sources of the real.
>
> (Rudrum and Stavris 2015, 300)

Similarly, in his 2006 article, Kirby wrote of the *trance* being the typical emotional state of pseudomodernism, that is the state of being 'swallowed up by your activity … pseudomodernism *takes the world away*' [Kirby's italics]. In an old-fashioned childhood (like my own) such a trance could be experienced reading a book of fiction, being engrossed, being taken away into the world/s of the story/ies. But that was a suspension of self and present reality into the others and times of the text given to you by the author, whereas the digimodernist text only comes into being with the insertion of the self in its present time. In Kirby's view, 'digimodernism is the state of being engulfed by the present real, so much so it has no room for anything beyond: what is, is all there is' (Rudrum and Stavris 2015, 301).

This book is about narrative worlds and the temporalities of stories that depict them. If the digimodernist text is not a finished product but exists in the moment of being produced, always open to further individual intervention, what are some of its stories? There are positive and negative attitudes to its possibilities. Turning to my local newspaper, *The Sydney Morning Herald,* I note a review of a newly released film, *In the Heights* (directed by Jon M. Chu) by Jake Wilson (2021). It's a 'Hollywood adaption of a Broadway musical' – a pre-digital finite cultural product that nonetheless appears to embrace the 'apparently real' values of digital culture – and its reviewer is not impressed. It fails to meet his pre-digimodernist criteria: 'for drama, you need conflict ... Or for lightness, you need comedy, which in turn would require an ironic perspective on the characters: again, not something that this team is willing or able to summon'. Of the 'apparently real', Kirby has written, '[It] comes without self-consciousness, without irony or self-interrogation'. Moreover, he says, despite the known manipulation of, for example, 'reality TV', 'we know it's not *totally* genuine, but if it utterly seems to be, then we will take it as such' (Rudrum and Stavris 2015, 296). The reviewer of *In the Heights* disagrees:

> The real problem isn't artifice as such, but the ersatz sincerity that goes along with it. This is a movie where a crowd at a rally chants 'Tell our stories! Tell our stories!' and where heaven is visualised as a light at the end of a subway tunnel covered in graffiti.

For a positive attitude to (apparently real?) 'genuineness' and 'sincerity' in the digimodernist text I turn to another article in *The Sydney Morning Herald*, 'Youngsters Turn Video Games into Financial Gains', by Amelia McGuire (2021). It tells of a 'wave of Australian creators building careers on social and streaming behemoths TikTok, YouTube, Discord and Twitch', and that while the average Netflix user spends about two hours a day on the platform, the average user on Twitch (a gaming live streaming platform) 'spends more than three [hours a day], with 73% under the age of 35'. A young woman 'creator on YouTube' tells McGuire, 'People feel more connected when they know there aren't layers of editing and production in between the person and audience. Now more than ever people want to feel connected'. And connectedness is of course marketable; as another interviewee says, 'less polished' creators present a relatable alternative that makes them more 'trustworthy' and 'therefore more appealing to brands'. The latter comment is made in the context of implying that 'Instagram influencers', who 'saturate social media platforms' are already more obviously produced and so less 'trustworthy'. Digimodernism may be in the present moment, but the technology of its practice is oriented to the future.

In summary, Kirby describes the 'present real' experience of digimodernist text as a human experience of time but not an experience of human higher-order consciousness. A strong caveat should be repeated here: previously, in discussing the temporalities particularly associated with postmodernism (Fraser's levels 1 and 2), I noted the temptation in some critical writing to reduce postmodernism to a culture of monotemporal 'becoming'. Similarly, one could note the danger of reducing post postmodernism to a culture of 'continuous present'. Rather, as Fraser insists, for humans time felt but unspeakable and time understood and spoken about and all the worlds associated with the extended human umwelt continue to exist, even though the dominance of one state or one world does not remain constant. For digimodernism, this co-existence of temporalities may be particularly traceable in gaming, as in the following final example that explores 'connectedness' through 'story'.

Jini Maxwell is *The Saturday Paper*'s 'games reviewer' (*The Saturday Paper* is a weekly Australian newspaper, first launched in 2014 in hard copy and online, and in mobile news format). In a review of the game *Mutazione*, they (Maxwell's preferred pronoun) write:

> With a structure modelled after a telenovela – rather than the typical hero's journey – *Mutazione* is an experiment in grounding a narrative in a community, not an individual. It's a story-telling approach that narrative lead Hannah Nicklin described as having 'multiple middles', compared with a typical narrative game that might offer the player multiple alternative endings.
>
> (Maxwell 2021)

The game involves collecting and cultivating plants for seven 'musical gardens'; each plant 'emits a different instrumental sound', which can vary from a seed's single note to a grown plant's arpeggio. Moreover, each of the gardens 'represents a different musical temperament and key'. As they gather more seeds, 'the player designs their own unique soundtracks to each emotionally charged space'. However, in the context of the game, this 'musical healing' is to restore a shattered community. Maxwell comments:

> What unfolds is an ecocentric narrative that looks unflinchingly at the effects of colonial trauma on the lives of the colonised both interpersonally and communally. The player encounters the story largely through conversations between Kai [a 16-year-old girl] and the richly imagined ensemble cast, whose desires, experiences, relationships, conflicts and decisions are presented and explored without judgement.

The reviewer is obviously impressed with the complexity of this narrative and, like the traditional reviewer of a highly valued book, encourages the gamer/reader to linger rather than rush through its sequence. The game 'could technically be played from start to finish in about six hours', Maxwell remarks, but, 'its musical gardens offer a creative dimension that deepens the experience well beyond the scope of the linear story'. The 'deepened experience' for this reviewer extends beyond the present moment of gaming; the review concludes:

> After I planted [the] garden, I needed a moment to myself. I let the melancholic soundtrack I had helped create spill into the living room. As I processed my thoughts, the delineation between my home in the real world and my experience of the game felt porous and open: a generative space, opening up room for something new to grow.

This nootemporal experience of aesthetic appreciation and ethical connectedness here described is surely an experience of 'higher-order consciousness'.

At the end of Chapter 3, I noted Fraser's opinion on the high value of the arts and letters and of science, which he described as 'the preoccupations of higher-order consciousness'. Fraser lists the continuing evolution of semiotic modes through dance, music, language, painting, sculpture, architecture, film ... what, from digital culture, can we now add to this list? Gaming, for example? Certainly, Fraser's evaluation of the sciences, quoted previously, resonates for me with Maxwell's review of *Mutazione*: '[the sciences] share with the humanities their spirit of exploration, their search for coherence by plot that is, by meaning (known as hypotheses) and their readiness to mine the imagination' (Fraser 2007, 265).

Moreover, as with the literary novels of print culture, already video games are reviewed, compared and evaluated for perceived differences in quality. From 2014, *The Games Awards*, created and produced by Geoff Keighley, have been held annually; in the words of its 'About' webpage: 'The Game Awards recognizes and upholds creative and technical excellence in the global video game industry' (Games Awards [about] 2022a). The immersion in the digimodernist experience, which so concerned Kirby, is part of what is evaluated positively; as the 'About' page explains, by bringing together 'a diverse group of game developers, game players and notable names from popular culture', the aim of the Awards is 'to celebrate and advance gaming's position as the most immersive, challenging and inspiring form of entertainment'.

At 'The Games Awards' of 2021, some categories of award sound familiar from film and literary occasions: '*Deathloop* led the show with nine nominations; it won Best Game Direction and Best Art Direction' and '*Marvel's Guardians of the Galaxy* was awarded Best Narrative' (Games Awards [wiki] 2022b). But recalling Ellis' axiom that 'categorization' precedes communication (Ellis 1993, 27), one anticipates different categories of discrimination will emerge in this new context of culture, even when the same wording is used. For example, Alex Stargame (so-called), in a short online piece, asks, 'What is narrative gaming?' and answers:

> The narrative in games consists of the plot, sounds, music, atmosphere, dialogues, player choices and, of course, gameplay. It creates the overall impression of a game and allows the player to feel like part of a story.
>
> (Stargame 2018)

Here we see a digimodernist meaning of story (recall the five definitions of story in print culture in Prince's *Dictionary of Narratology*, 2003, 93), compatible with Kirby's comments on the necessary involvement of the viewer/player in the production of a digimodern 'text'. This is patently 'text' as 'process', not finite product. Yet some old verities of story-telling persist. Stargame points out that 'everything has changed dramatically since mobile games became popular': the player has to be enticed back over longer periods of play and 'the story', 'the simple desire to know what will happen next' is a strong incentive. Stargame adds, 'Of course, a game, especially a casual one, is not a book or a movie, but people are still inclined to perceive it as a story'. 'What will happen next?' is a question of sequence and, as this book has suggested, sequence in story may be chaotic, probabilistic, reversible, chronological, associative, equative.

'Equative' is the coherent narrative sequence of the social world of sociotemporality and, in the global world of digimodernism, players in different public temporalities of clock time can connect sociotemporally. The young entrepreneurs previously quoted emphasized the importance of 'connectedness' as a value of the digimodernist experience. And in the final sentence of The Games Award 'About' page, one reads, 'We strive to recognize those who improve the wellbeing of the community and elevate voices that represent the future of the medium'. In contrast to the effacement of human temporal meanings in postmodern texts, to the escape from 'mechanization' and 'quantitative time' in modernist texts, this text foregrounds the inclusiveness of human participation and the importance of accommodating 'the medium'. In a sociotemporal assumption of shared values ('We strive ...'), a 'community' of players is brought into being, each interacting with each – rather than 'other' – through a technology that is oriented to the future. For me, this is at least an optimistic and open-ended projection of the extended human umwelt.

*****

Mythologically, being in a 'state of being engulfed by the present real' (Kirby's words) is a return to the Garden of Eden and the primary consciousness humans share with other animals. And then Eve bites into the apple (a founding story of misogyny). Ironically (a postmodern thought), the computer on which I am composing (typing) this authored text has exactly that bitten apple as its (Peircean) indexical sign. It is meant to signify, I presume, human access through the development of digital technology to the tree of knowledge – in Edelman's terms, the evolution of higher-order human consciousness; in Halliday's terms, the emergence of language as social semiotic. Halliday began his work on scientific English (which would lead to his theorizing the development of grammatical metaphor and 'spatialization' of language, discussed in Chapter 2) with the study of Isaac Newton's *Treatise on Opticks* (Halliday 2004, 145). Conversely, Halliday's work led me to think about the 'temporalization' of language in the telling of story, and the different social contexts of this telling through manuscript, print and digital culture. It seems appropriate then to end with the story of Newton, an apple, his moment of coming into knowledge, and the new availability of this record in digital form.

William Stukeley published his biography of Newton in 1752. In 2010, The Royal Society made his original manuscript available 'for the first time in a fully interactive digital form' (Gefter 2010; Moore 2012). As this manuscript records:

> After dinner, the weather being warm, we went into the garden and drank tea, under the shade of some apple trees ... he told me, he was just in the same situation, as when formerly, the notion of gravitation came into his mind. It was occasion'd by the fall of an apple, as he sat in contemplative mood. Why should that apple always descend perpendicularly to the ground, thought he to himself ...

References

Edelman, Gerald. 1994 [1992]. *Bright Air, Brilliant Fire: On the Matter of the Mind*, London: Penguin Books.

Ellis, John M. 1993. *Language, Thought, and Logic*. Evanston, IL: Northwestern University Press.

Fraser, J.T. 2007. *Time and Time Again, Reports from a Boundary of the Universe*. Leiden and Boston: Brill.

Funkhouser, Christopher. 2007. *Prehistoric Digital Poetry: An Archaeology of Forms, 1959–1995*. Tuscaloosa, Alabama: University of Alabama Press.

Games Awards, about. Accessed 15 January 2022a. https://thegameawards.com/about

Games Awards, wiki. Accessed 15 January 2022b. https://en.wikipedia.org/wiki/The_Game_Awards_2021

Gefter, Amanda. 2010. 'Newton's apple: The real story'. Accessed 25 June 2021. www.newscientist.com/article/2170052-newtons-apple-the-real-story/

Halliday, M.A.K. 2004. *The Language of Science*. Volume 5 in the Collected Works of M.A.K. Halliday, ed. Jonathan J. Webster. London and New York: Continuum.

Halliday, M.A.K. and Ruqaiya Hasan. 1976. *Cohesion in English*. London: Longman.

Huisman, 1998; 2000. *The Written Poem, Semiotic Conventions from Old to Modern English*. London and New York: Cassell; Continuum.

Kirby, Alan. 2006. 'The Death of Postmodernism and Beyond'. *Philosophy Now* 58 (Nov/Dec). Accessed 9 June 2021. https://philosophynow.org/issues/58/The_Death_of_Postmodernism_And_Beyond

Kirby, Alan. 2009. *Digimodernism: How New Technologies Dismantle the Postmodern and Reconfigure Our Culture*. London: Bloomsbury.

Maxwell, Jini. 2021. '*Mutazione*' (games review). *The Saturday Paper*, 26 June–2 July, No. 355: p 22.

McGuire, Amelia. 2021. 'Youngsters Turn Video Games into Financial Gains'. *The Sydney Morning Herald* (on-line and on paper), 25 June: p. 3.

McHale, Brian. 2015. *The Cambridge Introduction to Postmodernism*. Cambridge: Cambridge University Press.

Moore, Keith. 2012. 'Newton's apple tree'. Accessed 25 June 2021. https://royalsociety.org/blog/2012/02/newtons-apple-tree/

Prince, Gerald. 2003. *Dictionary of Narratology*. Lincoln and London: University of Nebraska Press.

Reddy, Michael. 1979. 'The Conduit Metaphor – A Case of Frame Conflict in Our Language about Language'. In *Metaphor and Thought*, edited by Andrew Ortony. Cambridge: Cambridge University Press.

Rudrum, David and Nicholas Stavris, editors. 2015. *Supplanting the Postmodern: An Anthology of Writings on the Arts and Culture of the Early 21st Century*. London: Bloomsbury Academic.

Stargame, Alex. 2018. 'What Games Narrative Is and What It Means in Casual Games'. accessed 16 January 2022. https://medium.com/@alexstargame/what-game-narrative-is-and-what-it-means-in-casual-games-67f35c191424

Visible Language. 1996. Special issue: 'New media poetry: poetic innovation and new technologies'. 30 (2).

Wilson, Jake. 2021. 'Sweet but sanitised story fails to soar', review of film *In the Heights*. *The Sydney Morning Herald* (on-line and on paper), 24 June: p. 15.

Zappavigna, Michelle. 2013. *Discourses of Twitter and Social Media: How We Use Language to Create Affiliation on the Web*. London: Bloomsbury.

Index

Note: Pages in *italics* refer figures, **bold** refer tables and pages followed by n refer notes.